Bright

Architectural Illumination and
Light Installations

Edited by
Clare Lowther,
Sarah Schultz

Frame Publishers,
Amsterdam

Contents

STATIC SECTION

 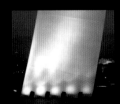  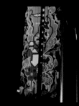  

008   016   024   032   040   048

056   064   072

DYNAMIC SECTION

082

090

098

106

114

122

130

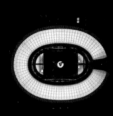
138

146

154

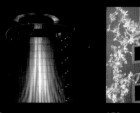
162

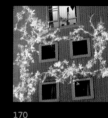
170

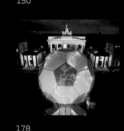
178

186

194

202

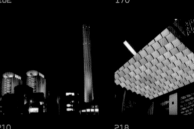
210

218

226

234

INTERACTIVE SECTION

244

252

260

268

276

284

292

300

308

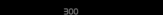

ABOUT ROGIER VAN DER HEIDE

ROGIER VAN DER HEIDE IS AN ARCHITEC-
TURAL LIGHTING DESIGNER AND DIRECTOR
WITH ARUP. HE IS THE GLOBAL LEADER
OF ARUP LIGHTING, AND HE HAS BEEN
RESPONSIBLE FOR INNOVATIVE, CREATIVE
AND WELL-EXECUTED PROJECTS ALL OVER
THE WORLD.
BEING A RECIPIENT OF THE PRESTIGIOUS
IALD RADIANCE AWARD, THE LIGHTING
DESIGNER OF THE YEAR AWARD, AN EDI-
SON AWARD OF EXCELLENCE, TWO EDISON
AWARDS OF MERIT, THREE INTERNATIONAL
ILLUMINATION DESIGN AWARDS AS WELL
AS A BRITISH LIGHTING DESIGN AWARD, HIS
WORK IS WIDELY RECOGNISED AS LEADING
IN THE FIELD OF CREATIVE AND INDEPEND-
ENT LIGHTING DESIGN.

Something out of Nothing

Text by Rogier van der Heide

Design is about creating 'something' out of 'nothing' - creating an experience that people would otherwise not have access to, or a product that, without design, would not exist. It is the impact that architecture has on retail clients. It is that which transcends a building's mere technical purpose. It is the excitement of using a music player that has been designed beyond functionality. Given this raison d'être of the design industry, it is clear that design is mission-critical to making your business a success. Lighting design goes one step further, setting moods and radiating aspirations. This book explores how the power to create something out of nothing can help organizations and businesses move forward, improve their bottom line and outshine competitors.

At the crossroads of business value - where customer experience meets environmental responsibility - design is the vehicle to a higher plane. Whether the project is a museum, a department store, a hospital or a public space; transportation to enlightenment can occur thanks to lighting design. No lighting design is successful unless it supports an underlying business strategy. However, this strategy must be more than just a plan; it must connect with reality. All the projects in this book use lighting design as a connector between abstract plans and the inspiring end-solutions that attract and bond with the users, passers-by or visitors.

I was amazed and enthused to see the previews of this book. All the projects demonstrate that these designers have a deep understanding of ownership. To reach out and touch their target audience, the lighting designer and client must together dive deep into the client's DNA. The foundations laid during this analytical stage serve as a base from which engaging concepts can grow.

Good lighting design must work on several key levels: functionality, sustainability and efficiency. Transforming brand data and values into a sensitive lighting design is an art. The hub of this creative form is the lighting design process which must strive to achieve total collaboration between client and lighting architect. Interaction means that a wealth of invaluable information becomes available, resulting in a much better understanding of a project. Cooperation is therefore vital to strategic design.

The focus of all design processes is the end user. Lighting is ultimately designed and made for people. A user-centred approach to spatial design not only means changes to an environment, but also a measurable impact on people as they go about their lives. Old, out-dated lighting design is dead. Long live the vision of exciting, vibrant lighting design. Now that drab, functionality-driven discipline is long gone. Perhaps the question facing the new breed of lighting designers is: 'Am I designing for tasks, or for experiences?'

However, the design profession is never simply black and white. The creation of value from design happens along a broad array of routes which span the distance between task-specific and experience-specific design. Experience design does not go without designing for a task, and museum lighting is a good example of where all these nuances must be combined into a single, integrated solution.

The lighting designers will often find themselves designing for a cumulative set of requirements in order to create true value. Nonetheless, the subtle degrees between task-driven design and experience-driven design can serve as an invaluable compass when trying to navigate a path to the solution for each new project.

The projects in this book represent a veritable cross section of today's creative vision and meaningfully presented as a collection of thoughts and concepts. The projects can be both a source of inspiration, and at the same time, a series of comments and statements on contemporary lighting design. Some are dramatic and experimental; others understated, functional or even shy. Throughout the diversity and range of possibility in this collection runs the continuum which we should all make central to our purpose: All lighting design can create value – and not just through experience.

THIS IS THE STATIC SECTION

MOTIONLESS AND CONSISTENT – REMAINING THE SAME WHILE RETAINING THEIR INITIAL POWER TO CAPTIVATE – THE STATIC LIGHTING PROJECTS IN THIS SECTION OF THE BOOK RELY ON FIXED COMPONENTS TO GENERATE FASCINATINGLY INNOVATIVE EFFECTS.

ROSS LOVEGROVE

LOVEGROVE STUDIO

ROSS LOVEGROVE
Staff: 10
Founded: 1986
Operates: Worldwide

AWARDS
Wallpaper Design Award, 2006
Time and CNN World Technology Award, 2005
Final Nomination for the Prince Philip Design Prize, 2004
JANUS Paris, 2004
Royal Designer for Industry by The Royal Society of Arts, 2004
'G' Mark Federal Design Prize Japan, 2002
D&AD Silver Medalist, 2002
Nominated 'Designer of the Year' by Architektur & Wohnen
magazine, 2001
ID magazine Good Design award, 2000
iF Industry Forum Design award, 1999
George Nelson award, 1998
Medaille de la Ville de Paris, 1998

KEY CLIENTS
Airbus Industries
Alias
Artemide
Apple
Cappellini
Ceccotti
Driade
Globetrotter
Hackman

Herman Miller
Idee
Issey Miyake
Japan Airlines
Kartell
KEF
Knoll
Luceplan
Moroso
Olympus
Peugeot
Tag Heuer
Toyo Ito Architects
VitrA
Yamagiwa Corporation

PROFILE
Ross Lovegrove has been working as an industrial designer since
the early 1980s, establishing his own practice in 1986, Lovegrove,
heavily influenced by science and technology, continues to bring
together industrial design and architecture, working on a diverse
spectrum of projects from small electrical products to lighting
systems and staircases.
The winner of numerous international awards, Lovegrove's work
has been extensively published and exhibited by internationally
recognized venues including the Museum of Modern Art in New
York, the Guggenheim Museum NY, Axis Centre Japan, Pompi-
dou Centre, Paris and the Design Museum, London, when in 1993
he curated the first Permanent Collection.

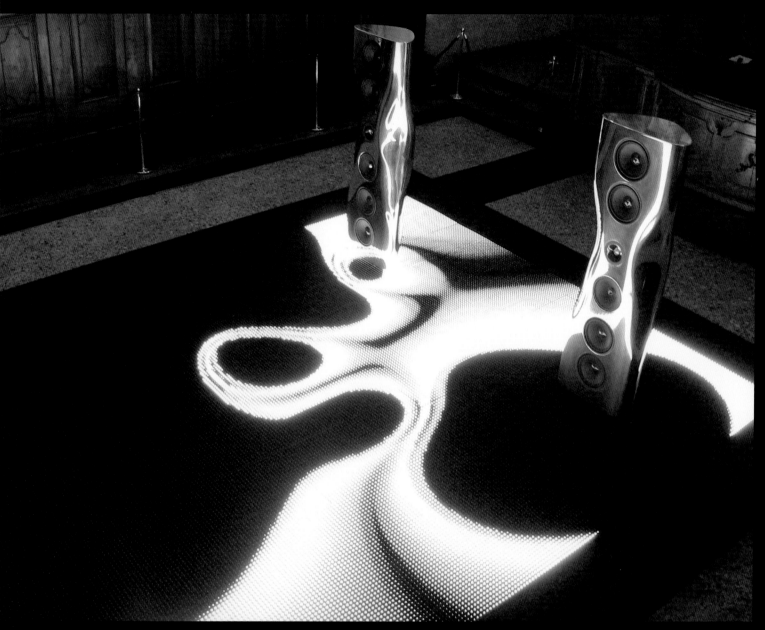

01

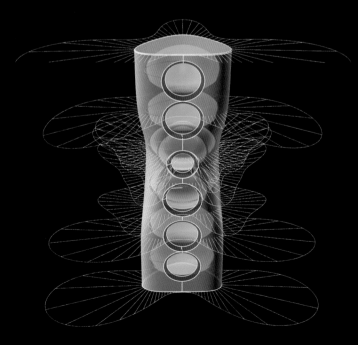

02

01 LAUNCHED AT THE MILAN
02 FURNITURE FAIR 2007,
LOVEGROVE'S MUON
SPEAKER FOR AUDIO FIRM
KEF WAS ACCOMPANIED
BY A RESPONSIVE LIGHT
INSTALLATION, COURTESY
OF MOVING BRANDS. A
VOLUMETRIC LIGHT
DISPLAY PROPORTIONATE
TO THE SOUND OF THE
SPEAKERS, THE LIGHT
INTENSITY AND SHAPES
OF THE INSTALLATION
CHANGED IN RESPONSE TO
AUDIO TRIGGERS.

A DIFFUSE POOL OF LIGHT
EMANATES FROM THE
SPACE-SHIPLIKE FLOWERS
POSITIONED ON THE TIPS
OF THE BRANCHES.

Solar Tree Vienna, Austria

CLIENT

MUSEUM FOR APPLIED
AND CONTEMPORARY ART

DESIGNER

ROSS LOVEGROVE

COMPLETION DATE

OCTOBER 2007

PHOTOGRAPHERS

LOVEGROVE STUDIO
WWW.ROSSLOVEGROVE.
COM

MAK / GERHARD KOLLER
WWW.GERHARDKOLLER.AT

MOVING BRANDS
WWW.MOVINGBRANDS.
COM

Solar Tree - an extraordinary symbiosis of pioneering design and cutting-edge solar technology - had its world premiere at the MAK Design Nite on Monday, 8 October 2007. The result of an urban design project initiated by Peter Noever, director at MAK – Vienna's Museum for Applied and Contemporary Art – Ross Lovegrove's prototype was unveiled to the public during Vienna's Design Weeks as a highlight of the city's first ever public design programme. Developed in co-operation with Artemide, the leading Italian specialist for innovation in lighting, and Sharp Solar, a high-tech company and global market leader for solar cells, Lovegrove's lighting unit offered a new perspective in urban design; considerate of social, cultural and changing ecological needs.

As the director of one of the city's creative institutions, Noever saw it as his duty to protest against the proposed installation of reproduction, historical street lamps on the city's Ringstraße Boulevard – in front of the MAK and the adjacent University of Applied Arts. Instead, supported by University Rector Gerald Bast, Noever managed to persuade the municipal administration (before the installation was complete) to let him present alternative innovative lighting concepts. 'What is needed', explains Noever 'is radically innovative and clear urban strategies. Urban planning is successful where tradition and experiment are juxtaposed in direct confrontation; where people dare to signal progressivism.'

Considered as one of the most important and innovative contemporary industrial designers, recognized for organic, fluid forms, Lovegrove was commissioned to design a concept more in-tune with twentieth-century design. Inspired by nature, Solar Tree follows the morphology of a tree, bringing a new and natural sensuality to grey urban-design reality. Positioned alongside the road, Solar Tree's illuminated trunks ascend skyward, sprouting individual stems that curve out to form clusters of spot lights. Emanating from the space-ship-like flowers positioned on the tips of the branches, a diffuse pool of light bathes the surrounding areas. The design meets both high standards in art and the imperatives of progressive ecological awareness. Based on cutting-edge solar technology, Lovegrove sees the tree as DNA – representing our times and the need to converge advanced technologies with the beautification of our collective environment. 'It brings nature to the greyness of urban environments and optimistically lifts our senses towards the future. It prompts us to consider how the physicality of all objects which surround us will inevitably change; either through need, enlightenment or simply through the celebration of new form in industrial art - it really complements the new quest for biological forms in architecture.' Lovegrove's 5.5-m-high prototypes will remain as a temporary installation whilst Noever enters negotiations over Solar Tree's permanent installation in front of the MAK and the University of Applied Arts. Seen by Lovegrove, Artemide, and Sharp Solar as the start of a worldwide expansion, it is hoped that the presentation of the Ringstraße project will convince other big cities to adapt innovative lighting concepts that use renewable sources for energy-intensive, urban street lighting.

'Ultimately the objective is to partner with other world-class art/culture cities who in turn will plant the trees in equal celebration of environmental progress in the urban condition', explains Lovegrove.

A suitable addition to the designer's solar-power themed introduction to Vienna's Design Weeks, the MAK Design Nite also presented Lovegrove's 'Swarovski Crystal Aerospace'. Designed by Lovegrove for the annual 'Swarovski Crystal Palace' – an initiative that presents new ideas for the integration of crystals with contemporary lighting technologies, the streamlined concept car consists of one-thousand Sharp solar cells, each with a specially made crystal in its centre. 'The design combines the intelligence of solar innovation with the optical, technological arm of Swarovski, prompting an exploration of the science behind the sparkle', says Lovegrove.

Illuminating designs that explore the synergies between alternative energy sources, Lovegrove's designs marry cutting-edge technologies with complex natural forms.

THE SOLAR TREE IN FRONT
OF THE MAK AND THE
UNIVERSITY OF APPLIED
ARTS.

RENDERING OF THE SOLAR
TREE.

THE 5.5-M-HIGH PROTO-
TYPE WILL REMAIN AS A
TEMPORARY INSTALLATI-
ON WHILST NEGOTIATIONS
OVER A PERMANENT IN-
STALLATION ARE HELD.

THE SOLAR TREE WAS
DEVELOPED IN CO-OPE-
RATION WITH LIGHTING
SPECIALIST ARTEMIDE
AND SHARP SOLAR, A
HIGH-TECH COMPANY FOR
SOLAR CELLS.

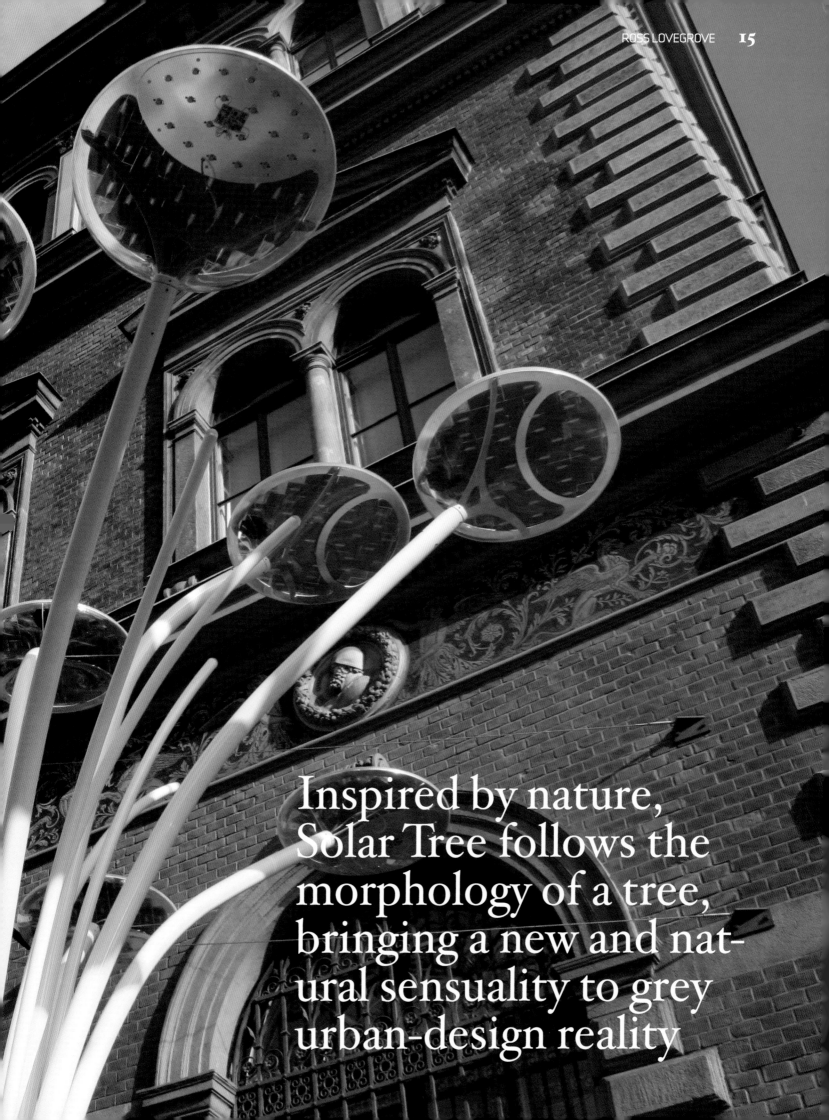

Inspired by nature, Solar Tree follows the morphology of a tree, bringing a new and natural sensuality to grey urban-design reality

ERCO
LEUCHTEN

BROCKHAUSER WEG 80–82
58507 LÜDENSCHEID
GERMANY

ERCO LEUCHTEN

Staff: 1080
Management: Tim Henrik Maack, Kay Pawlik, Mark Oliver Schreiter, Dr. Dirk Stahlschmidt
Founded: 1934
Operates: Worldwide

KEY PROJECTS

Grand Louvre, Paris/France, 1989/2005
BMW factory, Leipzig/Germany, 2005
Airport, Buenos Aires/Argentina, 2000
Airport, Dubai/UAE, 2000
Reichstag Building, Berlin/Germany, 1999
Adlon Hotel, Berlin/Germany, 1997
Guggenheim Museum, Bilbao/Spain, 1997
Airport, London-Stansted/UK, 1991
Pinacoteca Vaticana, Rome/Italy
Prado, Madrid/Spain

AWARDS

Numerous international awards for product and graphic design, marketing and corporate identity.

PROFILE

ERCO specializes in producing engineering hardware and software for architectural lighting. First and foremost, the company sees the product it sells as light and not as luminaires. This approach, which places the immaterial 'software' of light above the physical hardware of luminaires, has been the trademark of its work for many years, as well as the reason behind the name: ERCO, the Light Factory. ERCO's indoor luminaires, outdoor luminaires and lighting-control systems constitute an extensive range of lighting equipment for general, comprehensive, architectural lighting solutions.

01

02

03

01   THE GLASS PYRAMID OF
      THE LOUVRE IS A TRUE
      SYMBOL OF PARIS. THE
      LIGHTING CONCEPT, WHICH
      CLAUDE ENGLE AND
      ERCO DESIGNED ALMOST
      20 YEARS AGO, HAS
      RECENTLY BEEN UPDATED
      WITH CUTTING-EDGE
      TECHNOLOGY, ENERGY-
      SAVING METAL HALIDE
      LAMPS.

02   THE BARE CHASSIS
      SILENTLY MEANDER RIGHT
      THROUGH THE OFFICES
      AT THE BMW WORKS IN
      LEIPZIG: ZAHA HADID
      DESIGNED THIS SPECTACU-
      LAR LINK BUILDING BE-
      TWEEN THE SHOP FLOORS
      WHICH REFLECTS THE DY-
      NAMICS OF THE MARQUE
      IN BOTH ARCHITECTURE
      AND LIGHTING.

03   THE BRANDENBURG GATE,
      THE SYMBOL OF BERLIN,
      HAS BEEN RESTORED AND
      GIVEN A LIGHTING MAKEO-
      VER - USING LUMINAIRES
      FROM ERCO'S OUTDOOR
      PRODUCT RANGE.

BECAUSE THE SPIRES OF
THE AIR FORCE MEMORIAL
ARE MADE OF STAINLESS
STEEL, A COOL COLOUR
TEMPERATURE OF 4000K
WAS SELECTED TO EN-
HANCE THE MATERIAL IN
THE BEST WAY.

Air Force Memorial,
Washington, USA

CLIENT
AIR FORCE MEMORIAL
FOUNDATION
ARCHITECT
PEI COBB FREED &
PARTNERS
LIGHTING CONSULTANT
OFFICE FOR VISUAL
INTERACTION, JEAN SUN-
DIN, ENRIQUE PEINIGER
STRUCTURAL ENGINEER
OVE ARUP AND PARTNERS
LANDSCAPE
CONSULTANT
OLIN PARTNERSHIP
LIGHT SOURCES
ERCO BEAMER IV PROJEC-
TORS REF.NO. 34009.023
WITH MOUNTING PLATE
FOR T9.5 METAL HALIDE
LAMP, 250W
TOTAL SURFACE
4000 M²
TOTAL COST
US$ 37 MILLION
COMPLETION DATE
OCTOBER 2006

PHOTOGRAPHER
THOMAS MAYER
WWW.THOMAS-MAYER-
PHOTO.DE

The Air Force Memorial overlooks the Pentagon and 'monumental' Washington from the crest of a high-visibility promontory. It features three stainless-steel spires that soar skyward and reaches 82 metres at its highest point. Its array of arcs against the sky evokes a modern image of flight and is reminiscent of the precision 'bomb burst' manoeuvre performed by the United States Air Force Thunderbird Demonstration Team. The spires are asymmetric and dynamic, and each has a different height. As a result, the view of the memorial is different from every angle. The appearance of the arcs changes dynamically with the viewer's location, the weather, the season and the time of day.

The lighting scheme created by OVI lighting consultants features illumination that appears to emerge from within the memorial itself, enhancing the architectural qualities of the structure and conveying a feeling of inspiration at night. The challenge of illuminating the memorial lay in its unique design: each precisely crafted spire offered relatively small surfaces for catching and reflecting light. Each is a multifaceted, triangulated form with a unique footprint and a convex contour that turns away from the light. The spires can sway up to 18 degrees on a windy day. In addition, lighting had to meet Federal Aviation Association (FAA) requirements. To do so, normally red beacons would be required at the midpoint and top of each spire. After exploring numerous alternatives to these beacons, OVI developed a lighting scheme in which the upper third of the spires is illuminated to an average of 15FC, as required by the FAA. The spires are articulated, using this light level as a starting point. The lighting is balanced to achieve the appropriate shaping and aesthetic appearance of the spires, and all considerations – from splendour to safety – provided a firm basis for the lighting design.

Consequently, the upper portion of the spires is brilliantly illuminated with floodlights concealed behind the large granite inscription walls flanking the memorial, while a gradation of light is seen on the bases of the spires. This project demonstrates that a technical solution can be combined appropriately with aesthetics. To verify light levels, specialist 'climbers' from the UK took readings with hand-held light meters. As light sources had to be positioned far away from the surfaces to be illuminated, extensive lighting calculations were carried out using several lighting-software applications in order to determine optimal positions from which to aim the light, correct lamping/wattage solutions and the best product selection. Luminaires were given specific designations and aimed precisely at various positions along the contour of each spire. Generating the desired effect required very narrow beams and precision optics. Several manufacturers' lumi-

naires with different photometric data were studied. The ERCO Beamer series was chosen for its superior optical design and glare-shielding properties. Based on the photometric data and performance of the luminaire, positions and quantities were calculated and confirmed. Thanks to the performance of the Beamer projectors, the scheme required fewer luminaires than expected, resulting in lower cost and energy consumption.

The project had to be user-friendly and to work properly far into the future. The lamping logic was developed to utilize long-life light sources and one lamp type only with respect to FAA requirements, thus simplifying future maintenance. The luminaires have fully integrated, non-exposed cables as a standard design feature. The use of metal halide lamps was a prerequisite. The T-lamp currently offers the smallest lamp envelope, which in turn allows better optical control of the light beam and high peak intensity (cd) based on the combination of lamp and reflector technology. Because the spires are made of stainless steel, a cool colour temperature of 4000K was selected to enhance the material in the best way. The luminaires themselves are all equipped with integral anti-glare baffles. While the illumination of the spires was the central element of OVI's work, a pleasing balance of the spires with other key components of the memorial – granite inscription walls, glass contemplation panel, honour guard and luminous Air Force star – is key to the success of the overall lighting design.

THE UPPER PORTION OF
THE SPIRES IS ILLUMINAT-
ED WITH FLOODLIGHTS.

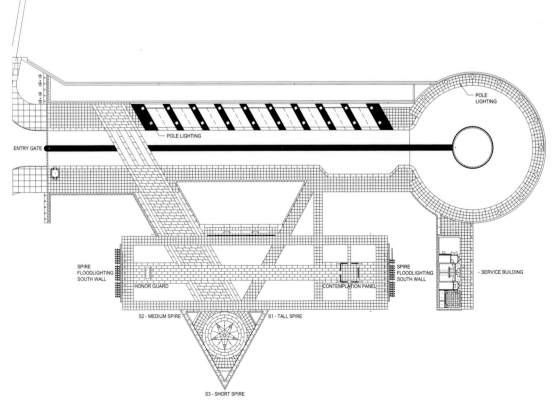

A GRADATION OF LIGHT IS
SEEN ON THE BASES OF
THE SPIRES.

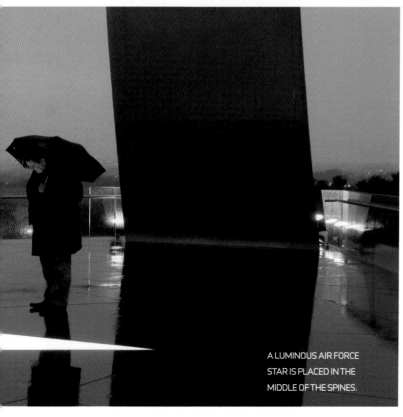

A LUMINOUS AIR FORCE
STAR IS PLACED IN THE
MIDDLE OF THE SPINES.

FLOODLIGHTS ARE
CONCEALED BEHIND THE
LARGE GRANITE INSCRIP-
TION WALLS FLANKING
THE MEMORIAL.

The memorial reaches 82
metres at its highest point

THE AIR FORCE MEMORIAL
IS VISIBLE FROM AFAR.

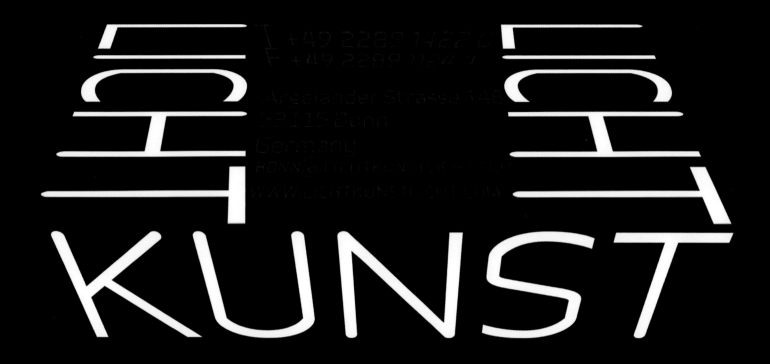

LICHT KUNST LICHT

Staff: 21
Management: Chairman Prof. Dipl.-Ing. Andreas Schulz
Founded: 1992
Operates: Worldwide
Memberships: IALD, IES, PLDA

AWARDS

Uniqa Tower, IALD, Award of Merit, 2007
Uniqa Tower, SEGD, Award of Merit, 2007
Uniqa Tower, IESNA, IIDA Award of Excellence, 2007
Coal Washer, IESNA, IIDA Award of Merit, 2007
Coal Washer, GE, Edison Award of Excellence, 2006
Novartis Pharma, Forum 3, GE, Edison Award of Merit, 2005
Novartis Pharma, Forum 3, Swiss Lighting Society, 3rd Price Prix Lumière
Marriot Hotel, IESNA, IIDA Award, 2005 Special Citation
Bertelsmann Representational Residence, IESNA, IIDA Award of Merit, 2005
Marie-Elisabeth Lüders Building, IESNA, IIDA Award of Merit, 2005
Marie-Elisabeth Lüders Building, GE, Edison Award of Merit, 2004
Centenary Hall, IESNA, IIDA Award of Merit, 2004
City Light House, IESNA, IIDA Award of Merit, 2004
Museum Schaefer, IALD, Compendium of Good Practice, 2001

KEY PROJECTS

Former Coal Washer Zollverein, Essen/Germany, 2007
Novartis Campus, Basel/Switzerland, 2006
Uniqa Tower, Vienna/Austria, 2006
Marie-Elisabeth Lüders Building, Berlin/Germany, 2004
Helmut Newton Foundation, Berlin/Germany, 2004
Jahrhunderthalle, Bochum/Germany, 2003
Federal Chancellery, Berlin/Germany, 2001
Old National Gallery - Alte Nationalgalerie, Berlin/Germany, 2001
Paul Löbe Building, Berlin/Germany, 2001

PROFILE

Filling architecture with light, setting the scene in buildings and creating space within space; the lighting design office of Licht Kunst Licht, led by Prof. Andreas Schulz, was founded in Bonn and Berlin in 1992 and is now one of the biggest names in its field in Germany. Licht Kunst Licht develops lighting sceneographies for museums, public buildings and private residences with open-minded and flexible solutions.

01

01 THE LIGHTING CONCEPT
FOR THE HELMUT NEWTON
FOUNDATION AT BERLIN'S
MUSEUM OF PHOTOG-
RAPHY GIVES GREAT
FLEXIBILITY, CHANGING
THE ATMOSPHERE FOR
DIFFERENT EXHIBITIONS.

02 AT THE NEW SEAT OF GOV-
ERNMENT IN BERLIN, THE
LIGHTING DESIGN NEEDED
TO RECONCILE THREE
DISPARATE DEMANDS:
THE REQUIREMENTS
OF THE CREATIVE AND
SCULPTURAL ARCHITEC-
TURE, STIPULATIONS OF
OFFICIAL REGULATIONS,
AND THE WISHES OF BOTH

Zollverein

Former Coal Washer Zollverein Essen, Germany

CLIENT
ENTWICKLUNGS-
GESELLSCHAFT
ZOLLVEREIN

ARCHITECT
HEINRICH BÖLL
ARCHITECTURAL
OFFICE, O.M.A.

LIGHTING DESIGN
LICHT KUNST LICHT

LIGHT SOURCES
DIMMABLE FLORESCENT
LUMINAIRES, PROFILE
PROJECTORS, PAR LAMP
PROJECTORS, VERTICAL
GLAZING LIGHTS, SUR-
FACE-MOUNTED DOWN-
LIGHTS, INDIRECT LED
EDGE LIGHTING, UPLIGHTS,
COLOURED ANODIZED
REFLECTORS

COMPLETION DATE
2007

PHOTOGRAPHERS
THOMAS MAYER
WWW.THOMASMAYERAR-
CHIVE.DE

LUC BERNARD
WWW.LICHTKUNSTLICHT.
COM

STEFAN MÜLLER

ULRICH SCHWARZ

The Coal Washer – with an area of approximately 90 x 30 m – was originally the first stage in the preparation and refining process for coal excavated from Pit XII at Essen's Zollverein Colliery. Some 20 years later and now retired from its industrial binds, the building hides behind an almost entirely new façade. Nowadays it houses modern, climatically-optimised exhibition spaces, illuminated by Licht Kunst Licht. Thanks to the rough ambience evoked by the lighting design, strong associations with its raw past of coal washing are nonetheless maintained. A mesh of 'light arteries' are integrated into the architecture of the building which create a uniform and diffuse luminous ceiling and generate a non-directional, artificially-lit atmosphere similar to that of the daylight which would have originally entered the space. Lighting units emit a cool white glow which is designed to illuminate the ceiling as evenly as possible. The luminaires become an integral part of the space as they visually recede into the background, to form silhouettes against the illuminated ceiling. To avoid the glaring white ceilings often associated with new buildings, all fluorescent luminaires can be dimmed and have been adapted to natural light levels, ensuring they don't become an intrusive element within the space.

To supplement this architectural illumination, a group of theatre projectors - profile projectors and PAR lamp projectors, both fitted with 35W ceramic metal halide lamps as well as cool, white dichroic glass filters and barn doors - were introduced where indirect light arteries could not be used. The same luminaire configuration was also used to illuminate the building's machinery, creating a diffuse 'luminous cloud'. Objects were lit from at least four directions, with low levels of light to avoid harsh shadows which would over-dramatize the subjects.

Installed as part of the preparations for the Ruhr Museum move - its permanent exhibition will relocate to this space in 2008 – tracks were integrated into the light arteries to accommodate spotlights for flexible, direct and accentuating illumination. Where the light arteries could not be suspended low enough, or in spaces where the tracks alone provided enough options, general illumination was integrated into wall niches or positioned directly on the tracks.

The international Visitors' Centre on level 24 - giving the public a further insight into the Ruhr district - now occupies the heart of the new Coal Washer. In addition to a three-lane light artery, projectors have been positioned high up and fitted with tubular glare shields to cast a laminar light onto the pedestrian pathways and machines. Meanwhile, vertical glazing lights on the large concrete wall point visitors discreetly towards the main stairwell.

External access to the Coal Washer is via a spectacular gangway. Echoing the route formerly taken by the coal, this gangway conducts visitors into and through the building. Just as conveyor belts used to transport the coal to the higher level where processing began, so people now progress up an exterior glass-enclosed escalator and arrive at the Visitors' Centre at a height of 24 m. At the front of the building are two 93-m-long escalators and 136 steps of steel staircase. This bold statement was deliberately chosen by the architects, rather than use the existing conveyor-belt structures, and the lighting concept has been designed to translate this into an overtly visible presence. Purposefully bypassing run-of-the-mill, functional illumination solutions - which could have been achieved with surface-mounted downlights - the use of light instead underlines the 100-m-long gangway's imposing geometry. This is achieved by backlighting the glazed flanks of both escalators. A colour gel, laminated into the safety-glass stair stringer, brings full colour to the fluorescent light behind, making the entire gangway emerge as a colour-saturated space. The result is a luminous interplay that bathes after-dusk visitors in tinted light and transforms them into colour-washed figures wandering amongst the scene. For people who cannot use the gangway, the ground level entrance has been steeped in warm light provided by surface-mounted downlights. A different scheme was required for the stairwell leading through the former storage bunker, so each step and handrail is illuminated by continuous, indirect LED edge lighting. The installation can be adapted for various requirements thanks to its dimming function. The building's vertical surfaces are highlighted by an exterior lighting concept which invites visitors to enjoy a walk through the site after dark. Uplights recessed in the ground give the warm-coloured brickwork a visual emphasis using a warm, white-light tone and a champagne-coloured anodized reflector. Inconspicuously integrated in and around the site, Licht Kunst Licht's laminar, homogeneous illumination breathes new life into this industrial monument.

A FLUORESCENT HUE EMANATES FROM THE IL- LUMINATED ESCALATORS BATHING THE BUILDING OPPOSITE IN A DIFFUSE POOL OF LIGHT.

HOME TO THE FORMER RAILWAY, A PASSAGE RUNS UNDER THE BUILD- ING LIT BY A SEQUENCE OF SPOTLIGHTS.

THE ROOMS ARE LIT WITH A COMBINATION OF LIGHT SOURCES INCLUDING, LIGHT ARTERIES, SPOT- LIGHTS AND UPLIGHTS.

ECHOING THE FORMER ROUTE TAKEN BY THE COAL, THE TWO 93-M ESCALATORS ARE BACKLIT TRANSFORMING THE BUILDINGS FUNCTIONAL ELEMENTS INTO A VISUAL SPECTACLE.

DIMMABLE LED EDGE LIGHTING GUIDES VISITORS DOWN THE STAIRWELL AND THROUGH THE FORMER STORAGE BUNKER.

THE IMPOSING GEOMETRY
OF THE 100-M GANGWAY IS
ENHANCED BY THE STRIK-
ING ILLUMINATION.

Just as conveyor belts used to transport the coal, so people now progress up an exterior glass-enclosed escalator

SFUNITED

Staff: 4-8
Management: Björn Klinger, Bella Sahin
Key designer: Chris Noelle
Founded: 2001
Operates: Worldwide

KEY CLIENTS

Osram
Sony
Tresor, Berlin
Metalheadz

KEY PROJECTS

wemix.tv, Berlin/Germany, 2007
Sony Bravia Visual-Insallation, Berlin/Germany, 2007
UrbanArtForms Festival, Vienna/Austria, 2006-2007
Metalheadz Tour, Hamburg/Germany, 2006
IAMX Europe Tour, Europe, 2005-2006

PROFILE

Founded in 2001 as an artistic network, sf united's work brings three distinct areas together: interactive live visuals, audiovisual collaborations and light-writing photography. Projects - both local and global - are based on youth and subculture, with themes of street and urban art inspiring audiovisual events, festivals and tours. The organization uses the term 'urban intelligence' to describe its work, which employs high-end technological and analogue skills to create special presentations, embedded architecture, motion graphics, illuminations, sound and design. Sf united operates with a special focus on below-the-line marketing.

01

03

02

01   MASK-LAYERING, MOTION
GRAPHICS AND TWO
BARCO PROJECTORS WERE
USED TO DISPLAY LIVE
VISUALS ON A CASTLE
DURING THE XI FESTIVAL
DELLE OMBRE.

02   A ROOM-LIGHTING SO-
03   LUTION FOR THE TRESOR
CLUB. PHOTOS OF THIS
SESSION WERE LATER
INSTALLED IN A 270°
PANEL PROJECTION. DELLE

CHANGING THE SURFACE
BY A NON-COMMERCIAL
SCREENING INSTEAD OF
BIG POSTER-BLOWUPS IS
NEW TO THE PUBLIC AND A
PERFECT WAY TO SUPPORT
ART.

IHZ-Tower Projection Berlin, Germany

CONSULTANTS
SKUDI OPTICS, GALLERIE TRISTESSE

ARTIST
TOFA - CHRIS NOELLE

MANUFACTURERS
PANIRAMA

LIGHT SOURCES
PANI PROJECTORS

TOTAL SURFACE
2,914 M²

DURATION OF CONSTRUCTION
12 DAYS

COMPLETION DATE
OCTOBER 2007

PHOTOGRAPHER
TOFA
WWW.METOFA.COM

In 2007, for Berlin's third consecutive Festival of Lights, light and media artists Skudi Optics presented the IHZ-Tower projection - a collaborative art project and part of the 'Berlin as canvas' PR campaign. The festival - Berlin's biggest cultural event for architectural illuminations - transforms more than 40 buildings into public screens displaying artwork and light-shows, igniting the city in an electronic glow.

Clean and functional by day, by night the tower becomes redundant; surrounded by only the dreary hue of dimmed lights. Skudi Optics decided to use the festival as an opportunity to transform the understated presence of this building into a site that would capture the attention of passers-by. Together with Gallerie Tristesse – an interdisciplinary platform based in the city – Skudi Optics invited 12 artists (1 for each night) to design a piece of 'art' for the tower.

Chris Noelle, one of sf united's key designers, was asked to create the look for the festival's grand opening. Located close to the banks of the River Spree, the colour range of the projection was designed to complement lighting emanating from the Nightliner - a boat hired by the festival organizers, equipped with mobile coloured-spotlights – which was to pass by every evening during the festival.

Adapting a familiar street-art style and pushing it into another dimension, sf united created a colourful piece of art using super-sized character illustration. Designed to appeal to everyone - regardless of age, the art was left open to interpretation. Noelle explains that 'showing a character in this size has a totally different effect on spectators and consequently their opinion of urban art,' he continues; 'We had spectators from the age of 10 to 80+ and their reactions were absolutely positive. We heard surprising comments. Older people who were not connected to the subculture look saw totally different things in it. It was an interesting experience to confront them with the projection and to see their reactions.'

Designed to catch people in transit, crowds coming straight out of the theatre and those trying to catch the subway were both encouraged to stop and view the super-sized character in all its glory.

With Skudi Opitcs handling the technical side of the installations, Noelle was left to concentrate on the composition. Due to the building's surface which has a black window stripe running down the middle, Noelle found that the colour choice was the most difficult aspect to prepare: 'Black outlines had to be inverted here and there to keep the character's expression,' explains Noelle. Pushing the contrast and 'pop-up' of the colours, the designer decided to use a black background for the image. Once on site, even the initial high-contrast artwork was washed out by lights from neighbouring buildings and abysmal weather. After making the final colour selection for the image, a remix of the projection was created using a special photo session with long-exposure, digital SLR technology. The light-writing elements were developed on a construction site close to the projection, so the full size picture could be seen in the background with the special effects in front of it. By using different LEDs and a mobile power converter for the integration of lasso lamps, sf united was able to create a unique light-illusion scenario – undoubtedly the most beautiful output of the installation.

For the final night, Skudi Optics organized an overview of the project. With all 12 artworks displayed consecutively, it was a chance for admirers of the project to see the whole output in one evening. For Noelle - who wanted to get a panoramic shot integrating the light-writing - the timing on the last night proved the biggest technical challenge of the entire event. However, despite a timeframe of only 30 minutes, the idea to work with 3D-characters and strobe lights to interact with the static projection and push the panoramic view deeper into the details was a success. Rain from the previous day even helped to achieve some additional special effects!

THE SUPER-SIZED CHA-
RACTER ILLUSTRATION
WAS DESIGNED TO APPEAL
TO EVERYONE, REGARD-
LESS OF AGE.

CHRIS NOELLE CREATED
THE STREET-ART LOOK
FOR THE GRAND OPENING
OF THE FESTIVAL OF
LIGHTS.

Adapting a familiar street-art style and pushing it into another dimension, sf united created a colourful piece of art using super-sized, character illustration

THE COLOUR CHOICE FOR
THE PROJECTION WAS THE
MOST DIFFICULT ASPECT
TO PREPARE, DUE TO THE
BLACK WINDOW STRIPE
THAT RUNS DOWN THE
MIDDLE OF THE BUILDING.

INGO MAURER

Staff: 60
Management: Ingo Maurer, Jenny Lau
Key designers: Ingo Maurer, with and without team
Founded: 1966
Operates: Worldwide

AWARDS

The Fifth Abitare Il Tempo prize, Abitare Il Tempo Fair, 2006
Honorary doctorate degree, the Royal College of Art, 2006
Royal Designer of Industry, The Royal Society of Arts, 2005
The Fourth Oribe Award, Design Academy Division, 2003
Georg Jensen Prize, 2002
Collab's Design Excellence Award, Philadelphia Museum of Art, 2002
Primavera del Disseny, 2000
Lucky Strike Designer Award 2000, Raymond Loewy Foundation
Chevalier des arts et des lettres, French Minister of Culture, 1986

KEY PROJECTS

Atomium, Brussels/Belgium, 2006
Kruisherenhotel, Maastricht/Netherlands, 2005
Dexia Banque Internationale de Luxembourg/
Luxembourg, 2007
Rockhal, Esch-Belval/Luxembourg, 2007
Lafayette Maison, Paris/France, 2004
US Fund for Unicef, New York/USA, 2004 and 2005
Issey Miyake Showroom and Installation for Fashion Show, London/UK, 1999
Subway Stations, Munich/Germany
Foundation Cartier pour l'art moderne,1997

PROFILE

Ingo Maurer (1932) has been designing exceptional lamps and lighting systems since 1966. His company, Ingo Maurer GmbH, manufactures and distributes these products worldwide. Manufactured primarily in low volumes, his best-known serial productions include his very first commission, Bulb (1966), the low-voltage system YaYaHo (1984), and the winged bulb Lucellino (1992). Moving beyond interior lighting, Maurer and his team began experimenting with LED technology in 1999. Since that time they have created unique pieces for both private clients and public spaces.

01 PIECES OF METAL, MUSI-
CAL INSTRUMENTS AND
OTHER OBJECTS FORM A
15-M STRUCTURE, MADE
FOR THE ROCKHAL. PART
OF THE OBJECT IS STILL
RECOGNISABLE AS A CAR,
BLOWN UP AS IN THE STILL
OF AN EXPLOSION. LIGHTS
FLASH AND FOG IS DRIF-
TING OUT, DIFFUSING THE
LIGHT IN AN INTRIGUING
WAY.

02 NINE PIECES OF 'BIG
03 DISH', WITH A DIAMETER
OF 230CM, LIGHT THE
LONG, HIGH HALL OF
THE KRUISHERENHOTEL.
THE INTENSITY OF LIGHT
AND ITS COLOUR CAN BE
VARIED FOR EACH LAMP.
IN THE COURTYARD, BUB-
BLES SWIRL AROUND IN
AN ILLUMINATED COLUMN
FILLED WITH WATER.

01

02   03

DESPITE A WEIGHT OF
APPROXIMATELY 1500 KG,
THE CHANDELIER RETAINS
AN AIR OF FRAGILITY,
APPEARING LIGHT AND
DELICATE AGAINST THE
ULTRA-URBAN SKYLINE
OF NEW YORK CITY.

UNICEF Crystal Snowflake New York, USA

CLIENT

UNITED STATES FUND FOR UNICEF

MANUFACTURERS

INGO MAURER, BACCARAT (CRYSTALS)

LIGHT SOURCES

16 HALOGEN METAL HA-LIDE SPOTS, 84 HALOGEN SPOTS, 24 STROBOSCO-PES, 300 LED BLINKERS

DURATION OF CONSTRUCTION

5 MONTHS

COMPLETION DATE

NOVEMBER 2005

PHOTOGRAPHERS

TOM VACK
WWW.TOMVACK.COM

JONATHAN B. RAGLE
WWW.JONATHANRAGLE.COM

NACASA & PARTNERS
WWW.NACASA.CO.JP

Gracing the intersection of Fifth Avenue and 57th Street in Manhattan, Ingo Maurer's giant snowflake shines bright. The light – the world's largest outdoor crystal chandelier – represents a new direction in the work of a man originally recognized for his small-scale products. Maurer calls the chandelier 'one of the biggest challenges of my career. It involved not only creativity but extensive technical engineering and a lot of handcraft.'

Invited by children's fund UNICEF to redesign the traditional symbol, Maurer created an apt addition to the city's artificial winter. UNICEF calls the object 'a beacon of hope, peace and compassion for vulnerable children around the world'. Installed in 2005, the crystal structure is 40 percent larger than its predecessor, also designed by Maurer, which illuminated the same spot in 2004. During construction, the new snowflake – consisting of 12 double-sided steel branches, with an overall diameter of 7 m – underwent several alterations. Each two-part section is adorned with crystals front and back, and is lined with an additional seven halogen spots that highlight the structure from within. Maurer's staff mounted nearly 16,000 crystals, manufactured by French company Baccarat, onto the frame before installing 16 halogen metal halide spots, 84 halogen spots, 24 stroboscopes and 300 LED blinkers, for a grand total of 7520 watts. They managed to meet the tight deadline, which the designer believes was eased by the noble cause. 'The snowflake involved months of intensive labour, often seven days a week, but everyone was most happy to contribute as much as possible to the cause. I am happy to continue my nonprofit work for the relief organization.'

The outdoor setting brought with it a fresh set of challenges for Maurer, who is more familiar with smaller-scale designs, generally aimed at indoor use. Here he had to create a product capable of withstanding the city's severe winter weather. At the same time, he needed technical components that would be as small as possible yet quite powerful – the finished product boasts an integrated cooling system. Building on the success of the first snowflake, which 'endured a blizzard with a wind speed of 110 mph without blackouts or loss of crystals, making us very proud', Maurer managed to install the second piece without any mishaps: all crystals remained intact throughout the entire installation process.

Despite the addition of 4000 extra crystal prisms and a weight of approximately 1500 kg, the chandelier retains an air of fragility, appearing light and delicate against the ultra-urban skyline of New York City. Positioned above an intersection that links two main thoroughfares, the snowflake glistens like a guiding light, thanks to a combination of focused spotlights and tiny flashing lights filling the air with movement. During the day, crystals catch the sunlight and play with reflections, while at night the clear glass prisms are emphasized by cold white light: a crisp refulgent contrast to the dim orange glow of the city. Spreading from the main beam in the middle, a diffusion of light illuminates the arms of the structure – defined at the ends with flashing blue tips. Elevating a section of the city, the snowflake draws the eye away from the claustrophobic grey landscape and invites the observer to consider the world beyond.

Grammy-winning musician and producer Quincy Jones lit the Snowflake for the first time on 28 November 2005. In conjunction with this lighting ceremony, UNICEF celebrated its second annual Snowflake Ball, organized by Baccarat, at the Waldorf-Astoria Hotel.

THE CRYSTAL SNOW-
FLAKE IS HELD TOGETHER
BY 20,000 SOLDERING
POINTS.

16,000 CRYSTALS, 16 HALOGEN METAL HA-LIDE SPOTS, 84 HALOGEN SPOTS, 24 STROBOSCOPES AND 300 LED BLINKERS, FORM A GRAND TOTAL OF 7520 WATTS.

'This challenge involved not only creativity but extensive technical engineering and a lot of handcraft' Ingo Maurer

THE SNOWFLAKE HAS A
7-M DIAMETER.

TROPP
LIGHTING
DESIGN

TROPP LIGHTING DESIGN

Staff: 4
Management: Clemens Tropp, Dipl.-Ing.
Founded: 2004, previously Werning Tropp and Partner
Operates: Europe

AWARDS

Hugo Häring Award BDA, 2003
Licht und Architektur Preis, Appreciation, 2003
Reward Advertising: Messe Frankfurt + Deutsches Architektur-
museum, 2003

KEY PROJECTS

Main Station Stuttgart S21, Stuttgart/Germany, Estimated
completion 2013
European Investment Bank, Luxembourg, Estimated comple-
tion 2008
McKinsey & Company, Munich/Germany, 2007
Lufthansa Aviation Center, Frankfurt/Germany, 2006
Burda Car Park, Offenburg/Germany, 2003
Main Station, Innsbruck/Austria 2003
RWE Headquarters, Essen/Germany, 1997

KEY CLIENTS

Audi
Deutsche Bahn
Deutsche Rentenversicherung Bund
European Investment Bank
Gira
Hubert Burda Media
McKinsey & Company
O2

PROFILE

Tropp Lighting Design plans natural and artificial lighting systems
for a range of architectural spaces, including temporary and
permanent buildings, exteriors, urban spaces and infrastructural
constructions. In close contact with principal architects and
other engineers, Tropp Lighting Design handles all phases of
construction, regardless of size. The company combines natural
and artificial light to create holistic architectural lighting concepts
– integral to the environments it produces. Tropp focuses on time-
less design rather than short-lived fashions.

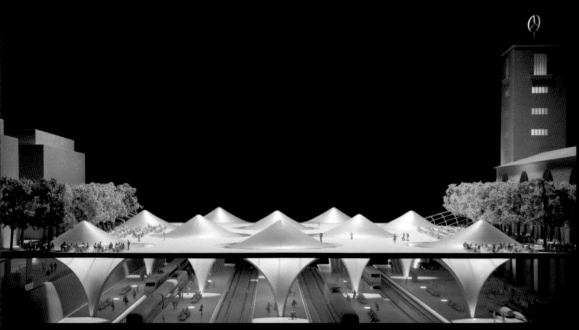

01

02

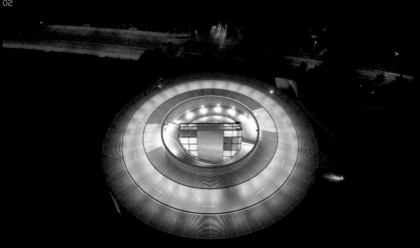

03

01 THE MAIN RAILWAY STA-
02 TION IN STUTTGART, GER-
MANY, DESIGNED BY IN-
GENHOVEN ARCHITECTS,
WILL BE COMPLETED IN
2013. INDIRECT LIGHTING
GIVES THE STRUCTURE
A SOFT AND PLEASANT
GLOW.

03 LIGHT GLOWS FROM THE
INSIDE WHEN THE BURDA
CAR PARK - BY INGEN-
HOVEN ARCHITECTS - IS IN
SERVICE, MAKING IT SEEM
TRANSPARENT. WHEN NOT
IN SERVICE THE STRUC-
TURE IS ILLUMINATED
FROM OUTSIDE ONLY AND
ITS VOLUME BECOMES
APPARENT.

THE ATRIUM BY NIGHT.

Lufthansa Aviation Centre Frankfurt, Germany

CLIENT

DEUTSCHE LUFTHANSA

ARCHITECT

INGENHOVEN ARCHITECTS

LIGHTING DESIGN

TROPP LIGHTING DESIGN

PROJECT MANAGEMENT

AYH HOMOLA

STRUCTURAL ENGINEER

WERNER SOBEK

INGENIEURE

LANDSCAPE

ARCHITECTS

INGENHOVEN

ARCHITECTS, WKM WEBER

KLEIN MAAS LAND-

SCHAFTSARCHITEKTEN

BUILDING PHYSICS

DS-PLAN

BUILDING SERVICES

BRENDEL INGENIEURE,

EBERT INGENIEURE,

HL-TECHNIK

FAÇADE PLANNING

DS-PLAN

MANUFACTURERS

ARTEMIDE, BEGA, ERCO,

SITECO

DURATION OF

CONSTRUCTION

3 YEARS

COMPLETION DATE

2006

PHOTOGRAPHERS

ERCO/FRIEDER BLICKLE

WWW.ERCO.COM

H.G. ESCH

WWW.HGESCH.DE

The new Lufhasa Aviation Centre is situated at one of the best developed locations in Europe for transport technology: between Frankfurt Airport, the motorway and the Inter City Express (ICE) high-speed track. Commissioned to create the lighting scheme for Christoph Ingenhoven's award-winning design, Tropp Lighting Design was faced with the challenge of realizing a high-quality, interactive office and working environment for an already-bustling site.

Shielded under the paraglider-styled roof - a pertinent reminder of the building's function - office areas fan out from the building's ten gardens which are each based on various continents' temperature zones. These wing-shaped structures emerge like a street of houses, forming an architectural backbone, or a connecting passageway that links the buildings' horizontal and vertical axes. Creating a more harmonious lighting scheme than those achieved with traditional strip lights, Tropp illuminated the 1,850 work stations with specially developed suspended luminaires containing micro-prism structures to eliminate glare and added flexible task lights.

Briefed to utilize the location of the headquarters – a highly-frequented traffic junction – as a marketing vehicle to represent the company by day and night, Tropp felt it imperative to enhance the exterior of the building for the hours of darkness. Two different lighting systems were used to illuminate this part of the building: narrow-beam, high-performance luminaires inserted into the roof beams and additional under-floor lighting. The arrangement, alignment and lighting angles for the atria, which serve to break up the total picture, were individually lit to coincide with their corresponding garden. Glowing from the inside out, the building appears pleasantly restrained in the dark of night. A conscious decision was made not to employ floodlighting or other artificial means of 'production' that would create glare and a wash of 'light scatter' on the façade. The designers therefore chose to light the eaves of the roof from below with Tesis in-ground luminaires. In order to meet the demands of the project, Tropp was required to develop new products, including strip lights with a micro-prism structure and integrated smoke detector (or the so-called TRM - modular technology frame system) and a new range of products that allowed several technical elements such as fire detectors, alarms, loud speakers and acoustic panels to be integrated neatly into the exposed concrete ceilings.

A continuation of Ingenhoven's crystalline, energy-efficient workplace, including the gardens that function as thermal buffer zones and provide fresh air to the office areas for Lufthansa employees, Tropp ensured the energy consumption of the building's lighting was kept to a minimum. Innovative lighting concepts, new lighting technologies, and the incorporation of intelligent lighting controls form the fundamental elements of this unique approach. To meet the client's demands for flexibility, the lighting concept is designed to be adjustable. A work place can be set up in any part of the building as each desk is equipped with a table lamp and is therefore mobile. The basic lighting for the offices measures a total of 300 lux. The 500 lux normally required for work places is achieved by the addition of these table lamps.

Free from the concerns of daylight, time of day and use, the lighting is automatically monitored and altered by the building's central control. This functionality also ensures that energy is only consumed when needed.

SILHOUETTES OF THE
ATRIUM PALMS.

HIGH-PERFOMANCE LU-
MINAIRES ARE INSERTED
INTO ROOF BEAMS.

ATRIUM 'CALIFORNIA
BEACH' AT NIGHT.

INGROUND LUMINAIRES
ILLUMINATE THE ROOF.

Glowing from the inside out, the building appears pleasantly restrained in the dark of night

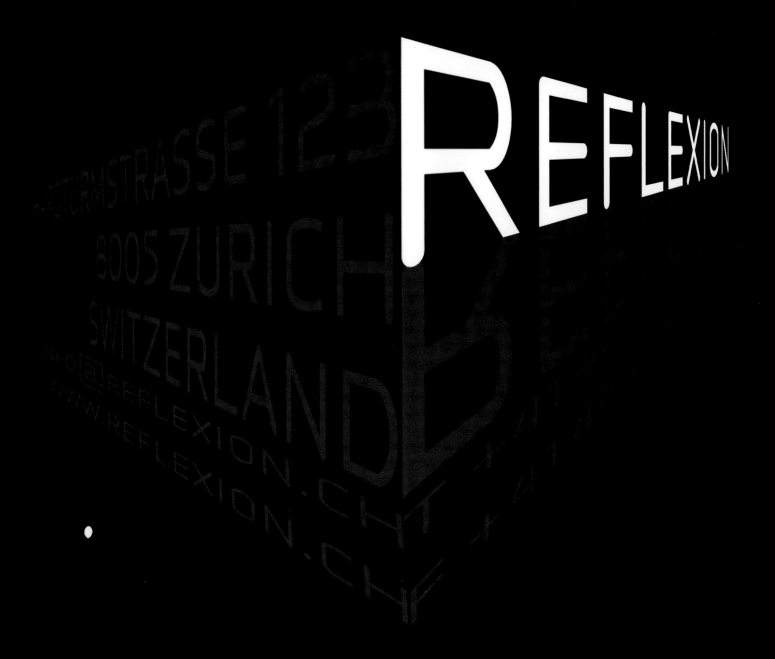

REFLEXION

TURMSTRASSE 123

8005 ZURICH

SWITZERLAND

INFO@REFLEXION.CH

WWW.REFLEXION.CH

REFLEXION

REFLEXION

Staff: 15
Management: Thomas Mika, Christian Burtolf, Oliver Königs, Claudia Widmer
Founded: 2001
Operates: Switzerland, Europe, Middle East
Memberships: PLDA, SLG

KEY PROJECTS

Löwenbräu Areal, Zürich/Switzerland, 2012
Philip Morris International, Neuchatel/Switzerland, 2010
Toni Areal, Zürich/Switzerland, 2011
Credit Suisse Branch Excellence, Switzerland, 2006 - 2010
The Paramount Sustainable City, Dubai, 2009
Sihlcity, Zürich/Switzerland, 2007
IWC Museum, Schaffhausen/Switzerland, 2007
The Murezzan, St. Moritz/Switzerland, 2006

Novartis Campus, Basel/Switzerland, 2006
Hugo Boss Concept Stores, Berlin, Stockholm and London, 2005/2006
Parkhaus Serletta, St. Moritz/Switzerland, 2004
Chesa Futura, St. Moritz/Switzerland, 2003
Migros Fitnesspark Puls5, Zürich/Switzerland, 2003

PROFILE

Zurich-based Reflexion combines Swiss engineering skills and design expertise with a profound knowledge of lighting effects. The company adopts a holistic approach, working in close contact with contractors, architects and clients, offering recommendations based solely on post-installation product performance, design, energy efficiency, environmental sustainability and atmosphere. Tailoring concepts to meet the individual demands of each brief, Reflexion works on both exterior and interior lighting schemes in Europe and the Middle East.

01

02

03

01 REDESIGNED IN 2007,
THE MUSEUM OF LUXURY
WATCHMAKER IWC
IN SCHAFFHAUSEN,
SWITZERLAND, WAS
GIVEN AN ATMOSPHERIC
ILLUMINATION SCHEME
BY REFLEXION, LIGHTING
BOTH EXHIBITION SPACES
AND SHOWCASES.

02 ILLUMINATING THE DOCK
AND SURROUNDING
AREA, REFLEXION GAVE
HARBOUR OF LACHEN
CLOSE TO ZURICH A NEW
FACE FOR ITS REOPENING
IN SUMMER 2007, IN A
DESIGN WHICH DRAWS IN
VISITORS AS WELL AS LO-
CAL INHABITANTS.

03 ACCENTUATING THE
ARCHITECTURE OF THE
MUREZZAN BUILDING
COMPLEX IN SWITZER-
LAND – DESIGNED BY
FOSTER & PARTNERS
ARCHITECTS – REFLEXION
DEVELOPED A LIGHTING
CONCEPT TO ENHANCE
BOTH THE FAÇADE AND
THE APARTMENT'S NEW
LOBBY.

KALANDAGASSE, THE
ONLY SHOPPING STREET
OF SIHLCITY. NIGHTLY AD-
VERTISING IS KEPT AT LOW
LEVEL TO ENHANCE THE
HORIZONTAL ILLUMINA-
TION OF THE ROOF.

Sihlcity Zurich, Switzerland

CLIENT

CREDIT SUISSE ASSET MANAGEMENT, KARL STEINER AG

ARCHITECT

THEO HOTZ

LIGHTING CONSULTANT

REFLEXION

ENGINEERS

KIWI SYSTEMINGENIEURE UND BERATER, THOMAS LÜEM UND PARTNER

MANUFACTURERS

ANTARES ILUMINACIÓN, NEURCO, IGUZZINI

LIGHT SOURCES

NEUCO LEDS AND OUTDOOR LIGHTING, IGUZZINI OUTDOOR LIGHTING, ANTARES ILUMINACIONE DOWNLIGHTS

TOTAL SURFACE

100,000 M²

TOTAL COST

€ 820,000

DURATION OF

CONSTRUCTION

3 YEARS

COMPLETION DATE

MARCH 2007

PHOTOGRAPHERS

RALPH BENSBERG

WWW.BENSBERG.CH

JONAS KUHN

WWW.JONASKUHN.CH

Opened in Spring 2007, Sihlcity is one of the largest private building projects to have taken place in Switzerland over the last few years. Dominating an area of 100,000 m² in the South-West of Zurich, it features an entire mirco-city; including shopping, entertainment, living, working, dining and leisure activities. The public areas are busy 24 hours a day so their lighting scheme plays a vital role in its dynamism and atmosphere.

An architectural concept designed by renowned architect Theo Hotz, the project preserves the industrial character of the location - a former paper factory - and adds wide spaces and large-scale buildings, unusual for densely-built Zurich. A blend of old and new buildings, the structures in Sihlcity vary from 1950s brick buildings to modern cubes with concrete façades and large-scale windows. Most buildings in Sihlcity are aligned along the North-South axis. To break this routine, Hotz also used the vertical axis, layering new elements over existing ones, which creates a unique impression of weightlessness.

Responsible for planning the illumination of all the public areas – namely the façades, the traffic areas in the shopping mall, the various entrance areas to Sihlcity, the main square (Kalanderplatz) and its adjoining street as well as the underground public transportation area - Reflexion was invited to join the project team in early 2004, with founder Thomas Mika and one of the company's head engineers, Oliver Königs, leading the proceedings.

Focusing on three main targets, their concept was to emphasize the large scale of the spaces and the layering of buildings, with a view to creating welcoming, atmospheric environments, and underlining the dialogue between old and new architectural elements.

Enhancing the spaces and shapes of Sihlcity, all outdoor areas were covered with a reflective type of asphalt. Utilizing this material to create façades that sparkled in the dark of night, Reflexion installed masts with dozens of bright spots, directed onto the surfaces in irregular patterns. Old buildings are illuminated with vertical, warm light, increasing the 3-dimensional appearance of their textured brick façades, whilst the new buildings with their smooth-surface structures are immersed in soft shades of cooler light. Contrastingly, one of the largest buildings in the centre of Sihlcity has no façade illumination. Instead it is framed by a ray of light at a height of over 10 m. This effect reflects the light on the roof, emphasizing the horizontal axis of the building and is achieved using specifically-developed, easy-to-service lights with shades that lie in a narrow canal around the façade.

The service functions of the complex are all located underground and are brightly illuminated. In order to optically separate the underground bus stop from the rest of the service area, Reflexion had it marked with dark pink rays of light and white illuminated advertising boards. This technique both highlighted the area and created a welcoming atmosphere for waiting passengers.

The core building of Sihlcity - the mall - borders Kalanderplatz to the South. It hosts over 70 shops and restaurants as well as a medical centre. : Daylight floods in through three large light-wells. Pointed lights fixed to their steel structure create the impression of a starry nights sky'. The oval balustrades between the mall's various floors are equipped with 2,700 LED lights and slowly fade into different colours. This lighting of the balustrades enhances the building's height and serves as a prominent indicator of the different levels. The sparkle of the lights gives an emotional contrast to the cool concrete of the balustrades and gives the impression of large chandeliers.

To ensure additions to Sihlcity's illumination remain considerate to the overall concept, Reflexion enforced a ban on neon shop advertising. As a result, to accommodate the needs of shops that require night-time advertising, a bespoke signage system was developed, made from standardized logo boards which hang on steel wires over the shopping street. Keeping the commercial signage in all outdoor areas at such a low level is intended to add to the charm and atmosphere of Sihlcity at night. However, there is one landmark which stands out and greets visitors far and wide. The two twin newels of the parking lot are illuminated with uplights in the parapets, giving them a nocturnal aura of weightlessness.

EVENING IMPRESSION OF
SIHLCITYS MAIN SQUARE
WITH OLD BUILDINGS
TO THE LEFT, THE PAPER
FACTORY CHIMNEY IN THE
MIDDLE AND THE NEW
CINEMA COMPLEX TO THE
RIGHT.

OVAL OPENINGS IN THE
MALL'S ROOF, ILLUMINA-
TED WITH LIGHT BANDS.

LIGHT MASTS ON THE
MAIN SQUARE.

1950'S BRICK BUILDINGS
WITH VERTICAL ILLUMI-
NATION.

Light creates a welcoming atmosphere in all public areas of the 100,000 m² Sihlcity complex

VIEW OF THE SIHLCITY
COMPLEX FROM THE
PUBLIC TRAIN STATION.
ORANGE RAYS OF LIGHT
HIGHLIGHT THE ENTRANCE
AREA.

WE-EF
LEUCHTEN

WE-EF LEUCHTEN

Staff: 350
Management: Stephan Fritzsche, Thomas Fritzsche
Founded: 1950
Operates: Worldwide

KEY PROJECTS

Sydney Opera House, Sydney/Australia, 2006
Southern Cross Station, Melbourne/Australia, 2006
Emirates Palace Hotel, Abu Dhabi/UAE, 2005
Royal Bank of Scotland, Edinburgh/Scotland, 2005
Staten Island September 11th Memorial, New York City/ USA, 2004
Marie Elisabeth Lüders Building, Berlin/Germany, 2004
Formula 1 racetrack, Shanghai/China, 2004

Airport Terminal 2, Munich/Germany, 2003
Chancellery of the Federal Republic of Germany, 2001
Various stadiums Olympic Games 2000, Sydney/Australia, 1999/2000
Sony Centre, Berlin/Germany, 1999

PROFILE

WE-EF, active in lighting innovation for over half a century, creates progressive and effective solutions for architectural lighting challenges worldwide. With an in-house lighting laboratory to develop high performance optical systems that merge cutting-edge technology with contemporary product design, WE-EF is internationally recognized for its reliability, longevity and outstanding quality design. Chosen by both internationally-renowned and young lighting designers as a reliable provider of lighting sources.

01

02

01   THE SYDNEY OPERA
      HOUSE IN AUSTRALIA.

02   THE SOUTHERN CROSS
      STATION IN MELBOURNE,
      VICTORIA, AUSTRALIA.

PRESENT EVEN IN THE
DARK OF NIGHT, THE
POSTCARD MEMORIAL
IN NEW YORK STANDS
TALL, PAYING TRIBUTE TO
THE 267 VICTIMS FROM
STATEN ISLAND.

Postcards Staten Island, New York, USA

CLIENT

THE CITY OF NEW YORK

ARCHITECTS

LAPSHAN FONG,

MASAYUKI SONO

ARTIST

TOSHIHIKO OKA

LIGHTING DESIGN

FISHER MARANTZ STONE

LIGHTING ENGINEER

WE-EF LEUCHTEN

INTERMEDIARY

COUNCIL ON THE ARTS &
HUMANITIES FOR STATEN
ISLAND

CIVIL ENGINEER

WEIDLINGER ASSOCIATES

LANDSCAPE ARCHITECT

MATHEWS NIELSEN
LANDSCAPE

ELECTRICAL PLANNING

PA COLLINS CONSULTING
ENGINEERS

GEOTECHNICAL
ENGINEER

HAN-PADRON
ASSOCIATES

GRAPHICS DESIGN

THAT'S NICE

LIGHT SOURCES

70W INGROUND UPLIGHTS,
CDM LAMPS

COMPLETION DATE

AUGUST 2004

PHOTOGRAPHERS

FRIEDER BLICKLE
WE-EF LEUCHTEN
WWW.WE-EF.COM

R.B. PHOTOGRAPHY
SHANNON MCGRATH
DOROTHEA SCHMID

Clearly visible on the Manhattan skyline, white, wing-like structures rise above the Staten Island Memorial – the monument that commemorates the 267 Staten Island residents killed in the terrorist attacks on the World Trade Centre of September 11, 2001. The victims' profiles are carved in granite, along with names, birth dates and occupations. The silhouettes provide a constant and very personal interpretation. In the twilight and by night, the finely tuned artificial light emphasizes the two-dimensionality of the profiles, giving them plasticity. Curved outwards, the two surfaces of the memorial frame Ground Zero, the former site of the World Trade Center, located on the St. George Esplanade across from New York Harbour. They form visual brackets that symbolize the twin towers and impart a vivid reminder of the horrific event.

The architects responsible for the project, Masayuki Sono and Lapshan Fong, decided to design a poignantly expressive memorial in honour of those who died, while at the same time creating a poetic place of personal encounter with the victims. In doing so, Sono remembered his own childhood, which he spent in Fort Lee, New Jersey while his father worked in Manhattan. Simply remembering the pain of losing him, just as so many lost their loved ones on September 11, gave Sono the idea of connecting the victims with their family members. This connection is represented by the two 14-m-high curved wing-like sculptures that serve as white postcards, enlarged 267 times, to the lost souls. The inward folds, reminiscent of origami, symbolize the preservation of privacy in personal messages. 'Postcards' is thus not only the theme, but also the title of the memorial. A touching tribute, the memorial shows the senselessness and arbitrariness of the victims' deaths.

Each of the 267 tablets symbolizes a commemorative stamp, with the profiles facing the harbour. When the sunlight hits one of the profiles, it casts a shadow on the granite in the background. Throughout the seasons, the sun backlights the profiles. At night, artificial light replaces the sun and allows the silhouettes to stand out. The direct effect on the viewer is strengthened by the plasticity of the faces. Many mock-ups and digital simulations were necessary before New York light designers Brian Mosbacher, Charles Stone, Kevin Fary and David Burya from the office of Fisher Marantz Stone were able to work out the best possible lighting solution. Seemingly simple things are often difficult to achieve. Such was the case with this concept, incorporating just two types of lighting. WE-EF inground uplights, each equipped with 70W CDM lamps, were mounted on the outsides of the curved folds to cast light on the silhouettes. Small LED luminaires, on the other hand, were installed as orientation lights between the walls of the postcards. Creating an evenly distributed illumination on the tablets also proved to be a challenge. By using extensive lighting calculations, the team became aware of shadows that disrupted the silhouette effect; they were then able to precisely define the position and beam distribution of the inground uplights. This has resulted in an extraordinary effect in which the inground light is directed from the outside to the inside, illuminating the horizontal profile.

WE-EF Leuchten Managing Director, Stephan Fritzsche, who firmly believes his responsibility is to provide lighting designers with tools that support architecture and its atmospheric effect through their technical and lighting-technical quality, explains the companies approach to Postcards. 'Standard luminaires have been used, with a lighting technique adapted to the type of problem involved. The soft transitions in the light/dark areas are especially well realized.'

Captivating visitors to the Staten Island Memorial, the white wing-like structures not only embody the remembrance of the victims, but also convey hope and consolation.

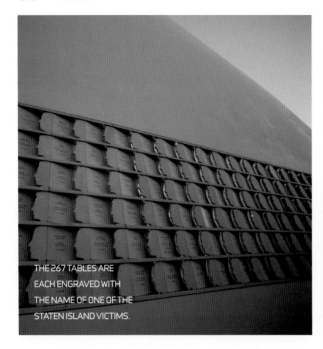

THE 267 TABLES ARE
EACH ENGRAVED WITH
THE NAME OF ONE OF THE
STATEN ISLAND VICTIMS.

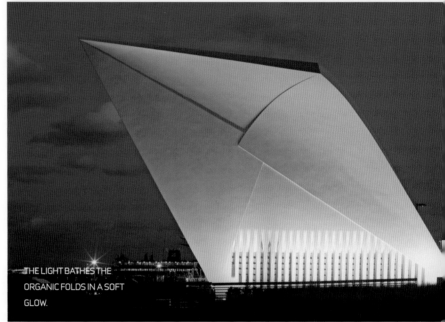

THE LIGHT BATHES THE
ORGANIC FOLDS IN A SOFT
GLOW.

AT NIGHT, REPLACING
THE SUNLIGHT, WE-EF
INGROUND UPLIGHTS
EACH EQUIPPED WITH 70W
CDM LAMPS, CAST LIGHT
ON THE SILHOUETTES.

Captivating visitors to the Staten Island Memorial, the white wing-like structures not only embody the remembrance of the victims, but also convey hope and consolation

CURVED OUTWARDS, THE
TWO SURFACES CREATE
VISUAL BRACKETS THAT
SYMBOLIZE THE TWIN
TOWERS.

ELECTRO

Level 2, 59 Hardware Lane
3000 Melbourne
Australia

ELECTROLIGHT
Staff: 7
Management: Paul Beale
Members: Paul Beale, Horatio Burton, John Ford, Jessica Payne,
Jess Perry, Larene Sullivan
Founded: 2004
Operates: Australia
Memberships: IALD, IESANZ

KEY PROJECTS
Centre Stage Theatre, Perth/Australia, 2008
Melbourne Recital Centre, Melbourne/Australia, 2008
MTC Theatre, Melbourne/Australia, 2008
Heide Gallery of Modern Art, Melbourne/Australia, 2006

PROFILE
Based in Melbourne, Australia, Electrolight is a lighting-design
firm whose staff represents a diverse range of backgrounds, including electrical engineering, theatrical lighting design, industrial design and interior design. Regarding light as the fourth dimension
of the built environment – a tool for creating a dynamic integral to
the experience of architecture – Electrolight is motivated by the
challenge of complex projects. The firm uses light and shadow to
enhance the architecture of a space and to make it visible on many
levels to users and occupants.

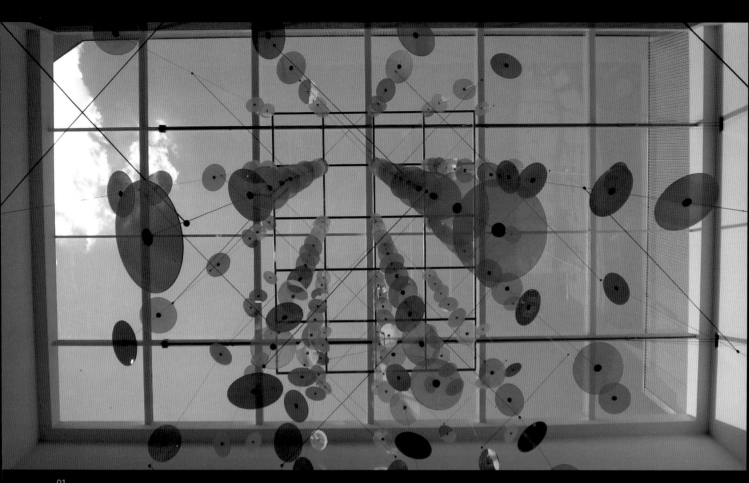

01

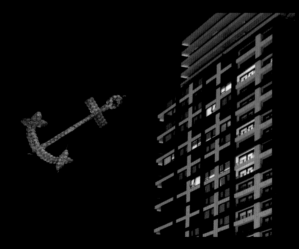

02

01   FABRICATED FROM 200 DICHROIC-GLASS DISCS, ELECTROLIGHT'S SECTION 84 LIGHT SCULPTURE TRANSMITS AND REFLECTS A MYRIAD OF COLOURS FROM DAYLIGHT ENTERING THROUGH A SKYLIGHT AT THE SHOPPING CENTRE OF THE SAME NAME.

02   IN MELBOURNE, THE ILLUMINATION OF ARTIST NEIL DAWSON'S ANCHOR SCULPTURE REVEALS THE TEXTURAL QUALITIES AND ACCENTUATES THE DIMENSIONAL ASPECTS OF A SEEMINGLY TWO-DIMENSIONAL WORK.

03   IN A SHOP AT THE ACMI (AUSTRALIAN CENTRE FOR THE MOVING IMAGE) IN MELBOURNE, TRANSLUCENT DISPLAY UNITS FEATURE CLEVERLY CONCEALED LIGHT SOURCES THAT CREATE A VIBRANT GLOW.

HEIDE MUSEUM OF
MODERN ART SITS WITHIN
LANDSCAPED PARKLAND
BESIDE MELBOURNE'S
YARRA RIVER. THE ORIGI-
NAL BRIEF TO THE ARCHI-
TECT WAS FOR A 'GALLERY
TO BE LIVED IN'.

Heide Museum of Modern Art Melbourne, Australia

CLIENT

HEIDE GALLERY

ARCHITECT

O'CONNOR AND HOULE

LIGHTING DESIGN

ELECTROLIGHT

ENGINEER

CONNELL WAGNER

MANUFACTURER

ERCO, IGUZZINI,

MOONLIGHT

COMPLETION DATE

2006

PHOTOGRAPHER

SHANNON MCGRATH

WWW.

SHANNONMCGRATH.COM

Heide Museum of Modern Art is a prominent Australian venue for the presentation of 20th-and 21st-century art. Originating as the home of John and Sunday Reed and the centre of a vibrant artistic community in the mid-20th century, Heide is now a public art museum that continues their legacy and promotes the practice of contemporary art. Now much larger than the Reed's original house, Heide comprises four galleries: Heide II, the award-winning 1960s modernist house/gallery by McGlashan and Everist; Peddle Thorp and Walker's Heide III, completed in 1993; and the Albert and Barbara Tucker Gallery, which O'Connor and Houle Architecture completed in 2006. Architects O'Connor and Houle were also asked to direct the redevelopment and extensive expansion of Heide III. Located in parkland in a far northeast suburb of Melbourne, the grounds extend to the banks of the Yarra River and include gardens filled with modernist sculptures. The brief given to the architects responsible for Heide II asked for a 'gallery to be lived in': a building that would create a framed experience of the estate from within. Heide II is recognized as a foremost example of Australian post-war modernist architecture.

Electrolight was commissioned to design a unique lighting scheme for both the redeveloped areas of Heide III and the new Tucker Gallery. Exploring the numerous parameters within the traditional formulaic pattern of lighting art displayed in galleries, the lighting designers illuminated the works of art – both two-dimensional pieces on walls and three-dimensional pieces on walls and floor – from favourable angles for optimal viewing. Electrolight's system transcends standard lighting techniques, however. Rather than focusing a single beam of light on each piece of art and leaving surrounding areas dark, Electrolight used a combination of wallwashers and spotlights, allowing the contrast between the art and the walls to be determined by curators on a show-by-show basis.

Integrating the scheme into an architecture which limited positions available for track lighting to lines that were neither parallel nor horizontal to the walls proved to be a challenge for the designers. As a result, track lighting follows the ridge-and-valley arrangement of the ceiling and runs diagonally across the room, initially creating problems for designers trying to achieve uniform wallwashed lighting and to attain ideal angles for illuminating artworks. Detailed computer models of the room were generated to determine the implications of mounting luminaires restricted to constrained positions. The models also assisted the lighting designers in selecting luminaires that would be well suited to the track-lighting locations.

Drawing daylight into the interior from the south,

the skewed sawtooth roof creates a pleasant environment for viewing exhibitions. In order to control the amount and quality of natural light entering the space, comprehensive daylight studies were performed prior to the installation of the roof. Fitted with blinds to control the ingress of daylight, the end wall of the Tucker Gallery features a large window, with views of the Sir Rupert Hamer Garden to the southwest. A landscaped sculpture plaza to the southeast of the new wing of Heide III houses numerous sculptures and water features and connects to the car park, located beside a landscaped embankment where Inge King's large sculpture, Rings of Saturn, stands. The area is lit with a series of glowing spheres that allude to the satellites of the King sculpture. The overall effect is subtle and avoids the use of floodlights. Utilizing the gallery's natural surroundings, exterior lighting was achieved by fixing lamps into a nearby eucalyptus tree, negating the need for poles. Atmospheric shadows are cast through the boughs and foliage, creating a dappled effect across the outdoor space with a strong distinction between the scene by day and by night. The lack of floodlights permitted Electrolight to play up distinct elements of the exterior environment with the use of delicate highlights.

A COMBINATION OF
WALLWASHERS AND
SPOTLIGHTS, ALLOWS
THE CONTRAST BETWEEN
THE ART AND THE WALLS
TO BE DETERMINED BY
CURATORS ON A SHOW-
BY-SHOW BASIS.

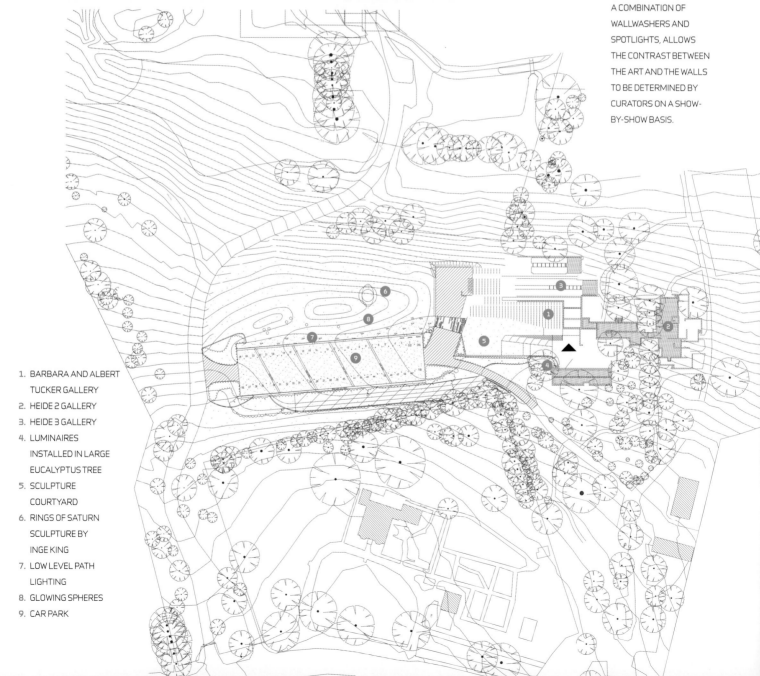

1. BARBARA AND ALBERT
   TUCKER GALLERY
2. HEIDE 2 GALLERY
3. HEIDE 3 GALLERY
4. LUMINAIRES
   INSTALLED IN LARGE
   EUCALYPTUS TREE
5. SCULPTURE
   COURTYARD
6. RINGS OF SATURN
   SCULPTURE BY
   INGE KING
7. LOW LEVEL PATH
   LIGHTING
8. GLOWING SPHERES
9. CAR PARK

UTILIZING THE GALLERY'S
NATURAL SURROUND-
INGS, EXTERIOR LIGHTING
WAS ACHIEVED BY FIXING
LAMPS INTO A NEARBY
EUCALYPTUS TREE.

THE OVERALL EFFECT OF
THE COURTYARD LIGHTING
IS SUBTLE AND AVOIDS
THE USE OF FLOODLIGHTS.

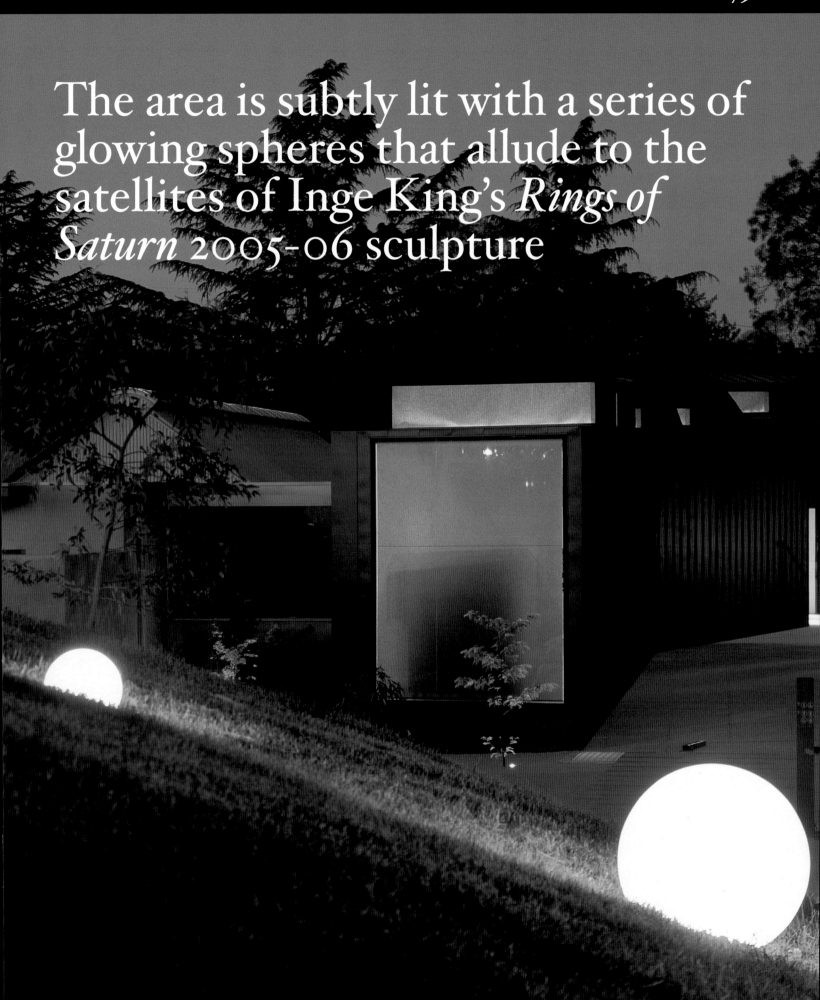

The area is subtly lit with a series of glowing spheres that allude to the satellites of Inge King's *Rings of Saturn* 2005-06 sculpture

THIS IS THE DYNAMIC SECTION

ENHANCING THE PROJECTS IN THIS SECTION OF THE BOOK ARE PRE-PROGRAMMED LIGHT SEQUENCES AND IMMENSE DIGI-TALLY CREATED IMAGES THAT CAN BE CONTROLLED VIA THE INTERNET: HIGH-TECH SOLUTIONS THAT OFFER DESIGNERS AN INFINITE NUMBER OF CREATIVE OPPORTUNITIES.

81

URBAN ALLIANCE

URBAN ALLIANCE

Management: Matthijs ten Berge, Jasper Klinkhamer,
Remco Wilcke, Hans van Helden
Key designers: Jasper Klinkhamer, Remco Wilcke
Founded: 2004
Operates: Worldwide

AWARDS

1st Prize, S1000C: Straat van 1000 Culturen
Competition, 2004
Voted Amsterdam's and the Province of North Holland Most Innovative Company, 2007

KEY PROJECTS

4th Wall, Amsterdam/Netherlands, 2008
Cruquius Landmark, Amsterdam/Netherlands, 2007
Moodwall, Amsterdam/Netherlands, 2007
The New Museum Line, Amsterdam/Netherlands, 2007

KEY CLIENTS

Gemeente Amsterdam
ING Real estate
MVRDV
Provast
Textielmuseum
VVKH Architecten

PROFILE

Urban Alliance is a company, specialized in creating interactive objects with moving images in public space. Utilizing state of the art media and light techniques, Urban Alliance combines their expertise and experience in design, content creation, engineering, implementation and construction to achieve an ultimate moving light experience. Urban alliance itself manages its projects from start to finish, from creative concept, content and engineering to final production and acceptance, and, if desired, even including maintenance and exploitation. With a portfolio that covers both indoor and outdoor projects for urban developers, governments and architects, Urban Alliance aims to integrate modern communication technologies into the urban environment by creating interactive moving images merged into architecturally-designed objects and buildings, both existing and new.

01

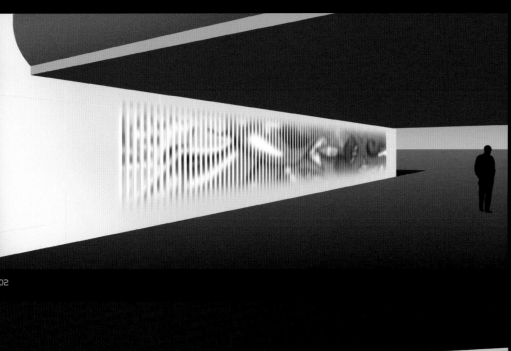

02

01 PLANNED FOR MUSEUM
SQUARE IN AMSTERDAM,
THE NEW MUSEUM LINE
WILL ILLUMINATE THE
CAPITAL'S HOTSPOT WITH A
400 M LONG INTERACTIVE
LIGHT LINE CONSTRUCTED
FROM OVER 400 INDIVIDU-
ALLY PROGRAMMABLE
LIGHTING TILES.

02 AS A PILOT PROJECT FOR
4TH WALL, URBAN ALLI-
ANCE PLANS TO INSTALL
MOODWALL – A 20 M,
INTERACTIVE VIDEO WALL
– INTO A PEDESTRIAN
TUNNEL IN THE BIJLMER,
AMSTERDAM IN SPRING
2008.

03 4TH WALL – WINNER OF

WITH IT'S 30 M IN HEIGHT,
6.500 INTEGRATED LEDS
AND A CONSTANT SUPPLY
OF NEW CONTENT, LED
LANDMARK CRUQUIUS IS
A 3-DIMENSIONAL SCREEN
AIMED TO CREATE A POSI-
TIVE ATMOSPHERE AT THE
SHOPPING CENTRE.

LED Landmark Cruquius
Cruquius, Netherlands

CLIENT
ING REAL ESTATE
CONSULTANTS
IBG OPTICS, KOMPLOT
MECHANICS, URBAN
ALLIANCE, VVKH
ARCHITECTEN
ENGINEERS
SORBA, URBAN ALLIANCE
MANUFACTURERS
IBG OPTICS, KOMPLOT
MECHANICS, OBDAM
STAALBOUW, PPG
SCHURGERS, URBAN
ALLIANCE
LIGHT SOURCES
COLOR KINETICS LED
TOTAL SURFACE
250 M²
TOTAL COST
€ 600,000
DURATION OF
CONSTRUCTION
15 MONTHS
COMPLETION DATE
MARCH 2007

PHOTOGRAPHER
URBAN ALLIANCE
WWW.URBANALLIANCE.NL

Few people will have heard of the picturesque hamlet of Cruquius before. However, all this may soon change thanks to Urban Alliance's LED Landmark Cruquius. Urban Alliance Partner, Remco Wilcke, had recently built a media object in Doetinchem called the D Tower (designed by NOX), and was subsequently asked to participate in the design and construction of LED Landmark Cruquius, which was designed by the architects of VVKH. It was during that time that Urban Alliance was starting to form its vision and mission statement; the opportunity of providing content for Landmark was to aid this forging process.

The result certainly turns heads. A 3-dimensional screen - approximately 30 m high - projects images aimed to enhance the atmosphere, promote the marketing of the area and create a positive environment for shopping.

Joining the project once wheels were already set in motion had both advantages and disadvantages. There were certain parameters to work within, a pre-determined budget, and most fundamentally the height and shape of VVKH's design had already been fixed. Wilke, together with VVKH and the construction team, was left to fine-tune the design; creating a skin that would let light through whilst still accommodating the various structural and physical demands of the landmark. The project began in January 2006 and the production of parts got underway the following summer, lasting throughout the autumn and winter. The final construction period spanned the four months between December 2006 and March 2007. The LED façade was completed shortly after, with 18 July 2007 marking the official celebration of the LED system. Although there have been large LED screens before, the curved, 3 dimensional screen and system produced for this installation remain unique to Europe.

Despite changes to the internal structure, the end result only differs slightly from the initial designs. The original plan was to have supporting elements close to the skin of LED Landmark Cruquius, whereas the final product had to change this to a supportive core to overcome constructional difficulties. Commonly used in ship building, the structure's skin is made out of a fibreglass and polyester mix, uniquely shaped into 100 panels. Each panel had a specific mould with preformed flanges and arrived at the site ready to be assembled. A truly advantageous material, not only does the fibreglass and polyester mix allow light to pass through, it also blurs pixels into a bigger smudge, resulting in better picture quality. The picture is constructed from 6,500 pixels, each made of six coloured LEDs.

Urban Alliance not only supervised the construction of the project but also developed the content - designed to fit the specific shape of the object. Although only basic content has been developed to date, Urban Alliance plans to stay involved with this aspect of the project. Shown in themed, 15-minute-long segments, content is followed by an animated interlude, after which another 15 minutes of animation are shown. Calming and quiet to begin with, the animations gradually escalate. One particular sequence starts with a campfire at the bottom of the screen which appears to gradually engulf the tower in a burst of flame. In order to keep this installation fresh and exciting, Urban Alliance will continue to produce and deliver a constant and systematic supply of new content. Endlessly repeating the original material, would 'defeat the whole purpose of building a landmark in the first place', explains an Urban Alliance spokesperson.

This ambitious project – which proved many naysayers wrong - is a testament to the fact that innovative structures can be built within limited time periods and restricted budgets.

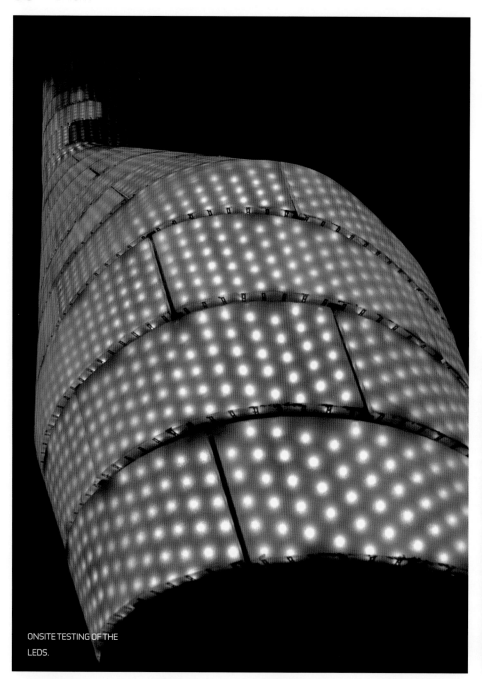

ONSITE TESTING OF THE
LEDS.

LIGHT DIFFUSION TEST OF
THE FIBERGLASS PANELS.

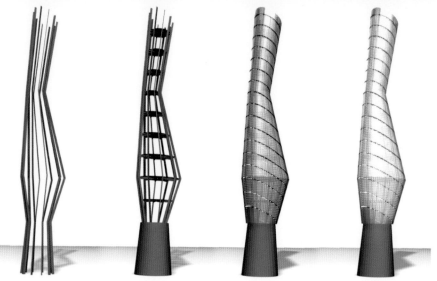

AN OVERVIEW OF THE
CONSTRUCTION PHASES
OF THE TOWER.

THE LANDMARK WITH
CONTENT CREATED FOR
THE OPENING CEREMONY
REFERRING TO THE
NEARBY FLOWER FIELDS.

LED LANDMARK
CRUQUIUS AGAINST THE
BACKGROUND OF SHOP-
PING CENTRE CRUQUIUS.

Endlessly repeating the original material, would defeat the whole purpose of building a landmark

MAGIC
MONKEY

5 RUE FRANZ MERJAY
1050 BRUSSELS BELGIUM
T +32 2 344 8484
F +32 2 347 7072
SOLUTIONS@MAGICMONKEY.NET
WWW.MAGICMONKEY.NET

MAGIC MONKEY

Staff: 8
Management: Daphné Delbeke, Marc Largent
Key designers: Daphné Delbeke, Marc Largent
Founded: 1995
Operates: Worldwide
Membership: Sofam

AWARD

Suez Innovation Award, 2006

KEY PROJECTS

**32nd America's Cup Endesa Monumental
Communication,** Valencia/Spain, 2007
Grand Lisboa Casino Lighting Design, Macao/China, 2007
KBC Boerentoren, Interactive Monumental Display, Antwerp/
Belgium, 2006
Toyota PRIUS European Launch, Brussels/Belgium, 2004
ING House World Headquarters, Amsterdam/ Netherlands,
2004

DEXIA BIL, Luxembourg City/Luxembourg, 2003
BBL Marnix Monumental Interactive RGB Matrix,
Brussels/Belgium, 1999-2001
Swatch Pavilion, Centennial Olympic Games, Atlanta/USA,
1996

PROFILE

Founded in 1995, Magic Monkey is a global innovator in urban
communication. Specializing in translating architecture and environments into monumental communication platforms, emotion
remains a key objective for Magic Monkey. Projects the company
works on elicit participation from the public, and generate true
emotional exchanges between brands, architecture and people.
Magic Monkey's main focus is on creating truly innovative designs
and meticulous implementation. The company has successfully
collaborated with famous architectural firms and prestigious
brands.

01

02

01 ENDESA, A SPONSOR OF
02 THE 32ND AMERICA'S CUP,
COMMISSIONED MAGIC
MONKEY TO CREATE A
MONUMENTAL INSTAL-
LATION ON THE PORT OF
THE AMERICA'S CUP IN
VALENCIA, SPAIN IN 2007.
THE 5.4 KM PERIMETER OF
THE PORT WAS INTE-
GRATED WITH POWER-
FUL SKY PROJECTIONS,
THOUSANDS OF RGB LEDS
AND PROJECTIONS ON
DAVID CHIPPERFIELD'S
VELES E VENTS BUILDING.
THOUSANDS OF LEDS,
POSITIONED ON HUN-
DREDS OF FLAG MASTS,
FOLLOWED THE WATER'S
EDGE AND CREATED A
GIGANTIC, TRANSPARENT
VIDEO DISPLAY, VISIBLE
FROM EVERY ANGLE OF
THE PORT.

IT TOOK TEN PROFESSION-
AL MOUNTAIN CLIMBERS
TWO MONTHS TO INSTALL
THE LIGHTS.

Electrabel Power Station
Drogenbos, Brussels

CLIENT

ELECTRABEL

LIGHTING DESIGN

MAGIC MONKEY

LIGHT SOURCES

8,032 LEDS

TOTAL SURFACE

18,000 M²

TOTAL COSTS

€ 600,000

DURATION OF
CONSTRUCTION

2 MONTHS

COMPLETION DATE

DECEMBER 2005

PHOTOGRAPHER

MAGIC MONKEY

WWW.MAGICMONKEY.NET

Colossal structures of functional concrete designed to feed man's unrelenting hunger for power - few things hijack the landscape more than a power station. Urban communicators, Magic Monkey, have proved that even these unsightly structures can be rejuvenated through the use of digital technology. Commissioned by energy giant Electrabel to create something 'exceptional' for the gas turbine station in Drogenbos - an eyesore that has dominated the South-Brussels skyline for over a decade, Magic Monkey transformed the 102-m-high cooling tower into a luminescent façade. A sequence of animated colours and imagery transform the 18,000 m² of reinforced concrete into an emotive light show, emulating autumnal colours in brown and green waves, speckled with falling leaves.

Born out of an on-going love affair with architecture, light, video and each other, the design process at Magic Monkey consists of husband and wife team, Marc Largent and Daphné Delbeke. The pair seduce one another with ideas of technical poetry, 'Each project is like a seductive dance. That's the magic part. We sit down and try to impress each other with ideas,' explains Largent. Founded 12 years ago, Magic Monkey was one of the first companies to experiment with splitting pixels to create large-scale video images. 'Many are apprehensive and don't believe an image or text will be legible when each pixel is several metres apart,' says Largent. 'But they are also the first to become true converts once the show is switched on and the precise balance between content-creation and pixel-placement is achieved.' Magic Monkey were selected for their impressive portfolio which includes projects such as the giant interactive screen at the Marnix building. This innovative project was actually the first RGB media façade – each window was lit up with individually controlled lights and the public were invited to upload their own creations on the internet. Electrabel's Brand Manager Benoit Crochlet, was confident that Magic Monkey would deliver a suitable result, 'There was no doubt who should do the project. We wanted them because we knew what they had done with other projects, especially the Marnix building.' says Crochlet.

Part of the company's global Living Architecture project for Electrabel - a design programme intended to bring to life five of the company's key buildings - the power station was fitted with a unique corset of 8,032 individually controllable RGB LED pixels. It took ten professional mountain climbers two months to install the lights - all performed without the possibility of turning the power off. The installation remains programmed from the heart of Magic Monkey – an office in central Brussels. The overall aim, says Largent, was to 'demystify the tower and turn it into something

beautiful'.

Compared to traditional projections where beams are directed at buildings, the LEDs used by Magic Monkey are visible from a far distance, creating crisp images that become seamlessly integrated into the building's architecture. However, Largent and Delbeke are careful not to be consumed by dazzling new technology, and remain adamant that light is just a 'tool'; 'Clients can be easily fascinated by the equipment and spend the entire budget on fancy electronics, forgetting the whole point of the project. The aim is to create something exceptional and engaging: something people look at, enjoy, engage in and never forget,' explains Largent.

To avoid becoming a show as monotonous as the daily commutes of those driving past, the tower has changeable content, which alters 15 times per year to reflect seasons and events such as national sporting celebrations, New Year's Eve and Valentine's Day.

Described by Delbeke as a 'gift to all passers-by', the power station is gradually evolving to fulfil its potential. A sneak preview of what's in store, current animations have eased the public into the futuristic possibilities of architecture. Visual effects in the coming years will include soaring peregrine falcons in homage to the rare birds of prey who have chosen to nest on top of the tower. Widening the audience beyond Brussels, the structure's metamorphosis can also be tracked daily via a website providing a live video feed of the tower. Committed to preventing the range and availability of technology leading to an influx of media-saturated architecture, where content would no longer be a priority, Largent is regularly involved in lectures and seminars. 'Otherwise' he explains, 'media façades are just going to be another trend; a flash in the pan.'

THE POWER STATION IS
EASILY SPOTTED ON BRUS-
SELS SKYLINE.

THE 102-M COOLING
TOWER WAS OUTFITTED
WITH 8,032 INDIVIDUALLY
CONTROLLABLE RGB LED
PIXELS.

THE TOWER HAS CHANGE-ABLE CONTENT, WHICH AL-TERS 15 TIMES PER YEAR TO REFLECT SEASONS AND EVENTS.

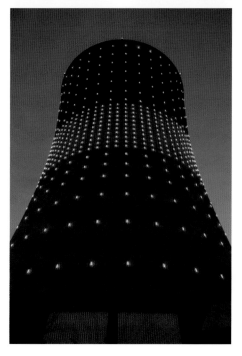

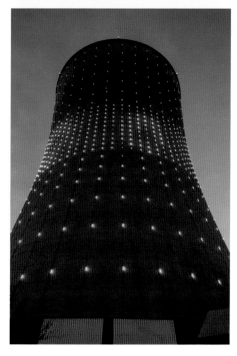

Colossal structures of functional concrete designed to feed man's unrelenting hunger for power - few things hijack the landscape more than a power station

THE CRISP IMAGES, CREATED BY SPLIT PIXELS, ARE SEAMLESSLY INTEGRATED INTO THE BUILDING'S ARCHITECTURE

JASON BRUGES STUDIO

Staff: 12
Management: Jason Bruges, Zena Bruges
Key designers: Gabby Shawcross, Tom Sloan, Jon Hodges, Tim Greatrex
Founded: 2001
Operates: Worldwide

PROFILE

Founded in 2001, Jason Bruges Studio develops and delivers interactive projects worldwide. The studio - a team of 12 - comprises experienced architects, project managers and lighting, interaction and industrial designers. Together they create surfaces, spaces and large-scale interventions for the worlds of architecture, installation art and interaction design. Combining innovative technologies with materials and fabrication techniques from the construction industry, the practice delivers engaging and robust solutions for a diverse range of briefs.

01

03

01   THIS PIECE WAS PART
     OF A CELEBRATION OF
     CULTURAL DIVERSITY IN
     THE CITY OF LEICESTER.
     BESPOKE COLOUR-CAP-
     TURING LIGHTING COL-
     UMNS LOCATED AROUND
     THE CITY CENTRE CREATE
     A CARNIVALESQUE
     SPIRIT; EMITTING A MIX
     OF COLOUR, FORM AND
     MOVEMENT.

02   BROADWICK HOUSE,
     LONDON. REFLECTING
     THE ACTIVITY OF ITS SITE,
     RECALL RECREATES LIFT
     MOVEMENT THROUGH
     KINETIC ARTWORK AND IS
     ILLUMINATED BY AMBER
     LIGHTING.

03   FOCUSING ON THE CRITI-
     CAL ISSUES OF CLIMATE
     CHANGE AND SUSTAINA-
     BILITY, WIND TO LIGHT VIS-
     UALIZES WIND MOVEMENT
     ACROSS THE BUILT FORM
     WITH THE USE OF MINI
     TURBINES AND LEDS. THE
     PROJECT WAS DESIGNED
     IN COLLABORATION WITH

THE BUILD-UP OF THE
FAÇADE IS COMPROMISED
OF GLASS DIAMONDS IN
FRONT OF THE LATTIC
STEEL WORK FRAME,
ALLOWING A VISUAL MIX
BETWEEN THE REFLECTI-
ONS OF THE ACTIVITY ON
BAKER STREET AND THE
GENERATED ART.

55 Baker Street London, UK

CLIENT
LONDON AND REGIONAL

ARCHITECT
MAKE ARCHITECTS

LIGHTING DESIGN
JASON BRUGES STUDIO

MANUFACTURER
MIKE SLOANE LIGHTING

LIGHT SOURCES
NARROW-BEAM LED
SPOTLIGHTS WITH CUS-
TOM OPTICS

COMPLETION DATE
NOVEMBER 2007

Three glass 'masks' span the voids between the existing blocks at 55 Baker Street in London – a 1950s office building. A new façade is thus created for the structure, which encloses a seven-storey atrium. Redeveloped and transformed by Make Architects, the project required a large-scale integrated public artwork that would create a unique and valuable contribution to both the Baker Street site and the local area in general. The Jason Bruges Studio's brief was to re-engage Michael House - the current name for number 55 - with the rest of Baker Street. The response to this brief would serve as a leading example of how public art can enhance an environment and change perceptions. Jason Bruges Studio developed an integrated proposal, considerate of the existing building's scale as well as the progressive and refined façade. Opting for an animated piece of art that would provide a visual prominence and encourage the public to enter the atrium spaces, Jason Bruges Studio worked closely with the main architectural design team and associated specialists. The lengthy design and development process resulted in the proposal of a bespoke project, tailored to complement the unique and site-specific architectural conditions.

From its central location on the main atrium, the artwork influences the two side masks and is designed to create a fluid and radiant continuity along the site. By working closely with the lead lighting designer for the redevelopment, Jason Bruges Studio was confident that the design would work well in cohesion with the project's other lighting schemes to create a fully integrated system. Fixed in front of the façade and made from a series of glass diamonds positioned on a steel lattice-work frame, the artwork is designed to reflect the activity on Baker Street alongside generated art to create a visual hybrid.

The concept of the mask as a representation of mood was the genesis of this piece. The art therefore needed to replay colour, movement and moods across the architectural skin. Iridescence - an optical phenomenon characterized by changes in surface hue according to the viewing angle – remains the designers' source of inspiration for the project. Working with the physical structure of these 'street masks', and taking into account the trajectories of pedestrians and motorists, Jason Bruges Studio were able to tune the artwork to the exact space and viewing requirements.

Due to frequent pedestrian and motor traffic, the proximity of neighbours and the building's current usage as offices, a crucial element in the development of the site was to ensure that light would remain 'captured' within the façade. It was necessary to avoid the creation of excessive light-spill or glare. This problem was overcome by utilizing high-quality, controllable light sources with tight beam angles to produce a wash of light across the façade without causing disturbance or distraction to people in the surrounding environment. To render the scheme accessible to as many people as possible, the trio of masks are illuminated. Particular emphasis is placed on the illumination of the central mask through which the public access the large atrium space. In addition to the distant views along Baker Street, significant consideration was likewise given to the more intimate scale of the viewer who is in close proximity to the façade. The proposal therefore aimed to offer equally impressive views from both sides of the façade.

The lighting of the main façade and that of the canopy are designed to function together as a method to entice members of the public to enter the newly created public atrium space. Developed with the aid of leading technical suppliers and manufacturers, the highly innovative proposal seeks to deliver a fully controllable lighting system for the otherwise steel structure of the façade.

The meticulously controlled artwork creates a variety of effects and offers a flexibility that had previously been all but impossible to achieve.

COLOUR SCHEME EXPERI-
MENT TO CREATE VARIOUS
MOODS.

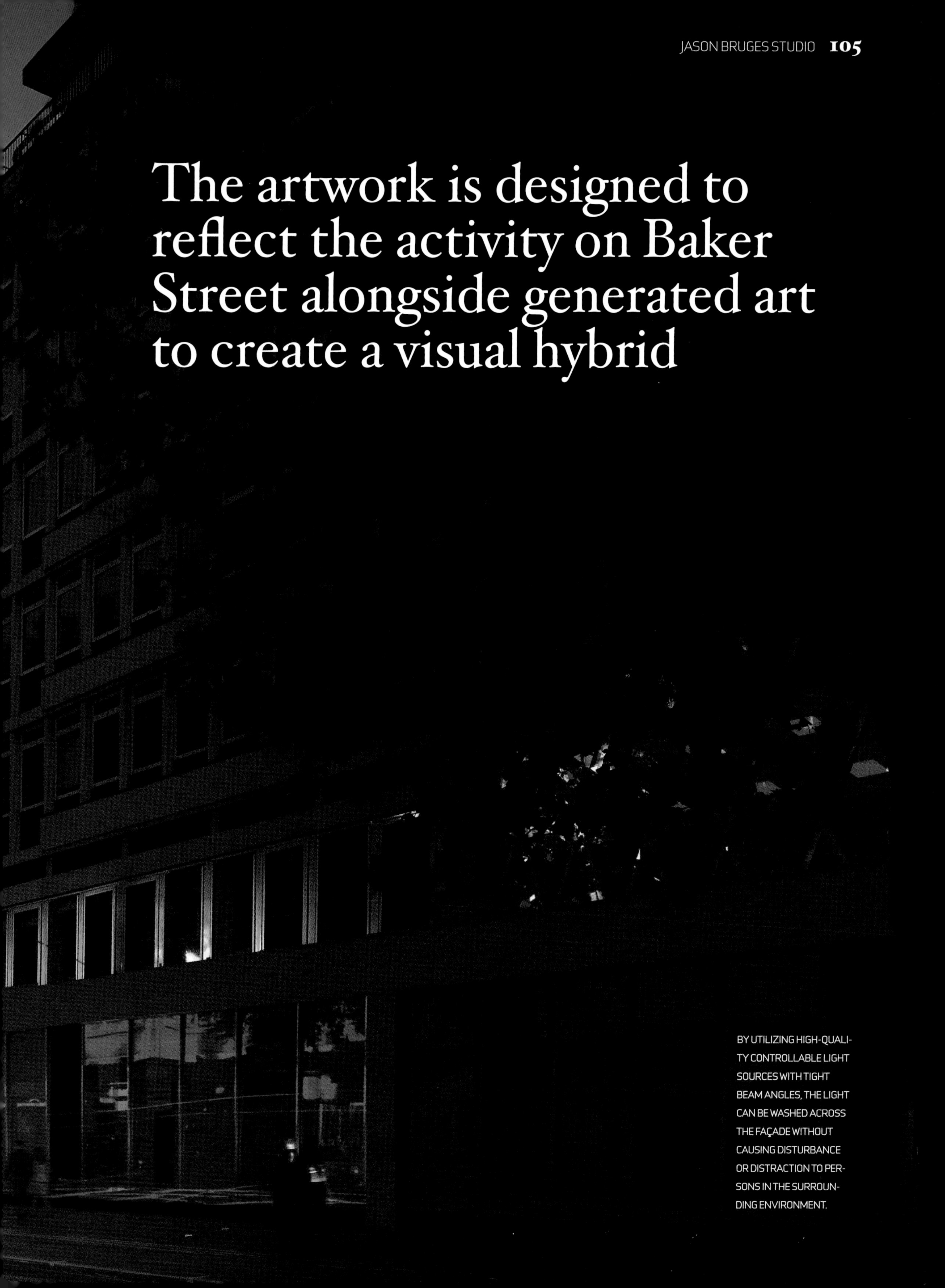

The artwork is designed to reflect the activity on Baker Street alongside generated art to create a visual hybrid

BY UTILIZING HIGH-QUALI-
TY CONTROLLABLE LIGHT
SOURCES WITH TIGHT
BEAM ANGLES, THE LIGHT
CAN BE WASHED ACROSS
THE FAÇADE WITHOUT
CAUSING DISTURBANCE
OR DISTRACTION TO PER-
SONS IN THE SURROUN-
DING ENVIRONMENT.

ARUP LIGHTING

Staff: 40 (Lighting Group), 9000 worldwide
Global leader: Rogier van der Heide
Key designers: Florence Lam, Rogier van der Heide, Brian Stacy, Jason Edling, Arfon Davies, Jeff Shaw
Founded: 1946
Operates: Worldwide

AWARDS

British Lighting Design Award: Commended, 2007
IALD Sustainability Award, 2006
International Lighting Design Award of Excellence, 2006
International Lighting Design Award of Excellence, 2005
IALD Radiance Award, 2005
IESNA Award of Merit, 2003
Edison Award of Excellence, 2002
Lighting Designer of the Year, 1999

PROFILE

Arup Lighting combines robust engineering skills, broad experience and award-winning creativity, flair and innovation. To provide a comprehensive architectural and natural lighting design service, Arup Lighting works closely with architects through all stages of a project. In fact, Arup Lighting considers light to be the fourth dimension of architecture; an element to give both visual comfort and quality. Incidental use of colour and a sense of theatrics enable Arup Lighting to extend the role of both natural and electric light beyond the typical boundaries of the lighting profession. Receiving the 2005 IALD Radiance Award has ranked Arup Lighting amongst the top creative lighting design firms in the world.

01

02

03

01   ARUP LIGHTING'S INNO-
02   VATIVE LIGHTING DESIGN
03   FOR AMSTERDAM'S NEW
       LIBRARY TOOK ADVAN-
       TAGE OF FLUORESCENT
       AND LED TECHNOLOGY,
       TO PROVIDE AN EFFICIENT
       SOLUTION WITH A POWER
       CONSUMPTION OF LESS
       THAN 12W PER M2.

THE PROJECT CONSISTS
OUT OF 275 TRANSLU-
CENT, 7-M-LONG, FIBER
GLASS TUBES WITH A
DIAMETER OF 15 CM.

The World's Largest Timepiece Zurich, Switzerland

CLIENT

JOINT VENTURE XMAS

ARCHITECTS

GRAMAZIO & KOHLER

LIGHTING DESIGN

ARUP LIGHTING,

GRAMAZIO & KOHLER

STRUCTURAL ENGINEER

ARUP

COMPLETION DATE

NOVEMBER 2005

PHOTOGRAPHERS

MICHAEL VAN OOSTEN

WWW.MICHAELVANOOST-
EN.NL

ROMAN KELLER

VZB

Zurich's Bahnhofstrasse, like London's Regent Street and New York City's Fifth Avenue, is famous for its elegant atmosphere; not least because of its holiday decor. In 1971, the city showcased its then revolutionary Christmas lighting - garlands of incandescent lamps suspended above the shopping route. After three decades of service, the cabling and fixtures of Willi Walter and Charlotte Schmid's creation (which included 215 light curtains, 20,640 lamps, and twelve 8-ft garlands consisting of 8 lamps each) was in need of repair, and a new scheme was required. Local shop owners organized and judged a design contest, inviting designers to create the new look. In addition they worked together to fund most of the US$1.85 million installation. 60 competition submissions were received from all over the world. Assisted by a board of non-voting experts including architectural and building professors, city planners and engineers, the Zurich Bahnofstrasse Association commissioned 11 teams to develop their proposals. Zurich-based architects Fabio Gramazio and Matthias Kohler realized the winning plan, which was inaugurated in Winter 2006. Beyond its decorative appeal, the winning design emphasizes the legendary street. A festive string of 275 light tubes winds its way from the train station to the shore of Lake Zurich. The installation's seasonal title - The World's Largest Timepiece - refers to the method controlling the patterns of light that flit along the 1-km stretch. Each 7-m-tall fibreglass tube is divided into 32 individually controllable segments illuminated with 28 white LEDs. The sections act like pixels, dimmed and brightened according to an algorithm determined by date and time. These sequences are transposed into 'shade' and 'shine', with patterns forming horizontal images that weave the tubes into one entity; a unified curtain of light which is both static and in motion. The beauty of the scheme is that it dares to be dark; the segmented tubes are simultaneously luminous and obscured as they convey their message of dynamic time and place interplay.

For this highly collaborative project, Arup Lighting was asked to oversee the project's lighting and engineering elements - a task which was not without its challenges. Suspended in a single row, directly above the existing tramlines, Arup Lighting had to create a stable yet supportive structure for the floating lighting sections, each weighing 30 kg. This structure underwent a lengthy installation process which had to take place during the few hours when the tram lines close. However, testament to a methodical approach, once Arup Lighting's energy efficient lighting system was successfully installed, it reduced the power consumption by 75 % over the previous display, without compromising Gramazio and Kohler's artistic vision. By extending the life of the structure to at least 25 years – each LED has a life expectancy in excess of 50,000 hours – theoretically, the fixtures will not have to be changed before 2030! The use of a glass fibre shell was also an intuitive decision by Arup Lighting, allowing the light to be evenly distributed along the entire tube within individual fibres. The highlights created by this choice of material added a sparkling effect to the texture.

Continuing their unique approach to festive lighting, instead of a predictable Christmas accompaniment, motion picture director Marc Schwarz synchronized music composed by Boris Blank – a member of popular Swiss electronica band Yello – with the lighting's animation.

Proud to play a part in such a bespoke lighting design, Florence Lam who headed the project says 'The Arup Lighting team is excited to see this project come to fruition. We have helped to form a new seasonal celebration for Zurich; something memorable and exciting for Christmases to come'. Let's just hope this 'timepiece' doesn't throw Santa off track!

EACH TUBE CONTAINS 32
LIGHT FIXTURES OF 28 LED
LIGHT SOURCES EACH.
THESE ARE CONTROLLA-
BLE TO CREATE DYNAMIC
LIGHT PROJECTIONS
ON THE SURFACE OF
THE TUBE. IN TOTAL,
THE PROJECT INCLUDES
NEARLY 4 MILLION LIGHT
EMITTING DIODES.

THE WORLD'S LARGEST TIMEPIECE CONTAINS SOFTWARE THAT SLOWLY CONTROLS THE BRIGHTNESS OF THE TUBES. PATTERN OF WAVES AND FLOWS ARE PROJECTED ALONG THE ENTIRE SERIES OF TUBES, THAT WAY CREATING AN IMAGE OF 1.1 KM LONG.

The beauty of the scheme is that it dares to be dark; the segmented tubes are simultaneously luminous and obscured

COMPARED TO THE PREVIOUS, TRADITIONAL CHRISTMAS LIGHTING OF THIS UPSCALE SHOPPING STREET, THE POWER CONSUMPTION IS APPROXIMATELY SIX TIMES LESS.

SEEDFACTORY
19, AVENUE DES VOLONTAIRES
1160 BRUSSELS
BELGIUM

T +32 2 453 0977
F +32 2 453 2851
info@act-design.com
www.act-design.com

ACT
Architectural Lighting Design

ACT-ARCHITECTURAL LIGHTING DESIGN

Staff: 8
Management: Koert Vermeulen, Bruno Demeester
Key designers: Koert Vermeulen, Bruno Demeester, Thomas Boets, Christophe Thomas, Andrea Mantello, Guillaume Escallier, Céline Deceuninck
Founded: 1995
Operates: Worldwide
Memberships: PLDA, IALD, ALD, TEA

KEY PROJECTS

Les Terrasses, Marseille/France, 2006 - 2009
Stargate Dubai, Dubai/UAE, 2006 - 2007
Espace Bethune, Lille/France, 2005 - 2007
Sainte-Waudru, Mons/Belgium, 2004 - 2006
Town Centre Ypenburg, Ypenburg/Netherlands, 2000 - 2006
Le Rêve, Wynn Hotel & Casino, Las Vegas/USA, 2005
De Klanderij, Enschede/Netherlands, 2005

Brel, le droit de rêver, Brussels/Belgium, 2003
Is dit Belgisch - C'est du Belge?, Place Poelaert, Brussels/ Belgium, 2003
Jeumont, Jeumont/France, 2002 and 2003

PROFILE

Independent lighting designers Koert Vermeulen and Bruno Demeester have worked together as ACT Lighting Design since 1995. Their aim is to combine a creative and sensitive approach to light with an understanding of its complex technical requirements. Filling the gap between professionals who use light as an expressive tool (stage lighting, photography) and those who integrate lighting technology into the built environment (building services), ACT brings together stage-lighting techniques (dynamic lighting, colour) and high-quality architectural lighting equipment (durability, glare control) to create schemes that reveal, modify and/or enhance the everyday environment.

01

01 URBAN AND ARCHITEC-
TURAL LIGHTING FOR
THE CITY CENTRE OF
YPENBURG IN THE NETH-
ERLANDS. FULL EXTERIOR
AND URBAN LIGHTING
DESIGN.

02 EXTERIOR ARCHITEC-
TURAL LIGHTING DESIGN
COMPETITION FOR THE
SPORT CITY TOWER OF
DOHA.

03 ARCHITECTURAL LIGHT-
ING DESIGN INTERIOR AND
FAÇADES OF A 43,000 M2
COMMERCIAL CENTRE IN
MONS IN BELGIUM, AND
THE 18HA OF EXTERIOR
URBAN PLANNING.

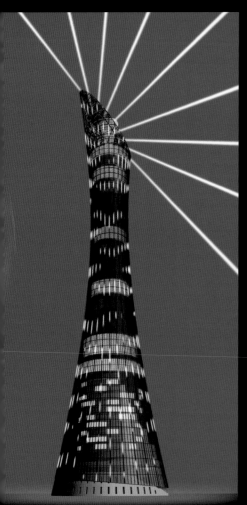

02   03

ATTACHED TO ACT'S TUBU-
LAR-STEEL KABOUTERS
WERE 20 LED TUBES, EACH
CONSISTING OF 12 RGB
PIXELS, AND A PIXELATED
LIGHT ANIMATION.

Opera de Lyon/Fête des Lumières Lyon, France

CLIENT

FÊTE DES LUMIÈRES

ARTIST

IN-SENSO

CHOREOGRAPHY

ENGINEER

PROCON

LIGHT SOURCES

LED TUBES, ETC PROFILE

X 12

DURATION OF

CONSTRUCTION

3 DAYS

COMPLETION DATE

DECEMBER 2006

PHOTOGRAPHERS

KOERT VERMEULEN

WWW.ACT-DESIGN.COM

ANDRÉS OTERO

ANDRESOTERO@

BLUEWIN.COM

Originating in 1852, when the people of Lyon refused to let a period of bad weather hinder plans for observing the addition of a new piece of sculpture to the city, Lyon's Fête des Lumières – an event that began with residents illuminating their homes and hosting official parties – marks the celebration of light and its potential for using architecture as a vehicle to stimulate social engagement. Over a century later, the festival has moved to a new level; running for four days in all districts of Lyon and calling for contributions from well-known artists, as well as from local initiators, the event is gradually gaining an international reputation. Selected from Lyon's Europe-wide competition to design a lighting installation, lighting and production company ACT Design was asked to realize its proposal for the 2006 festival. Koert Vermeulen of ACT explains how the nature of the project – free from the restraints of a brief – was dictated by the site, the Place Louis Pradel, address of the city's famous Opera House and City Hall. 'The square is very difficult,' he says. 'It's rather long, with no real sense of direction, and three major axes of pedestrian traffic meet at this point and flow through the square. Also, one side is about 3 m higher than the other, a discrepancy that suggested we do something in the air.'

Keen to use the Lyon Opera without compromising the aesthetics of the listed building, which is rapidly deteriorating despite renovation work completed ten years ago, Vermeulen created an undamaging installation. The sceneography, composed of three parts, united the building and its surroundings in an extravaganza of light, sound and space.

Electronic trees called Kabouters – five custom-made totems designed specifically for the festival – were dispersed throughout the space. Attached to ACT's tubular-steel Kabouters were 20 LED tubes, each consisting of 12 RGB pixels, and a pixelated light animation that was programmed to a 45-minute piece of music created for the project by Rami Khalifé. Sometimes sober, sometimes overwhelming, the dynamic lighting created a pixelated view of a digital world in which Vermeulen describes everything as becoming 'a pixel or a coordinate'. Covered with the same LED tube system, the façade of the Opera de Lyon was transformed into a field of 'light lines' similar to those on a low-resolution screen. Each of the 11 windows on the façade was equipped with 22 LED tubes. The visual rendition of the LED system was not composed of video images but programmed specifically as light sources, thus making full use of the saturation and composition of the colours. In addition to providing a solution sympathetic to the aged building, the system also cut down on the technological mess caused by big snarls of cable. Thanks to low-consumption LEDs and the digital control of fixtures, only three cables were needed to supply electricity to the installation: two power cables and one data cable.

To add an extra dimension to the scene, and in collaboration with Paris dance company In-SENSO, who specialize in dance voltige (vertical dance), Vermeulen and choreographer Odile Gheysens came up with a performance based on the interaction of dancers and light. Like moths to a flame, aerial dancers were drawn to the lights, working in pairs and alone to animate and occupy the illuminated space. 'We introduced human intervention,' says Vermeulen, 'to counterbalance all the technological violence.' Vermeulen's piece is an experimental project that transcends traditional lighting formats, such as big-format projection and big CMY colour changers, and borders on pixel art. Constructed from IP-rated LEDs, which are suitable for outdoor use, his was a relatively simple and inexpensive project. Using the least amount of power of all the festival's grade-A sites, it had an overall power consumption equal to one large-format projector – or 85 to 90 per cent less than most of the other projects. 'I like to take responsibility for my environment,' says Vermeulen.

THE FAÇADE WAS TRANS-
FORMED INTO A FIELD OF
'LIGHT LINES': 2 LED TUBES
PER WINDOW BLADE, 11
WINDOW BLADES AND 11
WINDOWS IN TOTAL.

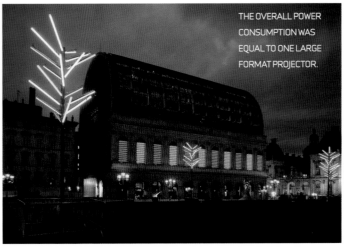

THE OVERALL POWER CONSUMPTION WAS EQUAL TO ONE LARGE FORMAT PROJECTOR.

THE TECHNICAL LAY-OUT OF THE 'KABOUTER'.

1.90m

5.08m

1.88m

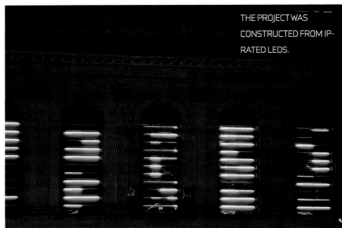

THE PROJECT WAS CONSTRUCTED FROM IP-RATED LEDS.

'We introduced human intervention to counterbalance all the technological violence' Koert Vermeulen

LIKE MOTHS TO A FLAME,
AERIAL DANCERS WERE
DRAWN TO THE LIGHTS,
WORKING IN PAIRS AND
ALONE TO ANIMATE AND
OCCUPY THE ILLUMINATED
SPACE.

T +1 212 947 6282
F +1 212 947 6289
admin@lightprojectsltd.com
www.lightprojectsltd.com

336 West 37th Street,
Studio 1410
New York, NY 10018 USA

LENI SCHWENDINGER
LIGHT PROJECTS

MARTIN

www.martin-architectural.com

info@martin.dk

+45 8740 0010

PROFESSIONAL

Olof Palmes Allé 18
8200 Aarhus
Denmark

MARTIN PROFESSIONAL

Staff: 1100
Management: Christian Engsted
Founded: 1987
Operates: Worldwide
Memberships: ALD, ELDA, ESTA, IALD, IESNA

KEY PROJECTS

Grand Mosque, Abu Dhabi/UAE, 2007
Branson Landing, Missouri/USA, 2006
Spinnaker Tower, Portsmouth/UK, 2006
Morongo Casino Resort & Spa, California/USA, 2005
Sony Center, Berlin/Germany, 2004
Post Tower, Bonn/Germany, 2004
HSBC, Hong Kong/China, 2004

PROFILE

Headquartered in Aarhus, Denmark, operates an extensive network of subsidiaries and distributors around the globe. Providing
exterior and interior colour-changing luminaires suitable for a
wide range of applications, Martin offers clients a product range
that is both functional and aesthetically pleasing.

LENI SCHWENDINGER LIGHT PROJECTS

Staff: 6
Management: Walter Ramin
Founded: 1992
Operates: Worldwide
Memberships: IALD, IESNA, WTS, CAUS

KEY PROJECTS

St. Louis Gateway Mall Masterplan, St. Louis/USA, 2007
HTO Park, Toronto/Canada, 2007
Hoboken Ferry Terminal, New York/USA, 2007
The Shops at Atlas Park, New York/USA, 2006
Marion O. McCaw Hall, Seattle/USA, 2003

PROFILE

Energizing sites with the ultimate objective of connecting people
to one another and to their surroundings, Leni Schwendinger
Light Projects works for both public and private clients to create
environments for architectural and public spaces all over the
world.

01

02

03

01 WORKING WITH MARTIN
02 ARCHITECTURAL, LENI
03 SCHWENDINGER LIGHT
PROJECTS TRANSFORMED
OVERLOOKED AREAS OF
THE KINGSTON BRIDGE
IN GLASGOW INTO
FUNCTIONAL DISPLAYS
THAT CONVEY DETAILS
ABOUT TRAFFIC AND TIDES
THROUGH A RIGOROUS
PALETTE OF COLOURED
LIGHT.

MOUNTED ON THE
CANOPY AND ITS SUP-
PORTING STRUCTURE
ARE LED FIXTURES, EACH
OF WHICH FEATURES A
CALIBRATED SET OF THREE
RED 1W DIODES.

Coney Island Parachute JumpNew York City, New York, USA

CLIENT

NYC ECONOMIC DEVELOP-

MENT CORPORATION

LIGHTING DESIGNER

LENI SCHWENDINGER

LIGHT PROJECTS

CONSULTANT

RON FOGEL AND

ASSOCIATES

PROGRAMMER

PAUL HUDSON

ENGINEER

STV

MANUFACTURERS

MARTIN PROFESSIONAL,

PHOSTER LIGHTING, ETC

LIGHT SOURCES

CUSTOM LED FIXTURES,

MARTIN ARCHITECTURAL

EXTERIOR 600 FLOOD-

LIGHTS

TOTAL SURFACE

80-M-HIGH

TOTAL COST

US$ 1.6 MILLION

COMPLETION DATE

2006

PHOTOGRAPHERS

ARCH PHOTO

WWW.ARCHPHOTO.COM

GLASGOW CITY COUNCIL

WWW.GLASGOW.GOV.UK

Declared an official landmark by New York City Landmark Preservation Commission in 1998, Coney Island's world-renowned Parachute Jump – constructed for the 1939 New York World's Fair as an amusement ride – has been transformed into a beacon of light. The same skies that had rendered the attraction virtually invisible for 37 years are now illuminated with a spectrum of colour.

Following the structural refurbishment of the 80-m-high tower in 2000, artist Leni Schwendinger and her firm, Light Projects, were asked to revitalize the structure. The idea was to create a lighting scheme that would reconcile Coney's garish boardwalk environment with the contrastingly engineered, modern steel icons that characterize the renovation of the nearby Stillwell Avenue subway station. Schwendinger envisioned a visual echo of the tower's vintage colours during the evening and night-time hours. In an attempt to convey the carnivalesque Coney Island spirit, Schwendinger developed choreographed lighting sequences meant to imply motion – to express the rise and fall of parachutes floating above the boardwalk. Establishing the objectives of a stakeholders' group that included the New York City Department of Parks and Recreation (owner of Coney Island), the Brooklyn Borough President's Office (funder) and the New York City Economic Development Corporation (coordinating agency) allowed the real design process to begin.

A collaborative decision to have the illumination serve as an internationally recognized beacon for the rejuvenated Coney Island drew inspiration from other illuminated icons, such as the recently relit Eiffel Tower and the Empire State Building, whose shifting colours mark public celebrations and special occasions, dividing urban day from night. Schwendinger envisioned a meeting of the popular and the mysterious – emanating from the openwork figure of the mushroom-shaped form. Uplights illuminate the attraction in four sections – lower, mid, high and tower canopy – to emphasize the sense of climbing and falling. The tower is equipped with Martin Architectural's Exterior 600 floodlights and a Martin internally automated colour-changing device for fluid sequencing.

To satisfy the client's request for an icon visible from multiple vantage points, including the Verrazano Bridge, Schwendinger and her team came up with an innovative solution. Mounted at regular intervals on the canopy and its supporting structure and aimed in several directions are LED fixtures (Phoster Industries), each of which features a calibrated set of three red 1W diodes. Programmed to produce six discrete scenarios, the lights mark notable days of the year – the start of the boardwalk season, full moon, holidays and so forth – with visual 'chimes' that announce the hour, on the hour. During Coney Island's boardwalk season, the lights reflect the atmosphere of the boardwalk with prominent reds, ambers and pinks – a fusion of colour that sparks memories of the historic Coney Island fires. At 8 p.m. on weekends, an hourly visual chime added to the weekday sequence features a fantastic canopy of LEDs and bright white pulses of light. Each hour is marked with a unique pattern of white light. An off-season display illuminates the structure with slowly undulating white, pale blue and cyan lights that reflect off the waves of the ocean. National and patriotic holidays are celebrated with a 72-hour wax-and-wane cycle, normally used on full-moon evenings, configured in red, white and blue and augmented by a red LED canopy chase.

Considerate of the environment, Schwendinger's light installation is programmed to start 30 minutes before sunset and to stop at midnight, except during autumn, winter and the migratory season for birds, when the lights are programmed to turn off at 11 p.m. as part of a 'Lights Out New York' initiative to save the lives of birds. Transforming the filigreed steel framework into a shimmering omni-directional icon for Coney Island and all of Brooklyn, the project represents Schwendinger's ability to interpret iconic urban-vernacular structures through light, time and movement.

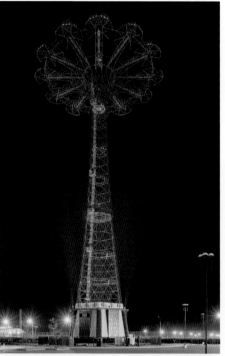

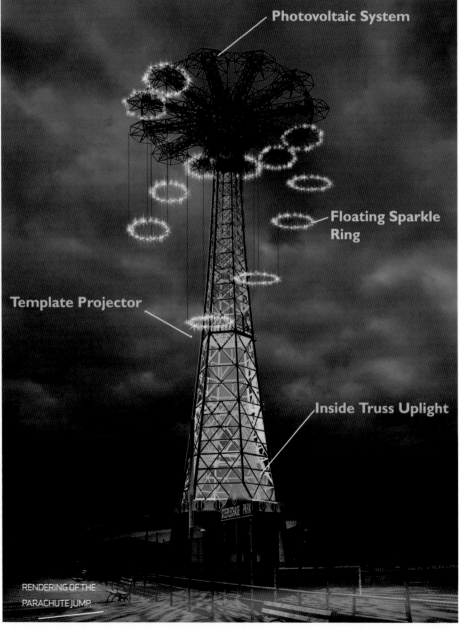

Photovoltaic System

Floating Sparkle Ring

Template Projector

Inside Truss Uplight

RENDERING OF THE
PARACHUTE JUMP

DESCRIPTION OF LIGHTING SCENARIOS

1. **OFF SEASON/TIDE CYCLES:** SLOWLY UNDULATING WHITE, PALE BLUE AND CYAN LIGHTS (NOT LEDS) REFLECT OFF THE WAVES OF THE OCEAN.

2. **IN SEASON/WEEKDAYS:** DURING CONEY ISLAND'S BOARDWALK SEASON, THE HOT SUMMER ATMOS-PHERE IS EXPRESSED THROUGH RED, AMBER AND PINK LIGHTS IN DISPLAYS THAT SPARK MEMORIES OF THE HISTORIC CONEY ISLAND FIRES.

3. **IN SEASON/WEEKENDS:** AN HOURLY VISUAL CHIME IS ADDED TO THE CONEY ISLAND BOARDWALK SEASON WEEKDAY SEQUENCE. FEATURED ARE A FANTASTIC LED CANOPY CHASE AND BRIGHT WHITE PULSES OF LIGHT. CHIMES START AT 8 P.M., AND EACH HOUR IS MARKED WITH A UNIQUE PATTERN OF WHITE LIGHT.

4. **FULL MOON/MONTHLY:** A 72-HOUR WAX-AND-WANE CYCLE BRIGHTLY MARKED WITH OPALESCENT WHITE

LIGHTS (NOT LEDS) CELEBRATES THE FULL MOON.

5. **AMERICANA:** ON NATIONAL AND PATRIOTIC HOLIDAYS DESIGNATED BY THE OWNERS, A LIGHTING SCENARIO COMPRISED OF RED, WHITE AND BLUE IS AUGMENTED BY A RED LED CANOPY CHASE.

6. **KALEIDOSCOPE:** A VIBRANT, STACCATO VISUAL DIS-PLAY ATTRACTS VISITORS ON HOLIDAYS AND SPECIAL OCCASIONS DESIGNATED BY THE OWNERS.

Leni Schwendinger envisioned a meeting of the popular and the mysterious

THE TOWER IS EQUIPPED
WITH MARTIN ARCHI-
TECTURAL'S EXTERIOR
600 FLOODLIGHTS AND
A MARTIN INTERNALLY
AUTOMATED COLOUR-
CHANGING DEVICE FOR
FLUID SEQUENCING.

REALITIES:UNITED

GLÜCKENSTEINSTRASSE 47-48 10997 BERLIN GERMANY

REALITIES:UNITED

Staff: 7 - 12
Management: Jan Edler, Tim Edler
Founded: 2000
Operates: Worldwide
Membership: BDA

AWARDS

ADC Awards Germany, Silver, 2007
Agency of the year for communication in space by ADC, 2007
'Inspire!' award by German T-Com, 2005
ADC Awards Germany, Gold, 2004
Hans Schaefers Award for young architects by BDA, Berlin/Germany, 2004

KEY PROJECTS

MuseumX, Mönchengladbach/Germany, 2006
SPOTS Light and Media Installation, Berlin/Germany, 2005
BIX Communicative Display Skin for the Kunsthaus
Graz/Austria, 2003

KEY CLIENTS

Art Center College of Design
Coop Himmelb(l)au Architects
European Central Bank
Foundation Bauhaus Dessau
Government of Andalucia, Spain
HVB Immobilien
Kunsthaus Graz
Museum Abteiberg

PROFILE

In 2000, brothers Tim Edler and Jan Edler founded realities:united - a studio for art, architecture and technology. Realities:united develops and supports architectural solutions, often incorporating new media and information technologies. The company provides conceptual design work, planning and research. Typical clients include museums, other architectural firms and enterprises. Realities:united has made a focus of the outward communicative capacity of architecture. Another key issue for realities:united is the quality of the user experience inside spaces, which is essentially augmented and changed in function and appearance by the addition of layers carrying information, media content and communication.

01

02

03

04

01 THE BIX COMMUNICATIVE
DISPLAY SKIN WAS THE
PRECURSOR TO SPOTS. A
MATRIX OF 930 FLUORES-
CENT FORMS A UNIQUE
COMMUNICATIVE MEDIUM
FOR THE KUNSTHAUS
GRAZ, THE PROJECT
ALSO AIMS TO RETRIEVE
SOME OF THE ORIGINAL
ARCHITECTURAL DESIGN
INTENTIONS.

02 THIS TEMPORARY INSTAL-
LATION – AN OUTCOME
OF THE MERGING OF
BILLBOARD, URBAN
REVITALIZATION, AND ART
SCULPTURE – ACTED AS
SURROGATE AND SOCIAL
PLACE-HOLDER FOR THE
FAMOUS ABTEIBERG
MUSEUM X IN MÖNCHEN-
GLADBACH WHILE IT WAS
CLOSED FOR RENOVATION.

03 SPROUTING LIKE ARTISTI-
04 CALLY ENGINEERED
PALM TREES, CLUSTERS
OF 24-M-HIGH POWER
PLANTS REACH SKYWARD,
GENTLY SWAYING IN THE
WIND AND SENDING OUT
PULSATING LIGHT WAVES.
THE OVERALL EFFECT IS
ONE WHICH EMBODIES
THE CITY OF PASADENA'S
ONGOING TRANSFORMA-
TION PROCESS.

DETAIL OF THE SPOTS IN-
STALLATION SHOWING THE
DIFFERENT LAMP TYPES
WHICH ARE ARRANGED
IN GRAPHICAL PATTERNS
SHIFTED BY 30° AND THE
VARYING TRANSPARENCY
OF THE COLOURED GRAP-
HIC LAYER ABOVE.

SPOTS Berlin, Germany

CLIENT

HVB IMMOBILIEN

ARTIST

REALITIES:UNITED

STRUCTURAL FIRE
PROTECTION

HPP BRAUNSCHWEIG

SOFTWARE
DEVELOPMENT

JOHN DEKRON, JEREMY
ROTSZTAIN

ELECTRICAL ENGINEER

BFI ANSORG + HORN

MANUFACTURER

SE LIGHTMANAGEMENT

LIGHT SOURCES

FLUORESCENT LIGHT
TUBES (1014 RING-
SHAPED AND 1520 BAR-
SHAPED)

TOTAL SURFACE

1,350 M²

DURATION OF
CONSTRUCTION

8 WEEKS

HOSTING OF
INSTALLATION

NOVEMBER 2005 -
MARCH 2007

PHOTOGRAPHERS

BERND HIEPE

HIEPE.B@T-ONLINE.DE

HARRY SCHIFFER

WWW.PHOTODESIGN.AT

NATALIE CZECH

WWW.NATALIECZECH.DE

REALITIES:UNITED

WWW.REALU.DE

From November 2005 until March 2007, the eleven-storey main façade of a building at Berlin's Potsdamer Platz in Berlin hosted the temporary light and media art installation SPOTS.

SPOTS comprised a light matrix of 1,774 ordinary fluorescent lamps that were integrated into the ventilated glass façade of the office building. A central computer controlled all the lamps individually; adjusting their brightness 20 times per second. As a result, graphics and animation sequences could be recreated on the façade as moving luminous images. The external shell of the building was transformed into a communicative membrane, which has been primarily used for displaying artistic material. Organized in curated exhibitions, international artists like Terry Gilliam, Carsten Nicolai, Jim Campbell or Rafael Lozano-Hemmer were commissioned to produce pieces, each to be screened for a period of four weeks. The works ranged from video productions to reactive or even interactive productions.

The motivation behind the SPOTS project is abstract: no specific message was to be broadcast to the surroundings; instead, a landmark was to be developed by fine-tuning the pre-existing, rather inconspicuous building complex on Potsdamer Platz. The long-term image of the real estate complex within its urban context was to be boosted through temporary artistic intervention. The brief indicated that this should not be achieved by revising the building or its structural elements per se, but rather by enhancing its perception within the surrounding public space.

Thus, the objective was to involve the building more actively to formulate meaningful urban spaces. The bilateral function of architecture, and especially of the façade, was to be strengthened to this end – as something that serves both inside and outside, and that creates a direct communication while also mediating between the various opposing requirements of the two sides. 'Communication' in this context is a metaphor for the interaction between the owners' proprietary interest in manifesting and expressing themselves, and the public's interest in a functional open space. This communication has to work both directly - through artistic light signs, and indirectly in the long term - through the building's evident efforts to actively enhance the larger urban landscape rather than exploiting it.

SPOTS was to be another element in a series of works researching the connections between architecture and visual media. What this canon of projects have in common is an attempt to explore the emerging phenomenon of superimposition from an architectural point of view – even if there is still no general consensus to date as to whether media surfaces on buildings should even be regarded as architecture.

The concept behind the SPOTS installation seeks involvement with the building's façade at a technical, functional and aesthetic level. The effects of the installation are developed not as a substitute, but as a complement to the façade's overall communication/mediation function. New communication levels – both static and dynamic – are added to the existing architecture by means of new constructional layers.

SPOTS was not designed to be a neutral carrier medium on which content is displayed. It is just as much a medium as it is a separate object whose structures influence the media content displayed on it. This character is created by 5 principal design techniques: 1) different types of lamps are arranged to form large graphic patterns, 2) a large, coloured graphic layer with varyingly transparent sections has been introduced, 3) the irregular outline of the illuminated field is divided over two separate screens, 4) the array of individual lamps is tilted to 30°, and finally 5) the lamps are kept as autonomous, individual objects.

Among the display's most striking attributes are the grainy resolution, the abandonment of colour, and its enormous overall size. Apart from economic considerations (energy efficiency of fluorescent lamps), the age-resistant, robust aesthetics of this older technology were deciding factors in choosing this solution. As in the BIX project (Graz 2003), the contrast between old-fashioned, individual components and the avant-garde appearance of the overall system was intentionally included as part of the design.

Besides the physical design, a great deal of importance was attached to the conception of specialized software tools for both the production of appropriate content as well as for the technical operation of the installation. In order to test their individual productions, artists were provided with real-time, 3D simulator software and additional assistants.

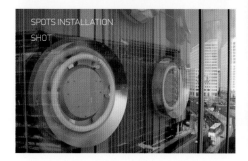

SPOTS INSTALLATION
SHOT

GRAPHICS AND ANIMA-
TION SEQUENCES COULD
BE RECREATED ON THE
FAÇADE AS MOVING LUMI-
NOUS IMAGES.

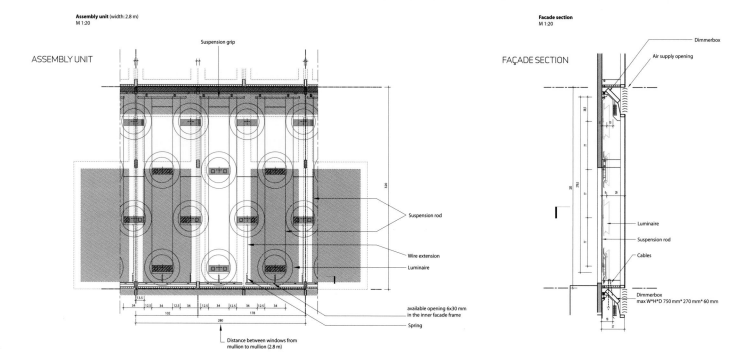

Assembly unit (width: 2.8 m)
M 1:20

ASSEMBLY UNIT

Suspension grip

Suspension rod

Wire extension

Luminaire

available opening 6x30 mm
in the inner facade frame

Spring

Distance between windows from
mullion to mullion (2.8 m)

Facade section
M 1:20

FAÇADE SECTION

Dimmerbox

Air supply opening

Luminaire

Suspension rod

Cables

Dimmerbox
max W*H*D 750 mm* 270 mm* 60 mm

SPOTS COMPRISED A LIGHT MATRIX OF 1,774 ORDINARY FLUORESCENT LAMPS THAT WERE INTEGRATED INTO THE VENTILATED GLASS FAÇADE OF AN OFFICE BUILDING AT BERLIN'S POTSDAMER PLATZ.

SPOTS FEATURING
MEXICAN-CANADIAN
ARTIST RAFAEL LOZANO-
HEMMER'S INTERACTIVE
PIECE '33 QUESTIONS PER
MINUTE'

The effects of the installation are developed not as a substitute, but as a complement to the façade's overall communication/mediation function

Key designers: Ettore Sottsass, Jean Michel Wilmotte, Engel
Founded: 1950
Operates: Worldwide

iF Design Award, Product Design + iF Gold Award, 2007
iF Design Award, Product Design, 2007
Winner Interior Luminaires, The Lighting Design Awards, 2005
reddot Design Award, Product Design, 2005
iF Design Award, Product Design, 2005
reddot Design Award, Product Design, 2004
Good Design Award, 2004
Internationaler Designpreis Baden-Württemberg, Focus: Balance, 2003
Winner, The Lighting Design Awards, 2002
Best Retail Lighting, FX Award, IIDA, 2002
Best Office Lighting, FX Award, IIDA, 1999
And numerous more awards throughout the years.

Victoria Garden, Melbourne/Australia, 2003

PROFILE

Zumtobel lighting - founded more than 50 years ago - remains committed to providing high-quality lighting solution concepts, and innovative technologies that improve communications and safety whilst placing high importance on environmental responsibility. With 50 company-owned sales organizations and commercial agencies in a total of 70 countries, Zumtobel shows international presence at the customer's site. It is also positioned as a global partner in international project management with investors and building developers, architects, lighting designers, electrical consultants, electricians, wholesalers and international distribution partners.

01

02

01 AN INTEGRATED LIGHTING
SOLUTION BY ZUMTOBEL
FORMED AN INTEGRAL
PART OF THE DESIGN CON-
CEPT FOR MERANS' NEW
HOTEL AND SPA RESORT.

02 THE FALLS LEISURE AND
WELLNESS CENTRE, IN
BELFAST, TAKES THE
STAGE AS AN ARCHITEC-
TURAL LANDMARK. THE
GLASS-FRONTED BUILD-
ING WHICH ALLOWS DIF-
FUSE SUNLIGHT TO SHINE
INTO THE SWIMMING POOL
AREAS BY DAY, IS TRANS-
FORMED AT NIGHT INTO
A LUMINOUS, COLOUR-
GRADED FAÇADE.

03 A COLLABORATIVE
PROJECT WITH ARCHI-
TECTS FROM THE BM+P
STUDIO, ZUMTOBEL
DEVELOPED A FUNC-
TION-SPECIFIC LIGHTING
SOLUTION FOR THE AUDI
CUSTOMER CENTRE IN
NECKARSULM, GERMANY.
THE RESULT PROVIDES
TREND-SETTING ACCENTS
FOR THE DRAMATIC LIGHT-

BERLIN'S OLYMPIC
STADIUM IS HOME TO
BERLIN'S TOP FOOTBALL
TEAM, HERTHA.

Olympic Stadium Berlin, Germany

CLIENT

SENAT DER STADT BERLIN

ARCHITECT

VON GERKAN, MARG +
PARTNER

LIGHTING DESIGN

CONCEPTLICHT HELMUT
ANGERER + RAINER TEIFEL

MANUFACTURER

ZUMTOBEL LIGHTING

LIGHT SOURCES

SPECIAL PENDANT LUMI-
NAIRES, SPECIAL IP-54
LUMINAIRE, LIGHTING
MANAGEMENT SYSTEM

COMPLETION DATE

2004

PHOTOGRAPHER

FRIEDRICH BUSAM/
ZUMTOBEL
WWW.ZUMBTOBEL.COM

Berlin's Olympic Stadium is a modernized high-tech arena and home to Berlin's top football team, Hertha. In 2006, it hosted the Fifa World Cup Final having been re-developed in 2004. It is now illuminated by an innovative lighting scheme. The task of the planning team at the von Gerkan, Marg & Partner architects' studio in Hamburg and the general contractor, Walter Bau, was to adapt the Olympic Stadium - a listed building - as sensitively as possible. Considerations included the requirements of a modern event arena, off-set by the strict rules of a monument conservation order.

Despite undergoing extensive modifications, by individually sandblasting each of the building's old natural stones, 70% of the existing historical structure was retained. The new roof design – which thrusts out 68 m over the stadium arena – is a fundamental change to the structure's existing appearance. However, even this was determined by the former design. Instead of a closed ring, the roof was made into a keyhole shape, allowing the historic opening at the Marathon Gate to be preserved. The undisturbed view of the Maifeld and the Bell Tower, requested by the Monument Conservation Authority, was also left untouched. Due to these construction restraints, the seemingly floating roof, forming a luminescent halo above the main building, is supported by 20 filigree-steel columns standing in the upper ring. The inside of the roof is integrated with some of the most advanced lighting technology to date, including glare-free floodlights and an audio system with a performance of more than 150,000 W. Translucent membranes and the glass rim of the upper and lower roofing lend the construction the lightness of a great, hovering canopy. Zumtobel were responsible for the lighting of this new roof in addition to the platforms and interiors of the modernized Olympic Stadium.

Designed to coincide with the idea devised by lighting designer Helmut Angerer of Concept Licht Angerer based in Traunreit, a special lighting solution was defined in co-operation with the Berlin lighting designer Edgar Schlaefle.

4,200 luminaires installed on the roof girders illuminate the upper, closed roof membrane, reflecting the light downwards. These lighting units ensure optimal basic lighting for the platforms and brighten the roof in a uniform way. Wired via seven-pin, plug-and-socket connections, the luminaires can be installed without any tools and easily maintained from the mounting level on the lower membrane. Moreover, the special light-ribbon concept operates far more efficiently than the individual luminaire solution originally planned by the client and designer. The wreath of light at the outer edge of the roof shines up against the underside of

the concrete counterweight of the roof construction. Reflected light elevates the mighty building in the public eye, rendering it visibile from afar, and making it tower above its urban surroundings. This building is thus given both buoyancy and a sense of the sublime. Light is precisely directed by TOL 1/58W T26 DALI moisture-proof, batten luminaires with swivelling, highly specular TTC reflectors, which are perfectly resistant against environmental influences. Two rows of dimmable luminaires, arranged one above the other, on the inside edge of the stadium roof transform it into the so-called 'ring of fire'. This configuration affords extra-fast lighting sequences, which are then accentuated further by acoustic effects, for instance a La Ola wave at the Football World Cup Final.

The VIP areas are enhanced by especially sophisticated luminaires: low-voltage down-lights and special pendant luminaires in a slim-line design. The lighting of the newly designed VIP stand and the adjoining VIP zone is striking. It features back-lit luminous glass ceilings, discreet cove lighting, and elegant glass pendant luminaires.

Two underground car parks were also newly constructed with over 600 parking places for prominent visitors. Moisture-proof batten luminaires with over-tubing installed on mounted tracks provide pleasant, bright light that is easily repositioned and guides visitors around the space.

Sending out its first 'light signals' in winter 2003/04, the Berlin Olympic Stadium has been host to an array of sporting events since the end of 2004. The modernized arena lives up to its promise of being far more than just a sports arena.

THE NEW ROOF CONSTRUC-
TION THRUSTS OUT 68 M
OVER THE STADIUM ARENA,
FUNDAMENTALLY CHANG-
ING ITS APPEARANCE.

THE REFLECTED LIGHT
ELEVATES THE MIGHTY
BUILDING INTO VISIBILITY
FROM FAR ABOVE THE UR-
BAN SOURROUNDINGS.

4,200 LUMINAIRES INSTALLED ON THE ROOF GIRDERS ILLUMINATE THE UPPER, CLOSED ROOF MEMBRANCE, REFLECTING THE LIGHT DOWNWARDS.

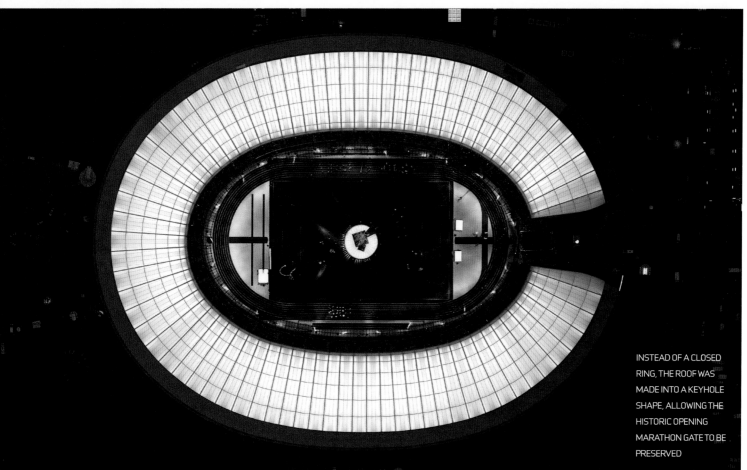

INSTEAD OF A CLOSED RING, THE ROOF WAS MADE INTO A KEYHOLE SHAPE, ALLOWING THE HISTORIC OPENING MARATHON GATE TO BE PRESERVED

DESPITE UNDERGOING
EXTENSIVE MODIFICATI-
ONS, 70% OF THE EXISTING
HISTORICAL STRUCTURE
WAS RETAINED.

The modernized arena lives up to its promise of being far more than just a sports arena

LED-ART
Staff: Project-based
Management: Paul Klotz
Founded: 2006
Operates: Worldwide

KEY PROJECTS
Concept design, MAF, Leeuwarden/Netherlands, 2007
Interactive light installation, Almelo/Netherlands, 2007
Hotel Mercure: Light plan & concept design, The Hague/
Netherlands, 2007
Streetgallery: Concept Design, Rotterdam/Netherlands,
2007
Generator: Interactive light installation, The Hague/Neth-
erlands, 2006
Foundation Kop: Interactive light installation, Breda/
Netherlands, 2006

Saxion University: Interactive installation, Enschede/Neth-
erlands, 2006

PROFILE
Founded by applied-art engineer and lighting designer Paul Klotz,
LED-Art creates light-based art installations designed to enrich
the consumer experience; both public and private. Specializing
in the manufacture of interactive, microcontroller-based installations, Klotz describes light as a variable that 'determines our state
of mind'. LED-Art combines interaction, art and architecture,
with the aim of creating a dialogue between the participant and
the installation. Visitor presence, environment and the desired
identity or emotion are elements used to steer the direction of
participants' experiences. The company strives to provide high
quality products and services for exterior and interior architecture.

02

01

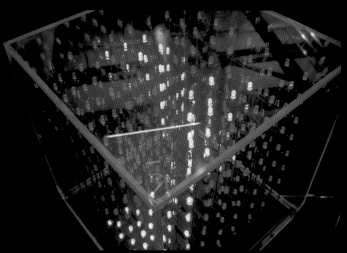

03

01 EQUIPPED WITH ITS OWN
IP AND MAC ADDRESS, IN-
TERACTIVE INSTALLATION
3D-MESSENGER DISPLAYS
MESSAGES POSTED ON A
WEBSITE, LETTER BY LET-
TER, IN ITS STRUCTURE.

02 CLIMATIC INSTALLATION
EL-37 (ECO-LINE 37) –
A 6-M-TALL MODULAR
THERMOMETER LOCATED
IN ALMELO – DISPLAYS
THE CITY'S TEMPERATURE
AND RESPONDS TO PASS-
ING TRAFFIC. THE PIECE
PROVIDES A VISUAL NAR-
RATIVE OF THE INFLUENCE
OF MANKIND.

03 FITTED WITH AN UL-
TRASONIC SENSOR TO
TRANSLATE THE DISTANCE
BETWEEN PEOPLE AND
ITS STRUCTURE INTO
LIGHT ANIMATIONS, LIGHT
INSTALLATION CUBLUE
RESEMBLES A STRAND
OF DNA RANDOMLY MU-
TATING AND CHANGING
DIRECTION.

EDD The Hague,
Netherlands

CLIENT
PROPOSAL FOR
GENERATOR
LIGHTING DESIGN
LED-ART
CONSULTANT
KITT ENGINEERING
VISUALIZATION
MILCHBAR
ENGINEER
LAGOTRONICS
MANUFACTURER
LAGOTRONICS
LIGHT SOURCES
DEKO-PANELS, DMXII
CONTROLLERS
TOTAL SURFACE
1200 M²

PHOTOGRAPHER
STEFAN VAN WEELE
WWW.STEFANVANWEELE.
NL

A proposal for Generator, LED-Art, headed by media artist Paul Klotz, used EDD – Embedded Data-texture Display – to offer a concept designed to transform the skin of a traditional building into a dynamic façade.

Initially developed for the Today's Art festival in The Hague, the proprietary concept was re-worked to fit the formulaic window structure and building frontage of The Hague's Hotel Mercure, situated in the city's central Spui Plaza. Prohibited from making alterations to the original architecture, Klotz was responsible for ensuring the project remained considerate to the building's primary function. The design therefore included considerations such as maintaining window transparency to allow hotel guests to see out. As an alternative to attaching external fixtures to the building, LED-Art decided to employ the use of LagoLED Deko panels. Providing a unique printed dot matrix, distributing light to the surface of a side-lit acrylic panel, the Deko panels were fitted with LagoLED RGB strips to guarantee a full RGB colour spectrum and strong, even light output. A high refresh rate was provided by DMXII controllers.

Inspired by the endless number of sequences in our natural environment, the artistic ideology behind the EDD is to take the sometimes hidden, dynamic patterns that surround us daily and translate these into abstract light animations. With this in mind, the content for the system is designed to continually change; specific themes are elaborated at the discretion of the curator-orientated art and content management system. In addition to the project's website providing information on current, future and previous concepts, Hotel Mercure and the Municipality of The Hague also have the option to become involved in the promotion and marketing of the façade.

Unlike other large-scale billboards that mask the front of buildings, by web-enabling the system, there are very few limitations concerning the input of data. Using sensors linked to small but powerful embedded systems, like the MRP developed by KITT engineering, the control units can process obtained data and transmit it via the internet to the main controller in The Hague. Desired data can also be retrieved from existing databases, accessible on the internet.

By combining an interactive visualization program with open-source accessibility allows the content provider or artist for each project to make a custom application and have it implemented by the system programmer.

Ensuring all plans presented are within the boundaries of the cultural policy is an important issue for EDD, enabling the curators to make appropriate selections. Applied themes can include social, cultural, environmental, political or educational issues. It is hoped that the beauty of these visual transformations will prompt people to question the ideas behind them and, in turn, increase their social awareness.

Concepts for the façade:
- An interactive display incorporating a camera interface to track people's activity on Spui Plaza. The idea is to encourage people on the street to move playfully and consciously communicate with the architecture to generate patterns. Movements captured would be instantly translated into colour traces on the panels.
- Animated natural phenomena, such as waves – a reference to The Hague's historic infrastructure and the recent floods occurring worldwide – supported by live sounds from the nearby seaside. This application would be reliant on real-time data such as wind force and sea levels to generate input variables.
- A global communication system, gathering data from multiple continents simultaneously to show visual transformations from a global point of view.

Keen to avoid illumination glare which could become a source of annoyance for people in the surrounding area, LED-Art intends the colours in the EDD's animated 'data-textures' to adapt in a gentle and smooth transition. Naturally, the actual speed of transition will depend on the concept written by the artist and can easily be adjusted for specific themes and events. For a festival for example, a more vivid, dynamic content can be generated in response to the visitors on the plaza.

LAGOLED DEKO PANELS
ARE USED AS AN ALTER-
NATIVE TO ATTACHING
EXTERNAL FIXTURES.

THE CONTENT OF THE
SYSTEM IS DESIGNED TO
CONTINUALLY CHANGE.
A HIGH REFRESH RATE
WAS PROVIDED BY DMXII
CONROLLERS.

The idea is to encourage people on the street to move playfully and consciously communicate with the architecture to generate patterns

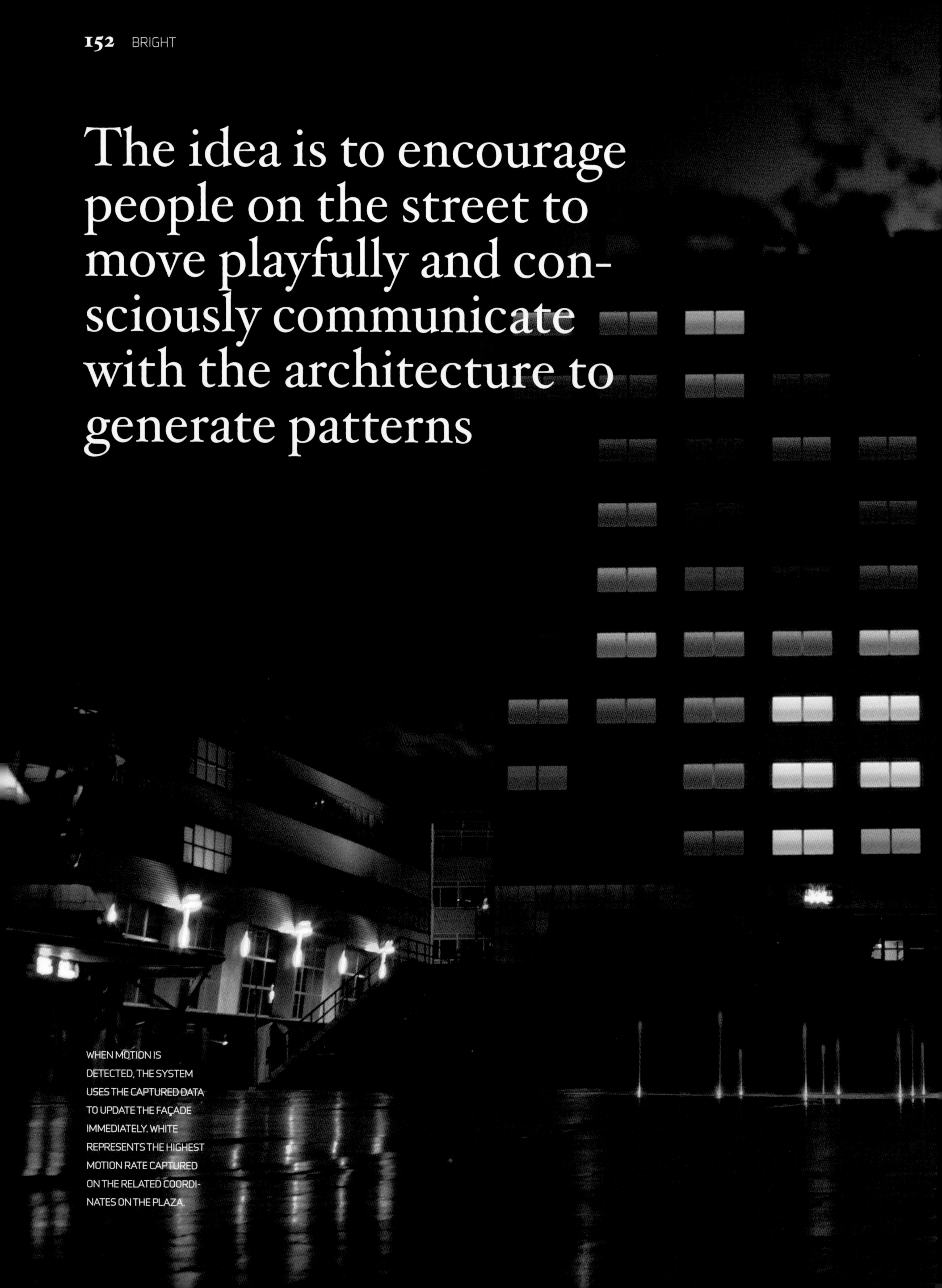

WHEN MOTION IS
DETECTED, THE SYSTEM
USES THE CAPTURED DATA
TO UPDATE THE FAÇADE
IMMEDIATELY. WHITE
REPRESENTS THE HIGHEST
MOTION RATE CAPTURED
ON THE RELATED COORDI-
NATES ON THE PLAZA.

XAL

Staff: 250
Management: Andreas Hierzer, Michael Engel,
Harald Dirnberger, Christian Schraml
Founded: 1989
Operates: Worldwide

AWARDS

Roeder award, 2005
Reddot award, 2004

KEY PROJECTS

Lotos Headquarters, Gdansk/Poland, 2006
Ferrero Research Center, Alba/Italy, 2006
Nivea House, Hamburg/Germany, 2006
Yahoo! Social Area, Munich/Germany, 2006
Vodafone Headquarters, Budapest/Hungary, 2005
Boeing, Washington DC/USA, 2004
Bloomberg Headquarters, New York/USA, 2004
T-Mobile Future House, Vienna/Italy, 2003

KEY CLIENTS

Arcotel
Boeing
C&A
Chanel
Cube
Fendi
Ferrero
Humanic
Hyatt
Intersport Eybl
Montblanc
RADO
Sheraton
Stiefelkönig
STRABAG
Versace
Yahoo!

PROFILE

Expert in designing, developing, producing and distributing high-end luminaires and light systems, Austrian company XAL operates worldwide through an international network of subsidiaries and distribution partners. Combining exceptional design and functionality to offer state-of-the-art solutions, XAL collaborates with renowned architects and lighting designers to deliver comprehensive architectural lighting concepts for shops, office buildings, hotels, restaurants and private residences. In-house production gives XAL a distinct edge over competitors, allowing the production of customized lighting solutions within short deadlines.

01

02

03

THE HEADQUARTERS OF
GRUPA LOTOS PRESENTS
ITSELF AS A LIGHT SCULP-
TURE OF EPIC PROPOR-
TIONS.

Grupa Lotos headquarters Gdansk, Poland

CLIENT
GRUPA LOTOS

ARCHITECT
ARCH-DECO

LIGHTING DESIGN
CANDELUX

LIGHTING ENGINEER
XAL

MANUFACTURER
XAL

LIGHT SOURCES
STILA RGB LUMINAIRES,
RGB STILA LED WALL
WASHER

COMPLETION DATE
DECEMBER 2006

PHOTOGRAPHERS
BEIERSDORF
WWW.BEIERSDORF.DE

PAUL GOSNEY
WWW.PAULGOSNEY.COM

RUPERT STEINER
WWW.RUPERTSTEINER.
COM

Integrating LED technology into architecture, global lighting firm XAL, worked with architects Arch-Deco to create a landmark with both structural and luminescent presence.

Complex architecture and glamorous light-plays, are not qualities often associated with oil refineries. However, the new office headquarters of Grupa Lotos – a leading oil refinery in Poland – are proof that industry and the art of lighting are in no way mutually exclusive. The new headquarters of Grupa Lotos in Gdansk, whose construction was required due to the rapid expansion of the company, presents itself both as an ultra-modern, functional building and a light sculpture of epic proportions. Visible for miles around, the building is situated on one of the main routes into Gdansk. Sharing a passion for lighting, XAL worked with Candelux - one of Poland's leading lighting designers - to develop a lighting concept that used the entire façade of the nine-storey building. After extensive discussions on how to illuminate the building in order to achieve the desired, 'glowing' effect, XAL drew on expertise in light control and previous experiences on similar, but smaller-scale projects, to create a system that went beyond single-colour, static lighting to offer a dynamic light show. The result is a sophisticated solution which exceeded the architects' initial expectations.

The main structure of the office building resembles a virtual paint pot, embellished with the company logo. It displays a variable succession of colours and formations. Single washes of colour, stripes, hand-picked rainbows, large-scale lettering and diffuse blends of colour can all be generated on the light surface, with the favoured corporate colours of yellow, blue and red appearing in countless combinations. The outer skin of the office tower is not only the radiant carrier of the corporate identity, but also a three-dimensional, multi-media screen on which complex digital control of STILA RGB luminaires constantly creates new patterns, structures and images. A prime example of digital artistry, this office building is also symbolic of new Polish economic dynamism.

The lighting concept uses the blinds of the double skin façade as a projection area for the RGB version of XAL's STILA LED wall washer, which is situated in each of the 500+ window segments of the building. Providing a powerful yet balanced illumination, each luminaire has two LED segments that are individually controllable. Generating one of the company's main corporate colours - yellow - proved a particular challenge for XAL. Amongst one of the most difficult colours to achieve with RGB LED lights, the lighting company's Research and Development team were only able to determine the perfect set-up and achieve the required colour spectrum after rigorous testing, involving numerous LED configurations.

Since the initial planning stages, the LED façade has been an integral part of the building's concept. The LED façade is part of architect Zbigniew Reszka's vision to create a 21st-century, illuminated beacon, visible from air, land and water. With its clear lines, the Grupa Lotos headquarters now provides a dominant contrast to the complex and interwoven network of pipes, tanks and chimneys found in the refinery area. The illumination concept is not only a visually captivating solution, but also benefits from the major advantages of LED technology in terms of efficiency and effectiveness. Demonstrating the potential applications of LEDs in innovative architectural lighting, the concept provides Lotos with not only an efficient and high-tech lighting solution, but also with an impressive and smart means of marketing; allowing Lotos to present its corporate identity on the exterior of the building, visible for miles.

The result of scrupulous planning, testing and development via computer simulations, the project only required minimal fine-tuning after its installation and initialization – which was completed in time for the building's opening ceremony in December 2006.

YELLOW, ONE OF THE MAIN CORPORATE COLOURS, IS AMONGST ONE OF THE MOST DIFFICULT COLOURS TO ACHIEVE WITH RGB LED LIGHTS AND PROVED A PARTICULAR CHALLENGE TO XAL.

THE BLINDS OF THE
DOUBLE SKIN FAÇADE ARE
USED AS A PROJECTION
AREA FOR THE RGB VER-
SION OF XAL'S STILA LED
WALL WASHER, WHICH IS
SITUATED IN EACH OF THE
500+ WINDOW SEGMENTS
OF THE BUILDING.

Complex architecture and glamorous light-plays, are not qualities often associated with oil refineries

USED LUMINARIES:
STILA 60 RGB OUTDOOR
LUMINAIRE
STILA 60 WHITE OUTDOOR
LUMINAIRE

Staff: 19
Management: Dirk Beiner, Jan Julius Miebach
Founded: 2002
Operates: Worldwide
Membership: PLASA

KEY PROJECTS

Grand Hotel LaStrada, Kassel/Germany, 2007
15th Asian Games, Doha/Qatar, 2006
Museums Bahnsteig, Oberhausen/Germany, 2006
Nova Eventis, Leipzig/Germany, 2005/2006
Red Bull Air Race, Berlin/Germany, 2006
Luminale, Frankfurt/Germany, 2006
WM-Globus, Germany, 2006
Nature One Rocket Base, Pydna/Macedonia, 2005
Railroad Museum, Netherlands, 2005
Business of Design Week, Hong Kong, 2005
Diesel Kid, Italy, 2005

Arctura, Östersund/Sweden, 2005
Philips Stand, IFA, 2005
Sisi Chapel, Vienna/Austria, 2005
Blue Night, Nürnberg/Germany, 2003
Libori, Paderborn/Germany, 2003
Rosenstolz Tour, Germany, 2002

PROFILE

e:cue is an engineering bureau for lighting control based in Germany with sales offices in Europe, Asia and USA and a worldwide expanding distribution network.

As a solution provider, e:cue offer a comprehensive range of products from software packages for designing shows, light- and media controllers, replay-units, terminals, DMX-ethernet-gateways, building automation systems up to integrated controller chip solutions for LED. Their mission, to invent, design and develop sophisticated and innovative professional lighting control solutions with versatile products and a powerful and unique software for controlling lights and media.

01

02

01 SETTING NEW STAND-
ARDS, THE LIGHTING
CONTROL OF THE GALERIA
STORE FAÇADE IN SEOUL
USED 16,000 DMX CHAN-
NELS. REJUVENATING THE
70'S STYLE CONCRETE
BUILDING WITH AN ILLUMI-
NATION THAT WRAPS THE
STRUCTURE IN ORGANIC
POOLS OF LIGHT.

02 AT THE FLICK OF A SWITCH
THE CEILING OF THE JET
NIGHTCLUB – AN L.A.
HOTSPOT LOCATED IN
THE MIRAGE HOTEL – CAN
BE TRANSFORMED INTO
A GIANT PROJECTOR.
DEVISED BY E:CUE THE
CLUBS LIGHTING CONTROL
INCLUDES 60 DMX UNI-
VERSES, LEDS, MOVING
LIGHTS AND HIPPOTIZER
MEDIASERVERS.

03 AN ARCHITECTURAL
ILLUMINATION PROPOR-
TIONATE TO THE BRAND
HOUSED WITHIN ITS
STRUCTURE, THE FAÇADE
OF THE LOUIS VUITTON
STORE IN SAR WAS TRANS-
FORMED INTO A COLOUR-
FUL BEACON OF LIGHT.

Arctura Tower Östersund,
Sweden

CLIENT

JÄMTKRAFT

ARCHITECT

HANS ALDEFELT. SWECO

LIGHTING DESIGNER

STEFAN WIKTORSSON

LIGHTING ENGINEER

E:CUE

MANUFACTURERS

E:CUE LIGHTING CONTROL,

PHILIPS

LIGHT SOURCES

MEDIA ENGINE LIGHT, 2X

E:COM, E:CUE PROGRAM-

MER, PHILIPS LEDLINE

SURFACE-MOUNTED

BCS722, PHILIPS LED-

FLOOD BCP73024 LED

1W ANALOGUE 0-10V,

LUXEON™LED, 1W &3W,

RGBW, LUMILEDS

TOTAL SURFACE

10,000 M²

DATE OF COMPLETION

2005

PHOTOGRAPHER

E:CUE

WWW.ECUE.TV

Every year Aurora Borealis, better known as the Northern Lights, attract thousands of visitors to Sweden and Scandinavia as a whole. This colourful event was the conceptual seed that client Jämtkraft -, a Swedish energy company and operator - brought forth for the lighting of a remote hot water tank in Östersund.

Sweden uses centralized systems to remotely heat its homes. Fossil fuel combustion is increasingly replaced by using waste heat from factories and energy pumps, as well as by burning household waste. Hot water is stored in giant tanks which are essentially over-sized 'thermos flasks'. The 65-m-high Arctura Tower is one such tank and has a diameter of 27 m. Its storage capacity of up to 26 million litres is enough to heat the whole town for several days.

Ljusdesign, sales representatives of lighting control firm e:cue, was contacted very early on in the project. Lighting designer Stefan Wiktorsson and SWECO's architect Hans Aldefelt met to come up with the breathtaking colour changes which would be a symbolic version of the Northern Lights. Lighting sequences needed to start two hours before sunset and end two hours before sunrise. The period of twilight, which takes several hours in Scandinavia, was to be the focus of attention.

For the technical realization, Ljusdesign decided to use an e:cue media engine. Consisting of a control and replay unit with internal DMX-output, network, SMPTE, RS232 and opto-isolated inputs, this was the ideal tool to handle the required timing and controlling of this kind of lighting, using an internal astronomical clock and sunrise timer.

The main scenario runs are fully automated, and vary according to the season, focusing on different colours; a bluish colour with slow changes in Autumn versus warm red colours in December. Special events like New Year's Eve are no problem for the e:cue programmer software which runs on the media engine. Any scenario of events can be programmed in advance.

The owner of the Arctura roof-top-restaurant wanted the option of manually changing the lighting scenarios. Therefore Wiktorsson decided to install an e:cue e:com remote terminal in the restaurant. This was then connected to the media engine which is installed in the technical room at the bottom of the tower. This easy-to-use terminal can recall predefined parts of the show on the e:cue media engine. The display on the terminal also shows the user which scenario is running at any given moment in time.

For the illumination, Ljusdesign chose to use LEDs. Architectural lighting with LEDs is already quite common in urban havens like Hong Kong, Seoul or New York, but is still a new lighting method in the relative wilderness of the Northern latitudes.

LEDs are installed at the top and bottom of the tower's façade, lighting a steel grid, distanced 2.5 m from the concrete wall. A decision had been made in favour of Philips LEDline² RGB luminaires. 198 of these fixtures, equipped with high-power LuxeonTM LEDs, were installed. To emphasize the steel grid, Wiktorsson decided to add a Philips LEDLine² luminaire with white-only LEDs.

LED lighting is used in a number of combinations to create the desired colour on the grey water tank and a flickering effect on the net that surrounds the building. One of the conclusions drawn from this installation was the difficulty of achieving acceptable yellow colours. This challenge was off-set by the advantage of a very cost-effective solution to illuminating such a huge building. When you consider that an area of 10,000 m² has been lit, the power consumption of 2500 W is negligible. Any other kind of luminaire would be hard-pressed to compete.

THE COLOUR CHANGES ARE
A SYMBOLIC VERSION OF
THE NORTHERN LIGHTS.

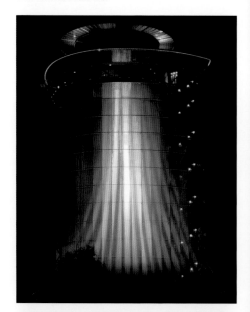

WHITE-ONLY LEDS EMPHA-
SIZE THE STEEL GRID.

A NET SURROUNDS THE
ENTIRE STRUCTURE.

VIEW OF THE ARCTURA
TOWER FROM BELOW.

When you consider that an area of 10,000 m² has been lit, the power consumption of 2500 W is negligible

THE STORAGE CAPACITY
OF THE ARCTURA TOWER
IS ENOUGH TO HEAT
THE WHOLE TOWN FOR
SEVERAL DAYS.

STICHTING PICOS DE EUROPA

STICHTING PICOS DE EUROPA

Staff: 1
Management: Noud Heerkens
Founded: 1993
Operates: Europe

KEY PROJECTS

Cineboards Guerilla, 2007
Cineboards, 2002, 2003, 2004, 2005, 2006
Global Attic film- en video Festival, 2002, 2000, 1998, 1997

PROFILE

Stichting Picos was founded in 1993 by film maker Noud Heerkens. The foundation is active in the fields of film and video art. The production and initiation of various film projects and productions is the major focus point. Picos searches for co-operations with other disciplines such as architecture, art, dance and theatre. When realizing projects a researching and reflecting attitude is

01

02

CINEBOARDS: VIDEO
PROJECTIONS IN PUBLIC
SPACES, IN THE CENTRE OF
THREE CITIES: ROTTER-
DAM, THE HAGUE, AND
EINDHOVEN WITH 'PUBLIC
SPACE' AS A THEME. THE
CURATORS ASSERT THAT
THE FUNCTION OF PUBLIC
SPACE HAS ALTERED IN
RECENT DECADES, FROM
BEING A PLACE WHERE
PEOPLE NEGOTIATE TO
A PLACE WHERE PEOPLE
SIMPLY ACT: PUBLIC
SPACE AS AN EXTENSION
OF THE PRIVATE AREA
OF INDIVIDUALS, SHOPS,
COMPANIES ETC.

PAULUSKERK BY URBI ET ORBI.

Cineboards Rotterdam,
Netherlands

CLIENT

ROTTERDAM 2007,
CITY OF ARCHITECTURE
(AMONG OTHERS)

CONSULTANTS

AV DWARSBUREAU, BEAM-
ERPLANET

ENGINEER

ERWIN VAN DEUTEKOM

LIGHT SOURCES

SANYO PLC-XF45 PROJEC-
TOR, 10.000 LUMEN

TOTAL SURFACE

APPROX. 100 M²

DURATION OF
CONSTRUCTION

2 DAYS

COMPLETION DATE

AUGUST 2007

PHOTOGRAPHERS

JAN ADRIAANS
ADRIAANS.JAN@GMAIL.
COM

RINIE BLEEKER
RBLEEKER@XS4ALL.NL

BAS CZERWINSKI
BCZ@XS4ALL.NL

CHRISTIAAN VAN DER
KOOIJ
WWW.CHRISTIAN-
VANDERKOOY.EU

In August 2007, Cineboards - an initiative organized by Rotterdam-based Stichting Picos de Europa - illuminated architectural façades in the centre of Rotterdam for the sixth consecutive year. The main focus was on films and animations that provide an impression of recent developments of international film and video art. The event's varied programme of surprising and widely accessible visual culture works, presented over a period of three weeks, brought images normally confined to the closed environments of museums, galleries and cinemas into the public domain. The hurdle of visitor punctuality was removed as passers-by were encouraged to stop and watch films which were shown on a loop and lasted no more than fifteen minutes. Inviting 14 makers including renowned artists Barbara Visser, Anouk de Clercq, and Floris Kaayk, the 2007 event explored the interface between architecture and animation.

Overcoming the main technical problems encountered during events in previous years, such as doubling the lucidity of the image to 10,000 lumens in order to compensate for the 'light noise' in the square, the 2007 event ran more smoothly than in previous years. Located around the Schouwburgplein (12,250 m2), a prominent site in the city and flanked by the municipal theatre, concert hall and central station, the location for the site was designed in 1996 by urban design and architecture practice West 8. A 10,000 lumen beamer was placed on the top of a ventilation tower situated in the square, with a long throw lens used to create a projection from the beamer to the screen which was positioned almost 50 m away. Out of view, the DVD player and sound installation were concealed in the ground floor of the tower.

Based on the notion of chance encounter, Cineboards showed the work of a different participant every evening for three weeks, from sunset to 1am. An examination and exploration of the boundaries between genres, design and presentation; the makers used animated, fictional imagery to make personal and sensually simulating statements on architecture and the urban structures that surround us in our daily lives. In a strange role reversal, the Schouwburgplein's Pathe cinema which usually projects films once visitors are inside, hosted the video content on its exterior. Content which included graphical pictograms forged together into a hallucinatory, modern-day tableau vivant. Large-format pencil drawings coalesced with advanced computer-aided designs, electrical insects and a monochromatic journey through the oppressive world of advertising. This collection, evoking a surrealistic architecture, made reference to visionary utopias and often futuristic fantasies. This work was inspired by contemporary urban scenarios, new buildings and famous statements such as 'A house is a machine for living in', uttered by architectural icon, Le Corbusier. In addition to the main programme of films, this year as part of Rotterdam 2007: City of Architecture, Stichting Picos added Cineboards Guerrilla. For the opening weekend, a number of Dutch film and video makers were each asked to create a new work for one of five allocated locations around the city. Works included lifecycles of organic ecosystems, an animated road-movie and an installation situated in the debris of Rotterdam's former Calypso cinema. Each piece was seemingly dictated by the architecture onto which it was projected. Despite being arranged more like an exhibition, the Guerrilla event, like Cineboards Schouwburgplein, was also a 'chance encounter'.

Noud Heerkens, Director of Stichting Picos, sees moving images as a vehicle to promote discussion on current sociological issues, and architecture can be used as the stage for this vehicle. 'Artists offer free interpretations of current affairs and encourage people to consider other perspectives', Heerkens explains. Cineboards is therefore an artistic counterpart to commercial image.

In a media-saturated society bombarded with visual stimuli, including the recent YouTube phenomena, Heerkens considers moving images as a basic form of communication next to the verbal and written language; an ideal way to connect to the masses.

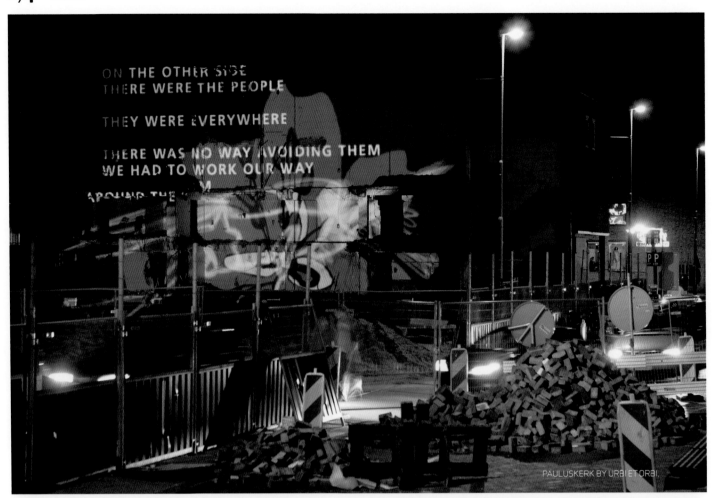

PAULUSKERK BY URBI ET ORBI.

PAULUSKERK BY URBI ET ORBI.

KAREL DOORMANSTRAAT BY JAN VAN NUENEN.

PAULUSKERK BY URBI ET ORBI.

CITY HALL ROTTERDAM BY FLOOR VAN KEULEN EN RENÉ OEY.

KRUISKADE BY THOMAS BAKKER.

'Artists offer free interpretations of current affairs and encourage people to consider other perspectives' Noud Heerkens

LIGHTLIFE

Staff: 9
Management: Antonius Quodt, Jan Julius Miebach
Key designer: Antonius Quodt
Founded: 1996
Operates: Worldwide
Memberships: ELDA, KölnDesign

AWARD
Kristina D., Luminaire of the Year, 2003

KEY PROJECTS
Kubik, Berlin/Germany, Barcelona/Spain, Lisboa/Portugal, ongoing
FIFA WM Globe, 2003-2006
Luminale, Frankfurt/Germany, 2006
VW-Pavilion, Car City, Wolfsburg/Germany, 2002
'Pharmacy', German Museum Munich, 2000
Art House, Bregenz/Austria, 1999
Swarovski Crystal World, Tirol/Austria, 1995 and 1998

PROFILE
Based in Cologne, LightLife is a German lighting-design firm that specializes in non-standard architectural lighting installations and artworks made with light. Most of LightLife's clients are architects, artists and designers.

02

01

01 IN A COMPREHENSIVE
SOLO EXHIBITION, THE
KUNSTHAUS BREGENZ
SHOWS EXAMPLES OF
KEITH SONNIER´S LARGE
SCULPTURES AND SPATIAL
INSTALLATIONS SINCE THE
LATE SIXTIES. THE FAÇADE
OF THE KUNSHAUS WAS
A BIG ARTWORK OF KEITH
SONNIER.

02 FOR 'BLUE NIGHT', A
LATE NIGHT OPENING OF
THE MUSEUMS, THREE
5-METER-TALL RINGS
CONSTRUCTED FROM
ALUMINUM PIPE WERE
POSITIONED ON THE MAIN
MARKETPLACE OF NÜRN-
BERG. EACH RING HAD 400
PIXELS WHICH COULD BE
INDIVIDUALLY CONTROL-
LED TO PRODUCE GRAPHIC
AND TEXT.

03 KUBIK WAS A TEMPORARY
LIGHT ROOM INSTALLA-
TION TO REVITALIZE A
FALLOW AREA RIGHT IN
THE CITY CENTRE. THE
INSTALLATION REMINDED
THE VIEWER OF A 3D TE-
TRIS GAME INTERACTING
WITH MUSIC.

03

THE FOOTBALL GLOBE
SEEN THROUGH THE
BRANDENBURGER GATE.

Football Globe/FIFA World Cup 2006, Germany

IDEA AND ARTIST
LEADING
ANDRÉ HELLER
PRODUCTION LEADING
STEFAN SEIGNER/
ARTEVENT
MANAGEMENT
STEFAN SEIGNER, ROBERT
HOFFERER/ARTEVENT
SCENOGRAPHY
DIETER BRELL/3DELUXE
INTERIOR DESIGN
3DELUXE
SOUND DESIGN
HAGÜ SCHMITZ/XOUND
MEDIA DESIGN AND
PROGRAMMING
MESO
INTERIOR
MANUFACTURER
GECCO
STEEL CONSTRUCTION
MERO
AIR PILLOWS
COVERTEX
SOUND SYSTEM
DYNACORD
LIGHT SOURCES
TRYKA LEDS, ETC SPOTS,
CLAY PAKY MOVING
LIGHTS, E:CUE LIGHTING
CONTROL SYSTEM
DURATION OF
CONSTRUCTION
6 WEEKS
COMPLETION DATE
2006

PHOTOGRAPHERS
FRANK ALEXANDER
RÜMMELE
WWW.F-A-R.COM

EMANUEL RAAB
WWW.EMANUELRAAB.DE

WOLFGANG STAHL
WWW.WOLFGANGSTAHL.
COM

By day, André Heller's creation took the form of a gigantic soccer ball, but after dark it became an illuminated globe. The 17.8-m-high sculpture was a 60-tonne mass of steel and technology. 'We wanted to flood the land with happiness and anticipation,' Heller recalls. The ambassadorial function of the project was two-fold. The main focus was the world championship event, of course, but the social and cultural aspects of soccer as a 'Volkssport' could not be overlooked. Organizers of the cultural programme invited visitors to view soccer from its many perspectives. Every evening, the globe was transformed into a 'stage' for a host of international guests that included politicians, musicians, artists, fans and media representatives.

Stefan Seigner, manager and director of the project, was more than happy to take responsibility for the artistic aspect of a presentation conceived by André Heller, his longtime friend and partner. Seigner's company, Artevent, coordinated the activities of contractors, experts and guests. The interior of the soccer ball comprised two levels and featured a multimedia presentation developed by 3deluxe. Highlighting the ground floor of the travelling exhibition was a display of cult memorabilia representing various soccer professionals. A 50-inch plasma display welcomed visitors, showing all current programme events and news surrounding the world championship. Stairs led to the second level, which was covered in Astroturf to generate the feel of a stadium and which had an interactive interface. Visitors could influence their surroundings with the use of three touch screens and four trackballs. They could play games as well.

At dusk, the huge soccer ball turned into a glowing globe, much to the delight of the public. To ensure that every eye was fixed on the brilliant orb, all exterior wiring had to be invisible. LightLife satisfied this requirement by attaching LED flexes to the exterior of the structure. These thin cords, with a diameter of only 13 mm, were enclosed within air pillows during manufacture. Furnished with six digital control channels, they could produce the individual continents of the world on command. This effect was synchronized with video projections. In addition to the continental lighting scheme, the soccer ball was equipped with a 'light-dress' that took its form from light sources located in 20 white fields. With the use of RGB LED technology developed by Tryka, light designer Antonius Quodt installed these light sources between two layers of air pillows. Exterior projections aimed from three positions relied on panoramic projection and film drives. Synchronization of lighting and video projections was implemented by means of a network controlled with the use of e:cue media-engine software. Design office Meso was tasked with developing media systems inside the globe. Meso was responsible for planning, developing and producing the computer technology for the highly complex graphic designs. The interior was outfitted with a 360° video projection screen and supplied with ten 3000 ANSI lumen video projectors. The panorama was 12 m in diameter and had a picture quality of 10240 x 768 pixels. The extremely complex 360° projection included various 3D and 2D objects, which necessitated a render controller that functioned with a 3D coordinate mapping system. The composition level included videos, interactive clips and animated cartoon characters and, at the graphic level, additional 3D animated globes. All effects were rendered live in 3D. Thanks to lighting and colours that changed continually, the atmosphere inside the globe altered constantly as well. Fourteen standard PCs supported the projectors with high-end gaming graphic cards, and 14 others took care of additional film material in both terminals and display cases. All computer power combined in one render farm united 500,000 MHz of processor power and 1 terabyte of disc space. Owing to live links to the internet at DSL speed, the editors were able to update text, video and news at a moment's notice.

THE INTERIOR WAS OUT-
FITTED WITH A 360° VIDEO
PROJECTION SCREEN AND
SUPPLIED WITH TEN 3000
ANSI LUMEN VIDEO PRO-
JECTORS. THE PANORAMA
WAS 12 M IN DIAMETER
AND HAD A PICTURE
QUALITY OF 10240 X 768
PIXELS.

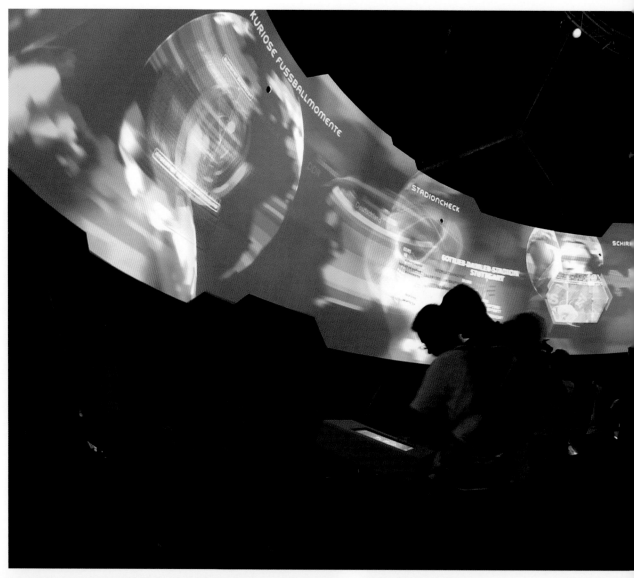

AFTER DARK THE SOCCER
BALL BECAME AN ILLUMI-
NATED GLOBE.

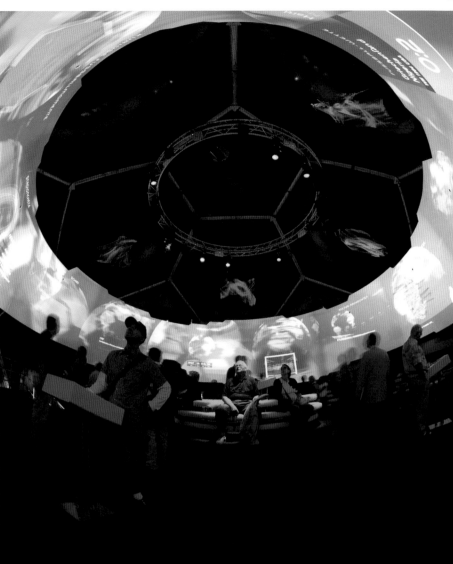

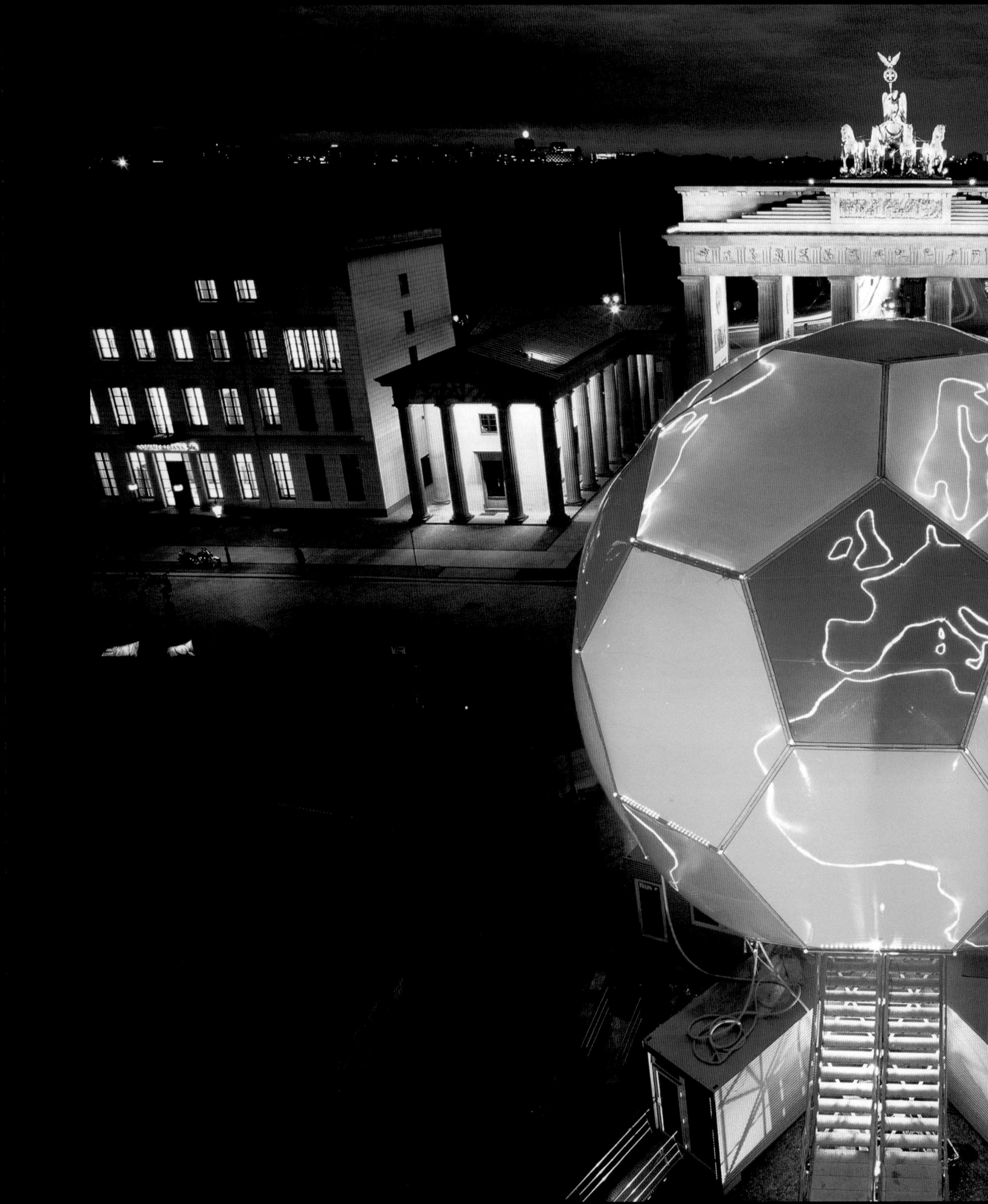

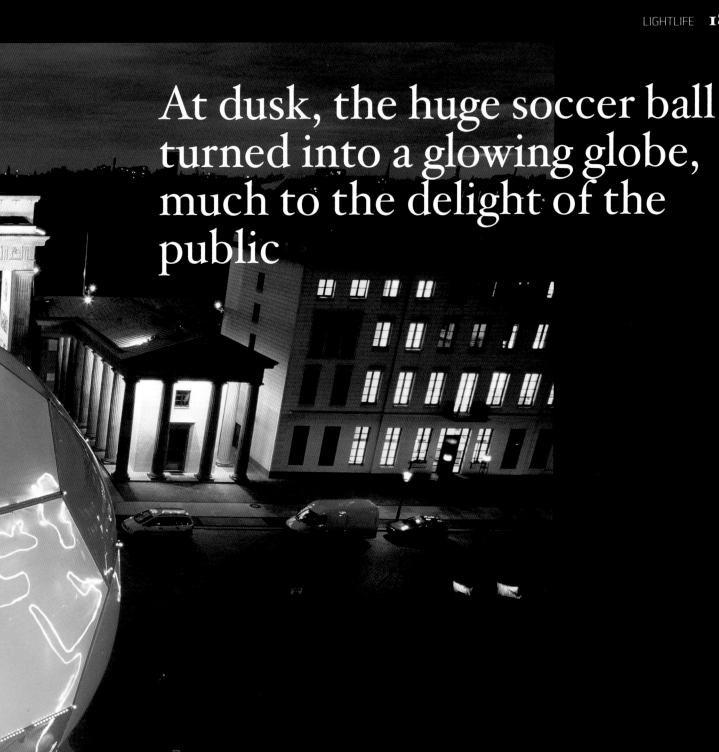

At dusk, the huge soccer ball turned into a glowing globe, much to the delight of the public

LED LIGHT ROPES WERE
FITTED TO THE EXTE-
RIOR OF THE CONSTRUC-
TION. THIS EFFECT WAS
SYNCHRONISED WITH A
VIDEO PROJECTION USING
THE E:CUE MEDIA-ENGINE
SOFTWARE.

SCENARIO LICHT- UND KLANGKONZEPTE

SCENARIO LICHT- UND KLANGKONZEPTE

Staff: 2
Management: Tobias Link
Key designers: Tobias Link, Oliver Jene
Founded: 1993
Operates: Europe
Membership: PDLA

AWARDS

Nominated for German Bundes-Designpreis, 2008
Goldene Flamme, 2006

KEY PROJECTS

Nova Eventis, Günthersdorf/Germany, 2006
The Living Seas, Günthersdorf/Germany, 2006

KEY CLIENTS

Bilfinger Berger
Bretz
Commerzbank
ECE Projektmanagement
Gasanstalt
GIU Flächenmanagement
Vitra

PROFILE

Calling themselves Scenario, Tobias Link and Oliver Jene are lighting designers and artists who take an artistic approach to highly complex projects. They use not only lighting tools but also acoustic, video, graphic and multimedia elements, turning architectural space into an experience by adding contours and depth to the structure in question. Scenario looks at architecture as though it were sculpture, accentuating its complexity, enhancing its nuances and emphasizing, animating and conveying the architect's theme through lighting.

01

02

01 LOCATED AT OVAL AM
BASELER PLATZ IN
FRANKFURT, SCENARIO'S
OPUS LUMIS COMBINED
ARCHITECTURE WITH
LIGHT IN A SCHEME BASED
ON 'EARTH AND FIRE'. THE
INSTALLATION, WHICH
OCCUPIED A COURTYARD,
GENERATED A SOUND AND
LIGHT EXPERIENCE THAT
TRANSFORMED STATIC
ELEMENTS INTO A RADI-
ANT LIGHTSCAPE.

02 AN OUTDOOR SHOPPING
CENTRE BECOMES A
CANVAS FOR A DRAMATIC
LIGHTING INSTALLATION,
A COLOURFUL 'NIGHT-
DRESS' OF LIGHT AND
COLOUR DESIGNED TO BE
WORN BY ARCHITECTURE.

THE GLOBES ACRYLIC 'FISH
SCALE' SKIN, SEEN FROM
THE INSIDE.

Nova Eventis Günthersdorf, Germany

CLIENT

ECE PROJEKTMANAGE-
MENT

LIGHTING DESIGNER

SCENARIO LICHT- UND
KLANGKONZEPTE

MANUFACTURERS

HIGHEND SYSTEMS,
IGUZZINI, INSTA ELEKTRO,
MARTIN PROFESSIONAL,
PR LIGHTING

LIGHT SOURCES

MOVING LIGHTS (XSPOT
XTREME FOR PROJEC-
TIONS), COLOUR-CHANG-
ING UPLIGHTS (WALL-
WASHERS), COLOUR-
CHANGING SPOTS, LED
CONTOURS, LED SPOTS

**DURATION OF
CONSTRUCTION**

3 MONTHS

COMPLETION DATE

SEPTEMBER 2006

PHOTOGRAPHERS

OLIVER JENE
WWW.SCENARIO.IL

PETER FRANKE
WWW.PUNCTUM.NET

Nova Eventis is the first 'event mall' realized by shopping centre planning and development company ECE, whose aim was to give visitors an extraordinary experience. In planning the mall, ECE paid special attention to activities and events that would encourage visitors to stay longer and to have a good time. The firm took an all-embracing approach to the emotional and sensory side of shopping, inviting visitors to interact, thus intensifying their experience at Nova Eventis.

ECE's vision included a major role for lighting. Tobias Link and Oliver Jene of Scenario were asked to come up with a scenographic lighting design for the interior of the mall, as well as the main entrance and the 'scenery façade'. To create a dynamic, comprehensive lighting design, they developed a concept based on changing colours and strategically placed light sources: a scheme geared to both seasonal changes and the time of day.

The lighting generates an ambience that reflects the season of the year and is perceptible as a basic theme throughout the public zones. Four lighting systems that provide dynamics, colours and graphic elements rely on the use of a media controller. The entire colour-and-illumination network, which is based on DMX, operates as an extension of the building's EIB control system. On its own, EIB – a certified system for the automation of a building's mechanical installations – would have been unable to cope with the various tasks required to control Scenario's highly dynamic lighting production, particularly the high-frequency aspects.

The scenery façade comprises two levels and a geometric kaleidoscope of brightly lit blocks and rectangles. The exterior lighting scheme also includes a parking garage to the rear. In illuminating the façade, Link accentuated the character of the individual areas. Numerous colour-changing uplights and spots make it possible to completely alter the look of each section of the façade and thus to redefine the architecture through lighting. The result is a fragmented skin – the designers refer to 'nested architecture' – in which each part of the façade retains its individual character. Winter, characterized by white and blue, features the projection of ice crystals on parts of the façade. Green and yellow mixed with winter's cool blue announce the arrival of spring. Orange and red convey the warmth of summer. And autumn is the most colourful season, not only in nature but also at Nova Eventis.

Three staircases lend access to the parking garage, whose exterior is wrapped in a stainless-steel mesh and accentuated with contours created by white LEDs. The background is illuminated with blue-filtered, dimmable fluorescent lamps that function separately for each floor. In combination with the steel mesh, the lamps form a lantern-like object. Shoppers on the stairs are 'silhouetted actors' in a play of light.

Moving head projectors mounted in waterproof, air-conditioned, outdoor housings produce graphics on the walls. At Christmas time, for example, Santa smiles from the façade and stars sparkle everywhere. Special shutter gobos allowed the designers to highlight various structural elements in such a way that they seem to have built-in lighting. Outlining selected structures are built-in red and white LEDs that form a counterpart to the wallwashed elements.

A spectacular attraction at Nova Eventis is a water feature composed of nine circular fountains. Lighting here consists of underwater LED luminaires that make individual cascades and water curtains stand out vividly. In Scenario's clever scheme, the media controller manages not only every aspect of the overall lighting design, but also the control circuits of pumps for these fountains. Lighting effects above the water feature merge with lighting on the scenery façade to provide an active, animated element that complements the static architecture.

The pièce de résistance is the glass façade of the service building, which forms a cyclorama for the large globe in front of it. Both façade and globe are illuminated with LEDs, which are concealed within the steel wall and thus invisible to people approaching this side of the mall, with its cheerful, welcoming entrance. Architecturally, the globe communicates with a huge steel volume opposite the scenery façade; this structure forms a monumental wave on which the globe 'dances' like a ball on water. Link covered the façade in an acrylic 'fish scale' skin that looks great by day and lights up after dark, thanks to 372 specially designed LED spots, one behind each scale. Each spot can be accessed separately, like a pixel, to make the scenery façade a pageant of light against the night sky.

THE MEDIA CONTROLLER
MANAGES THE LIGHTING
AS WELL AS THE PUMPS
FOR THE FOUNTAINS.

GRAPHICS ARE PROJECTED
ON THE WALL ACCORDING
TO CURRENT EVENTS.

THE ENTRANCE OF THE
SHOPPING MALL.

THE COLOURS OF THE
FAÇADE LIGHTING CHANGE
WITH THE SEASONS OF
THE YEAR.

THE LIGHTING OF THE
FOUNTAINS CONSISTS
OF UNDERWATER LED
LUMINARIES.

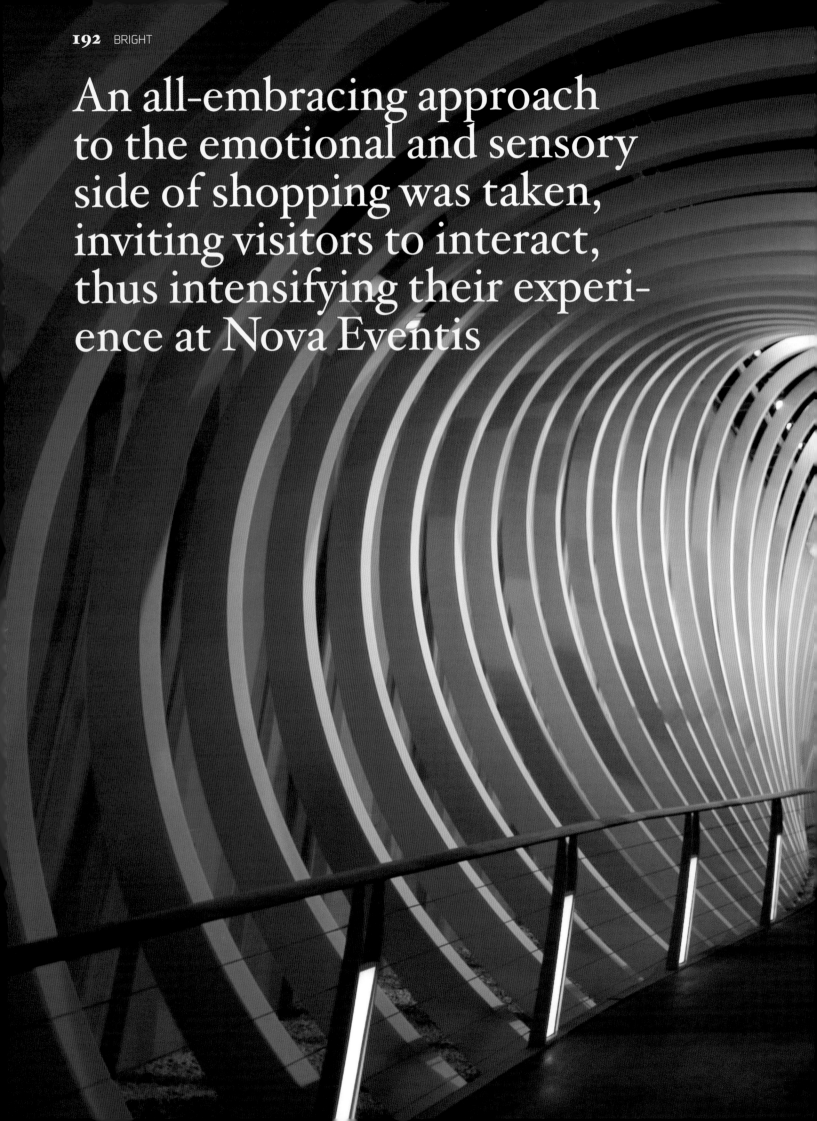

An all-embracing approach to the emotional and sensory side of shopping was taken, inviting visitors to interact, thus intensifying their experience at Nova Eventis

THE ENTRANCE STRUC-
TURE IS LIT UP BY 150W
COLOUR CHANGING WASH-
LIGHTS.

STUDIO VAN ENGELENBURG
PLEINMUSEUM FOUNDATION

STUDIO VAN ENGELENBURG/PLEINMUSEUM FOUNDATION

Staff: 3
Management/Design: René van Engelenburg
Curators: Meta Knol, Edwin Jacobs
Founded: 2004
Operates: Worldwide

KEY PROJECTS

Dropstuff.nl, various locations/Netherlands, 2008-2009
Pleinmuseum, various locations, 2004 - 2007
Limes@Flumina, Utrecht/Netherlands, 2005
ZOET!, Amsterdam/Netherlands, 2005
Inflate the Rietveld!, Amsterdam/Netherlands, 2002

PROFILE

René van Engelenburg designs installations and performances in public spaces and temporary architectural objects. His projects aim to create an overall experience in which the exhibition or presentation is viewed as a pre-eminently communicative act. He therefore concentrates on creating the conditions that make a specific interaction with the public possible. Van Engelenburg's work is multidisciplinary and straddles the boundaries between visual art, architecture and design.

In 2004 he started Pleinmuseum Foundation. The Pleinmuseum Foundation has initiated and curated new platforms for contemporary art and design. Focusing on the relationship between art and public, Pleinmuseum develops projects which are for the most part mobile, temporary and boast open architectural structures that forge dynamic relationships with public space. Activating public space is the key physical and conceptual parameter for the ideas of participating designers and artists.

01

02

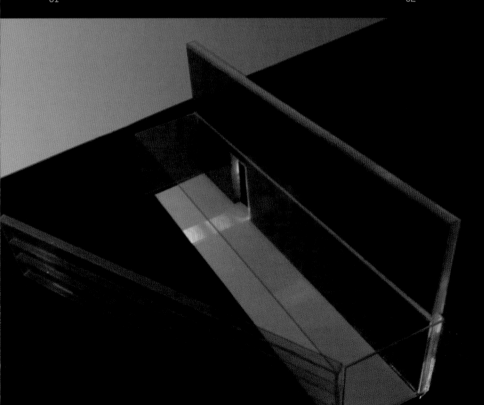

01   ZOET! DIFFERENT COL-
OURS ARE PROJECTED
ON WHITE CANDY AT THE
"COLOUR FAIR" FOR THE
SIKKENS FOUNDATION.

02   LIMES@FLUMINA IS
A 40-M-LONG VIDEO
PROJECTION ON A BRIDGE
IN UTRECHT, SHOWING SIX
DIFFERENT LANDSCAPES.

03   DROPSTUFF.NL IS A MO-
BILE PAVILION THAT OF-
FERS A STATE-OF-THE-ART
DIGITAL COMMUNICATION
PLATFORM FOR YOUNG
PEOPLE. TOURING 12 CIT-
IES IN THE NETHERLANDS
THROUGHOUT 2008 AND
2009, THE PAVILION FUNC-
TIONS AS AN INTERACTIVE
INTERNET CAFÉ. YOUNG
PEOPLE ARE INVITED TO
PRESENT THEIR PERSONAL

AMIR ADMONI - GREAT
SLEEPING GIANT, PARIS/
FRANCE

Pleinmuseum Venice,
Italy

SPONSORS

MONDRIAAN FOUNDA-
TION, VSB FOUNDATION,
STIMULERINGSFONDS
BNG, BOUWFONDS
CULTUURFONDS,
PRINS BERNHARD
CULTUURFONDS

AUDIO VISUAL
CONSULTANTS

HECLA PROFESSIONAL

ENGINEER

CAROTTE ENGINEERING

MANUFACTURER

SILCA APPARATENBOUW

TRANSPORT,
CONSTRUCTION/
DE-CONSTRUCTION

MONTAGEPARTNERS

LIGHT SOURCES

PANASONIC PT-5500 DLP
PROJECTORS

TOTAL SURFACE

125 M²

TOTAL COST

€235,000

DURATION OF
CONSTRUCTION

3 MONTHS

COMPLETION DATE

JUNE 2005

PHOTOGRAPHERS

COEN BOUMAN/KEY-
FRAMES
WWW.KEYFRAMES.NL

RENÉ VAN ENGELENBURG
WWW.PLEINMUSEUM.ORG

MARC VERHILLE / MAIRIE
DE PARIS

In Summer 2007, the Venice Biennale, Documenta, Munster and Istanbul Art fairs – four of the world's most prestigious and influential arts events - aligned for the first time in a decade.

To coincide with this occasion, and to challenge and stimulate the international arts scene, the International Curators Forum (ICF) launched Pan European Encounters - a symposium exploring the themes of Race and Diaspora. Curated by David A. Bailey and Mike Phillips, the initiative gave a group of Britain's most promising curators from Asian, African and Caribbean backgrounds an opportunity to develop their professional experiences and expertise.

Located on the waterfront between the Arsenale (the city's historic Dockyard which only opens during the biennale), and the Giardini (parkland which hosts approximately 30 pavilions each year), Pleinmuseum - a mobile exhibition pavilion - that has occupied the central squares of various cities since 2004, showed a selection of works from its international collection. Presented by the Arts Council England during the opening days of the Venice Biennale, the Pleinmuseum was used as a practical case study for the symposium and as part of the collateral programme of the British Pavilion. The piece provided a necessary platform for critical dialogue on emerging tropes of representation within the accelerated globalization of culture. Used to illustrate the idea of the 'migrating museum', Pleinmuseum encouraged discussion surrounding curatorial changes throughout the international art world.

A radical and progressive alternative to other contemporary art museums, Pleinmuseum is a new concept: an open and flexible museum that is easily approachable and accessible, forming a natural part of urban life. Set up as the opposite of 'Museumplein', the cultural heart of the Netherlands which is home to big established institutes such as the Van Gogh Museum, the Rijksmuseum and the Stedelijk Museum, Pleinmuseum displays the work of artists that are able to develop innovative and diverse collaborations within the context of public life. Director of Pleinmuseum, René van Engelenburg, describes the role of the project in the curation of contemporary art: 'The project is a statement about the changing position many contemporary artists take for themselves; many don't want to be dependent on traditional museums or galleries any longer. They are searching for better platforms to communicate with a bigger audience who may not ordinarily visit museums'.

During daytime, the pavilion remains closed, making a symbolic reference to the 'white cube'; a paradigmatic model of the modernist museum. After sunset, the computer-generated system is activated and the cube opens itself hydraulically, forming a dynamic architectural installation - a 3-dimensional digital canvas that celebrates contemporary art and embraces space. Approximately 15 m long and 5 m high, Pleinmuseum, although substantially smaller than traditional museums, is striking nonetheless. Transformed into projector screens, the white walls are illuminated with images and videos via Panasonic PT-5500 DLP projectors, housed within specially developed climatized and 'damage-proof' boxes. Like the skin of a chameleon, the appearance of the screens, which artists Driessens and Verstappen describe as 'an animated membrane stretched over an asymmetrical frame', continuously change, becoming a temporary stage for visual communication and the platform through which artists and designers can communicate with a broad audience. The selection shown at the Biennale included works from Driessens and Verstappen, Peter Missotten, Amir Admoni, Niels Schrader, Ladds and Trash. A diverse body of work which contains films endlessly looping, rough-cut animations, a 1:1 scale multimedia Chinese Circus, and a digitalized flood, ensured that the audience were entertained regardless of the time of evening they walked past.

In cooperation with Edwin Jacobs, director ot the Municipal Museum 'de Lakenhal' in Leiden, Pleinmuseum continues to invite artists, whose work is interdisciplinary and context-oriented, to develop innovative and diverse collaborations that forge a dynamic relationship with public space, activating the space as the key physical and conceptual parameter for their ideas. Undeterred by the potential problems of working in the public domain, van Engelenburg is also developing a new project entitled 'Dropstuff.nl': a mobile pavilion that will provide young people with a state-of-the-art digital communication platform. The new pavilion tours cities in the Netherlands throughout 2008 and 2009.

PETER MISSOTTEN-
EXPECT POISON FROM
STANDING WATER IV.

PIET ROGIE - CORPO
LIQUIDO.

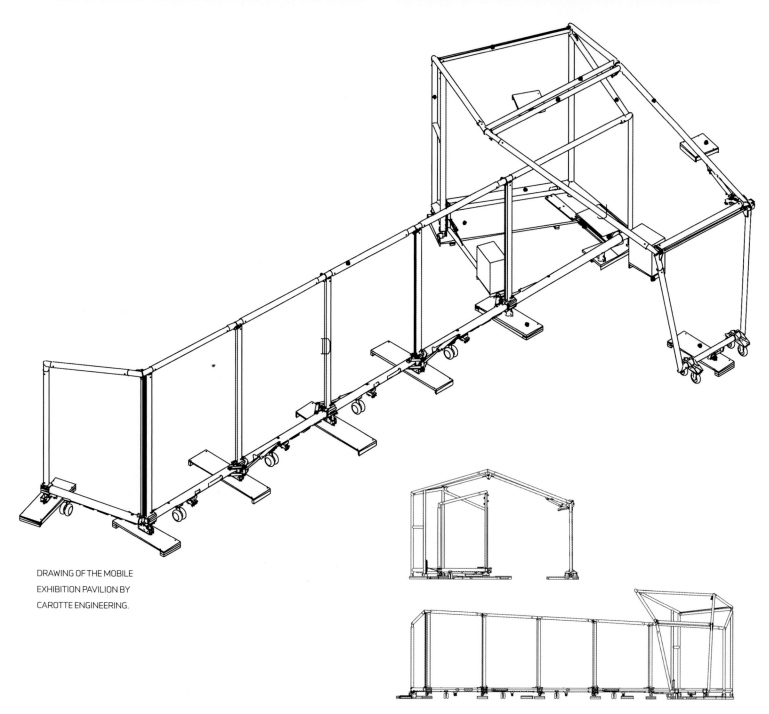

DRAWING OF THE MOBILE
EXHIBITION PAVILION BY
CAROTTE ENGINEERING.

PETER MISSOTTEN-
EXPECT POISON FROM
STANDING WATER IV.

DRIESSENS/VERSTAPPEN-
MEMBRANE.

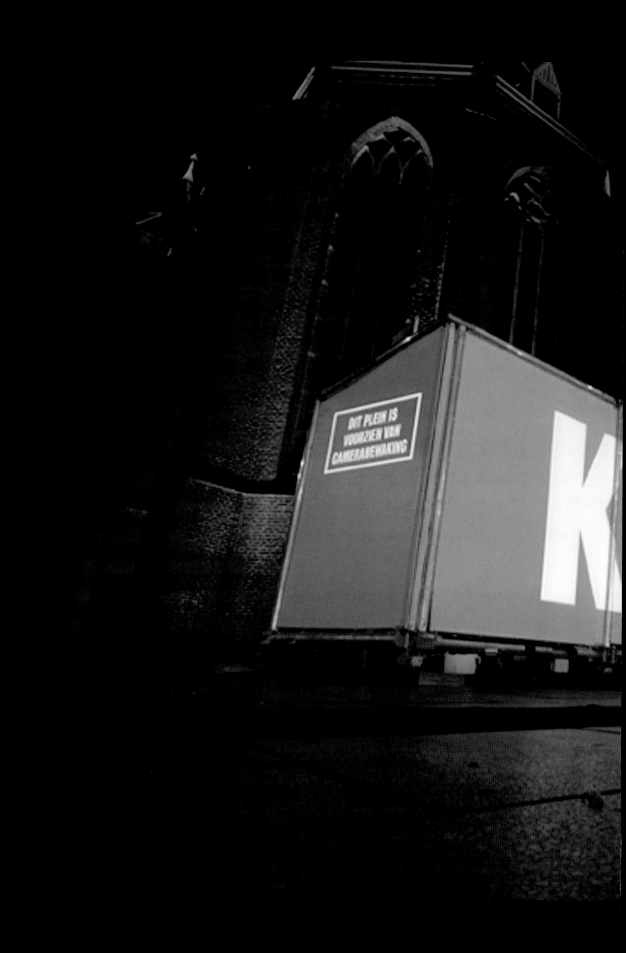

DIT PLEIN IS
VOORZIEN VAN
CAMERABEWAKING

'The project is a statement about the changing position many contemporary artists take for themselves; many don't want to be dependent on traditional museums or galleries any longer'

René van Engelenburg

MADER
STUBLIC
WIERMANN

SENEFELDERSTRASSE
10437 BERLIN
GERMANY
T +49 30 417 22 958
ATELIER@WEBBLICK.DE
WWW.WEBBLICK.DE

MADER STUBLIC WIERMANN

Staff: 3
Artists and architect: Holger Mader, Alexander Stublic, Heike Wiermann
Founded: 2001
Operates: Worldwide

AWARD

Segd Award, Uniqa Tower, Vienna/Austria, 2007
IALD Award, Uniqa Tower, Vienna/Austria

KEY PROJECTS

Media Façade, Reykjavik/Iceland, 2008
Twists and Turns, Uniqa Tower, Vienna/Austria, 2006
Reprojected, Osram Seven Screens, Munich/Germany, 2006

PROFILE
Artistic media and architectural design company Mader Stublic Wiermann, researches human perception through projects exploring the conflict between reality and simulation. Creating a new reality, the company generates spatial contexts by opening up traditional architecture as a means of space-creation to incorporate the temporal media of light, video and sound. While the projection for the Uniqa Tower in Vienna and the planned media façade in Reykjavik are about the intensification and deconstruction of architectural form, the real spatial situation of the Munich location for Reprojected was processed and absorbed into a simulation.

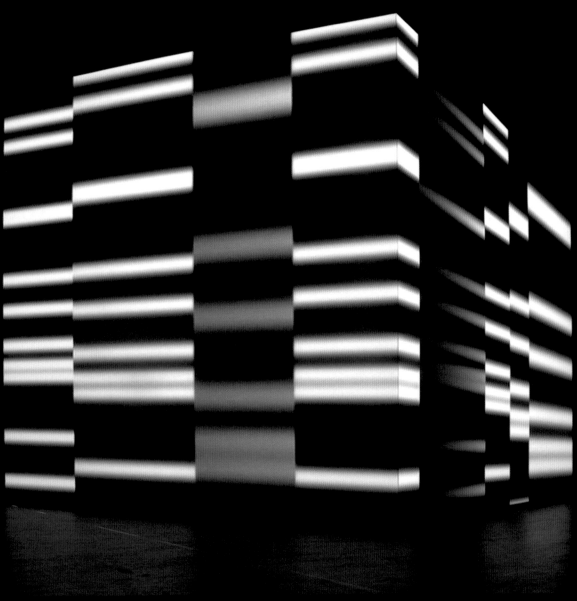

01

02

01   CUBE, A TEMPORARY
      INSTALLATION, USED
      TWO-DIMENSIONAL VIDEO
      PROJECTION OF BLACK
      AND WHITE PICTURES TO
      INTERACT WITH A REAL
      OBJECT, SIMULATING
      THREE-DIMENSIONAL
      SPATIAL AREAS.

02   THE MEDIA FAÇADE FOR
      ORKUVEITAN REYKJA-
      VIK COMMUNICATES A
      DYNAMIC FORM OF ARCHI-
      TECTURE ANALOGOUS TO
      THE EXISTING BUILDING
      BY DEVELOPING MOVING
      LINES AND GRID CONSTEL-
      LATIONS TAKEN FROM THE
      BUILDING'S STRUCTURE.

Reprojected Munich,
Germany

CLIENT

OSRAM

LIGHTING CONSULTANT

OSRAM / MICHAEL

REITHMEIER

CURATOR

DR. CHRISTIAN SCHOEN

PR

GOLDMANN

ENGINEER

OSRAM

MANUFACTURER

OSRAM

LIGHT SOURCE

HIGH-CAPACITY LEDS

TOTAL SURFACE

84 M²

DURATION OF

CONSTRUCTION

3 MONTHS

COMPLETION DATE

OCTOBER 2006

PHOTOGRAPHER

MADER STUBLIC

WIERMANN

WWW.WEBBLICK.DE

In 2006, lighting giant Osram celebrated its centenary year and the 40th anniversary of the Osram gallery by installing a new platform for art in the public domain. Situated in front of the company's Munich headquarters building, which itself is a luminescent piece of art containing over three million RGB, high-brightness LEDs. This 'Seven Screens' site consists of seven 6 m high light steles. Osram CEO, Martin Goetzeler, describes the objectives of the project: 'We want to use it to make the general public aware of the fascinating possibilities that new lighting sources can offer – and show that the Osram brand today still stands for innovation, as it did 100 years ago'.

Kick starting the digital art platform – changing twice a year to display the work of different young artists – Mader Stublic Wiermann created the installation's initial content, a video projection entitled 'Reprojected'. Catering for the site's central location on the middle ring road in Munich, the designers were asked to create a concept which would be swift and direct in its communication with the passing viewer. Mader Stublic Wiermann developed a concept that would re-define the normally flat or two-dimensional video picture with simple and reduced forms, abandoning the cinematic approaches of narration or illustrative film in favour of a more architectural condition. Blending film and life on the same stage, Reprojected uses virtual elements congruent with real space. The lucent columns stand tall, like portals to another dimension, and appear to capture Osram employees in transit from the office. Created by reconstructing the real situation to scale and in three-dimensions on a computer, computer-generated people were then tracked as they moved through a space of virtual lights. Their movements were translated into shadows as they brushed past the computerized steles. These various spatial scenarios were then extracted from the steles in Mader Stublic Wiermann's virtual environment and used to create the main video content for the installation. The end-result is one in which real space and simulated space are superimposed.

Unlike normal film, nothing is portrayed. Instead the picture surfaces become parts of a scene, with the spaces between them providing the location of the (virtual) event. The shadow of a real person can therefore be seen numerous times or can move across the steles with a time-delay. The overall vantage point is somewhat distanced and focuses exclusively on the shadows of computer-generated people who become visible only by means of a light source. Reprojected plays with the perception of 'the space between', introducing a distance between events and the installation. For the viewer, the piece creates the impression of simultaneity in real and virtual space, with the steles acting as a link between the two. This complex, two-way programming suggests an artificial form of reality located not beyond physical reality but right in its midst. To generate these impressions, Reprojected interprets video as light. Light art is therefore more finely meshed – and becomes video art.

Allowing the Seven Screens to project both static and moving pictures, seven masts are equipped with Osram's latest, double-sided LED light technology. Controlled from a central computer via fibre optics, tubes are fitted at a grid distance of 10 mm with 55,296 LEDs per light surface, and over 750,000 RGB, high-capacity LEDs.

SECTION OF THE LIGHT
STELES.

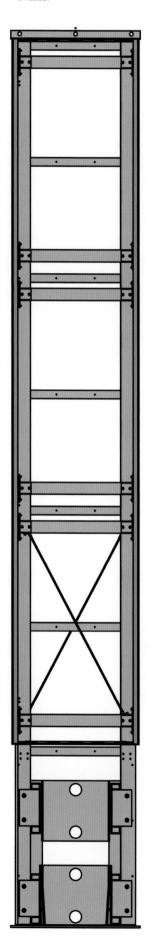

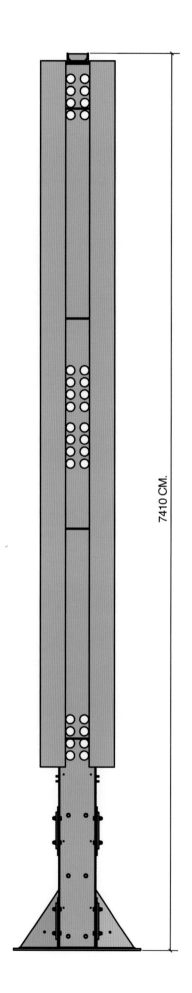

7410 CM.

THE TUBES ARE EQUIPPED
WITH OVER THREE-QUAR-
TERS OF A MILLION RGB
HIGH-CAPACITY LEDS,
WHICH CAN BE CONTROL-
LED FROM A CENTRAL
COMPUTER VIA OPTIC
FIBRES.

The lucent columns stand tall, like portals to another dimension

LDE BELZNER HOLMES

BELZNER HOLMES, ARCHITEKTUR - LICHT - BÜHNE
Staff: 16
Principals: Uwe Belzner, Andrew Holmes
Founded: 1992
Operates: Europe, Asia
Memberships: LDE, ELDA

AWARDS
IALD Award of Merit, 2002
Architekturlicht Preis, 2002
IALD Award of Merit, 2000
Renault Traffic Award, 2000
Mention in Architekturlicht Preis, 2000

KEY PROJECTS
Lightplan, Hammerfest, Norway, in progress
Congress Center, Rosengarten, Mannheim/Germany, 2007
Shanghai Automotive Museum, China, 2006

Market Square Coburg, Germany, 2005
Church Center Munich Riem, Germany, 2004
Erco Highbay Warehouse, Lüdenscheid/Germany, 2001
Garten der Erinnerung, Duisburg/Germany, 1999

PROFILE
Belzner Holmes is a design studio based in Heidelberg, Germany. Primary design areas for the company are lighting on all scales from interior (architectural, exhibition, theatre, event), to exterior (architectural and landscape lighting and urban spaces). Additional design fields include interior and set design, trade-fair and event design as well as speciality in-theatre technology. Both Uwe Belzner and Andrew Holmes are architects and urban planners with substantial theatre-lighting backgrounds. This combination gives the company a sound basis from which to tackle most challenges in architectural lighting and its related fields. Belzner Holmes is founding member of the Light Design Engineering network (www.lde-net.com).

01

02

03

01 SCULPTURAL LIGHTING OF
    AN ART NOUVEAU WATER
    TOWER – WASSERTURM
    MANNHEIM – CLEARLY DE-
    LINEATES THE ARCHITEC-
    TURAL COMPONENTS.

02 KURPARK BAD AIBLING:
    DRAMATIC LIGHTING OF
    THE KURPARK.

03 ERCO P3 IS AN AWARD-
    WINNING WAREHOUSE
    WHICH HAS BEEN DYNAMI-
    CALLY LIT. ARCHITECTS:
    SCHNEIDER SCHUMACH-
    ER, FRANKFURT.

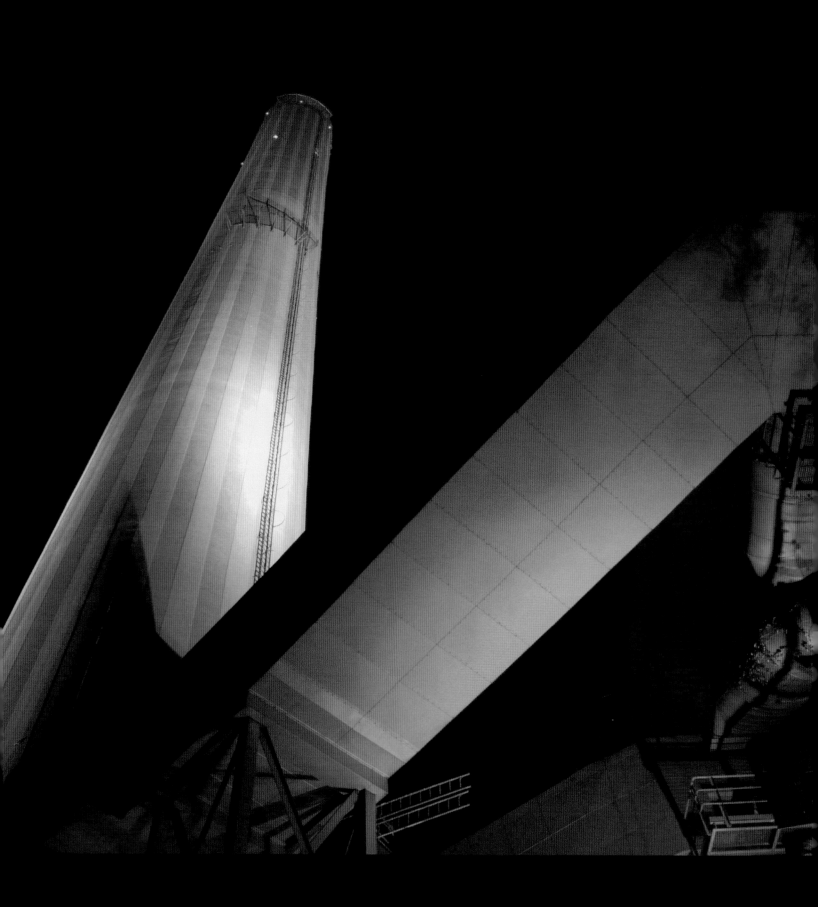

CLOSE-UP OF ELEMENTS.

Westhafen Power Station Frankfurt, Germany

CLIENTS

IGUZZINI, MAINOVA

CONCEPT

BELZNER HOLMES

CONSULTANT

SL-LICHT FOR IGUZZINI

TECHNICAL PROJECT

MANAGER

JOHANNES BÄHR FOR

BELZNER HOLMES

MANUFACTURER

IGUZZINI

LIGHT SOURCES

4 COLOR WOODY 250W HIT,

4 COLOR WOODY 400 W HIT,

16 MAXI WOODY MEDIUM

400W HIT WITH GLASS

FILTER, 7 MAXI WOODY

SUPERSPOT 400 W HIT

WITH GLASS FILTER

4 MAXI WOODY SPOT 250 W

HIT WITH GLASS FILTER, 20

PLATEA FLOOD 70W WITH

GLASS FILTER, 65 BLUE

FLUORESCENT TUBES 36W,

65 BLUE FLUORESCENT

TUBES 58W

TOTAL SURFACE

FAÇADE AND CHIMNEY

20,000 M²

TOTAL COST

€ 100,000

DURATION OF

CONSTRUCTION

2 WEEKS

COMPLETION DATE

APRIL 2006

PHOTOGRAPHERS

JÖRG HEMPEL (ERCO P3)

WWW.JOERG-HEMPEL.COM

ANTJE SCHMIDT

ANDREW HOLMES

WWW.LED-NET.COM

In Autumn 2005, Frankfurt representatives of lighting manufacturer iGuzzini contacted Belzner Holmes. They asked for a concept and support for their contribution to 'Luminale – the Lighting and Culture Spectacle', which would take place parallel to the Light+Building Trade Fair in Frankfurt in April 2006. The basic idea of Luminale is 'to take the themes of lighting and architecture featured at Light+Building and bring them to the City.' The idea was originally to illuminate the river-facing façade of a centrally-located, large museum on the southern bank of the Main, for whom Belzner Holmes had just completed a festive illumination of the east wing courtyard façade and grounds continuing through to the garden patio. The illumination of the main façade was negotiated with the director, whose term unfortunately finished at the end of the year. The new director felt that 'the art is in the house – not the house itself!' – meaning no lighting of the building after all.

Meanwhile, the organizers of Luminale had been propagating the Illumination of the museum as one of the highlights of this spectacular event which takes place once every two years. So another equally prominent object had to be found. After a brief phase of scouting, an alternative was found: the Westhafen Power Station. Fortunately the owners – Mainova (Frankfurt's municipal works) – were enthusiastic about the project and even joined as sponsor.

By happy coincidence, the power station turned out to be a more apt choice for this project. Due to its size and location, the power station in Westhafen (the western docks) is visible for long distances, both along the entire length of the southern bank of the river Main and from the exhibition area itself to the north and beyond. All trains that travel to or from Frankfurt's main station pass directly by the power station. Previous to the lighting project, the power station had been largely neglected in the cityscape and certainly hadn't been perceived as the landmark it was to become.

The lighting concept is based on various narrative intentions. The first, on an urban scale, was to create an apex for the inner city where the skyline is dominated by high-rise office buildings. The purpose of this was to create a reflective symmetry between this area and the Frankfurt Dome of similar proportions, about 3 km to the east, for which Belzner Holmes is just planning the illumination with Thomas Emde. Second was to show the main structure of the plant in the city's nightscape. The two 72-m-high main boiler houses and the two chimneys, which are up to 125 m high, were all to be illuminated. The colour choice for illumination was based on the original colour scheme of the structure, namely bright red and ochre which, over

the past decades, has faded to dull aubergine and grey tones. Using different colours for the different parts of the building clearly contrasts the post-modern, barrel-shaped roofs from the main body. To make the actual scale of the boiler houses more understandable, the escape staircase platforms were illuminated in blue. To exemplify what happens in the buildings (the burning of coal) and to draw attention to the chimneys, dynamic colour changes were installed suggesting the glowing embers of a fire. Though the chosen colours may seem exaggerated, the fade into each new colour is very subtle and scarcely perceivable.

A large selection of iGuzzini architectural spotlights were installed in positions on and around the rooftops and escape galleries of adjacent buildings. The majority were equipped with pre-selected colour filters. Blue tubes replaced the fluorescent lighting of the standard white escape route. The dynamic 'amber-glow' lighting effect was achieved with programmable colour-changing spotlights. Implementation was divided as follows: iGuzzini provided and installed the equipment; Mainova supplied energy, the building, electrical connections and general support.

The installation was a huge success and became a highlight of Luminale. After the event, Mainova decided to keep the illumination as a permanent feature. Now the power station lights up at the western end of downtown Frankfurt every night and is a large beacon for everyone approaching Frankfurt from the west.

LIGHT AND REFLECTION
ON THE GROUNDS OF THE
POWER PLANT.

LONG DISTANCE VIEW OF
LIGHTED PLANT, SILHOU-
ETTING THE BUILDINGS IN
THE FOREGROUND.

LIGHT AND CONTRAST
FROM THE POWER PLANT.

LIGHT AND CONTRAST
FROM THE GROUNDS OF
THE POWER PLANT.

The power station lights up at the western end of downtown Frankfurt every night and is a large beacon for everyone approaching Frankfurt

AWA LIGHTING DESIGNERS
Staff: 18
Management: Reeta Gyamlani
Key designers: Abhay Wadhwa, Wai Mun Chui, Courtney Mark
Founded: 2002
Operates: Worldwide
Memberships: IESNA, USGBC, AIA, LEED AP

KEY PROJECTS
U-Bora Towers, Dubai/UAE, under construction
Mumbai International Airport, Mumbai/India, 2007
Peak Tower, Hong Kong/China, 2006
Mumbai University, Mumbai/India, 2006
Port Authority Bus Terminal, NY-NJ/USA, 2004

KEY CLIENTS
Aedas
Architect Hafeez Contractor
Arcop
Contemporary Urban
Design Cell Studio
FXFowle Architects
H3 Hardy Design Collaborative
Hong Kong and Shanghai Hotel Group
Kiss + Cathcart Architects
Point B Design
Port Authority of NY and NJ

PROFILE
Founded by Abhay Wadhwa, AWA is a New York City-based international architectural lighting design firm. The company creates solutions which evoke a sense of place rather than mere space. The lighting solutions the company has designed and implemented have been used in commercial, civic and residential projects alike. A unique worldwide service is provided through AWA's offices in New York, Mumbai, Hong Kong and Dubai. Each of these offices operates independently, but uniform standards infuse the same spirit of inquiry and collaborative energy. This work ethos ensures that all projects, regardless of location, are the subject of the highest levels of quality control.

AWA LIGHTING DESIGNERS

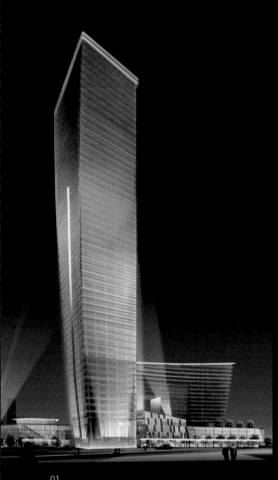

01

02

01   THE U-BORA TOWER IN
       DUBAI

02   COMMEMORATING
       MUMBAI UNIVERSITY'S
       150TH ANNIVERSARY IN
       2006, AWA INSTALLED
       THE BUILDING'S FIRST
       EVER ELECTRICAL LIGHT-
       ING SYSTEM USED FOR
       EVENING EVENTS. ALL IN-
       STALLATION PROCEDURES
       AND FIXTURES CHOSEN
       WERE SYMPATHETIC TO
       THE ARCHITECTURAL
       BEAUTY OF THE EXISTING
       STRUCTURE.

03   LEDS PROGRAMMED TO
       CHANGE COLOUR AT DIF-
       FERENT SPEEDS TRANS-
       FORMED 3 WEST 13TH
       STREET, NEW YORK INTO A
       DIGITALIZED WATER TANK.
       AWA'S BESPOKE LIGHTING
       PROGRAMME GIVES A
       DYNAMIC STREET SCULP-
       TURE WHICH APPEARS
       TO FILL WITH COLOURED
       WATER, BEFORE DRAINING
       OUT AGAIN.

AWA LIGHTING DESIGNERS
DESIGNED A LIGHTING SY-
STEM FOR THE BUILDING'S
INTERIOR AND FAÇADE.

Peak Tower Hong Kong Island, China

CLIENT

HONG KONG & SHANGHAI
HOTEL GROUP

ARCHITECT

RONALD LU & PARTNERS

LIGHTING DESIGN

AWA

LIGHT SOURCES

DOWN-LIGHTS, UP-LIGHTS,
LED PANELS

TOTAL SURFACE

152,400 M²

DURATION OF

CONSTRUCTION

2 YEARS

COMPLETION DATE

NOVEMBER 2006

PHOTOGRAPHERS

ABHAY WADHWA
WWW.AWALIGHTINGDE-
SIGNERS.COM

MARCEL LAM
WWW.MARCELLAM.COM

At 552 m above sea level, the Peak is the highest mountain on Hong Kong Island. Renowned for its spectacular views of the city and harbour, Peak Mountain has become a popular tourist destination, attracting approximately seven million visitors each year.
156 m below the summit of Victoria Peak lies Victoria gap - a dip along a line of hills at an elevation of 396 m - and the auspicious location of the Peak Tower. Proportionate to its neighbouring landscape, the tower stands 428 m above sea level. Since its original construction in 1971, the building has undergone a series of regeneration projects. Initially transformed from restaurants, and coffee shops into a new retail and entertainment complex in 1997, at the cost of HK$ 500 million, the tower eventually achieved its latest reincarnation – through an extensive revitalization process – in 2005. The iconic boat-shaped structure, designed by architect Terry Farrell, which includes features such as a solid base, open podium and a magnificent floating roof with up-swept eaves - typical of traditional Chinese architecture - was retained during the latest architectural interventions. Illuminated by AWA Architectural Lighting Designers in 2006, the newly renovated building now boasts an additional floor and roof-top viewing terrace. Briefed by Hong Kong & Shanghai Hotel Group – owners of both Peak Tower and Peak Tram – to design a lighting system for the building's interior and façade, Abhay Wadhwa, principal of AWA Architectural Lighting explains the company's approach: 'We are engaged in dynamic, technologically sophisticated design that reflects the vision of the architect. Whether it is an historical renovation or a new building altogether, our design is carefully tailored to enhance the site and its uses'. To draw focus to the iconic nature of the building, the company chose advanced technology systems that create colourful special effects and scenes. These features are all programmable through one central system. The lighting of Peak Tower is therefore both dynamic and functional.

Visible from almost anywhere in Hong Kong, AWA explored the tower's setting and surrounding environment to create a lighting concept to address both the distant viewer and visitors interacting personally on site. The result is also carefully interwoven with the architecture.

Coordinated with lighting elements throughout the building, the ceiling - a luminous sky - consists of 700 individual panels, fixed in a grid, with each pixel individually lit and controlled through flash files. The curvature for each pixel was carefully calculated to eliminate colour-bleed between pixels whilst still maintaining an even wash and colour mix over each pixel.

The two parts - a 55-minute sequence and a five-minute 'Showtime' script - illuminate the pixelated ceiling, crystal ceiling and underside of the boat and are synchronized so 'the whole building sings and dances together', as Wadhwa explains. The colours from the five-minute 'Showtime' display - which reads 'Welcome to Peak Tower' in both English and Chinese - are repeated on the pixelated ceiling and on the underside of the boat. Transitions (cuts, sweeps, irises, fades) and colour-changes between the various video images are also synchronized across these three areas. The visitor experience is likewise enhanced through movement within Peak Tower; additional lights were built into the railings and the underside of escalators to create an environment that AWA describes as both 'welcoming and exciting'. Like a champagne cork popping out of a bottle-neck, the escalator which connects a selection of high-end restaurants on the building's upper floors is surrounded by a bespoke lighting effect that resembles rising bubbles. This feature is a prime example of how AWA tailored this diverse lighting scheme to match the venue's varying clientele.
For the upper Peak Tram terminal, also housed within Peak Tower, AWA installed colour-changing LEDs which display different patterns to indicate the arrival and departure of trams, thus providing a source of entertainment for the 11,000 people who use the tram each day.

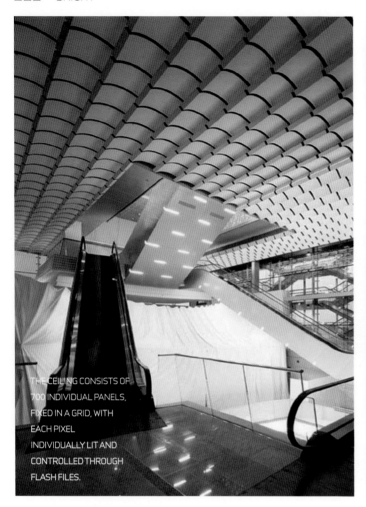

THE CEILING CONSISTS OF 700 INDIVIDUAL PANELS, FIXED IN A GRID, WITH EACH PIXEL INDIVIDUALLY LIT AND CONTROLLED THROUGH FLASH FILES.

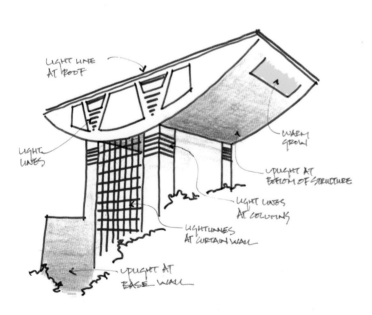

SKETCH OF THE EXTERNAL LIGHTING PLAN.

THE ESCALATOR SURROUNDED BY A BESPOKE LIGHTING EFFECT THAT RESEMBLES RISING BUBBLES.

THE PEAK TOWER STANDS
428 M ABOVE SEA LEVEL.

'The whole building sings and dances together' Abhay Wadhwa

THE CURVATURE FOR
EACH PIXEL ON THE
CEILING WAS CAREFULLY
DESIGNED TO ELIMINATE
COLOR BLEED BETWEEN
PIXELS, WHILE MAINTAI-
NING AN EVEN WASH AND
COLOR MIX OVER EACH
PIXEL.

PANIRAMA

PANIRAMA

Staff: 3
Management: Kai-Uwe Schwenck, Thomas Treubel
Key designers: Kai-Uwe Schwenck, Ingo Dietzel
Founded: 2005
Operates: Europe

PROFILE

Lighting manufacturing and design company Panirama was
established in 2005 by lighting designer Kai-Uwe Schwenck and
businessman Thomas Treubel. In this joint venture to pursue their
passion professionally, the duo each contribute years of experience
in their respective industries to create a business-savvy, artistically
led company. Projects have included lighting schemes for architecture, festivals and marketing events, with the advertising industry
making ever-increasing use of their mobile, lit signboards.

01

02

03

01   FOR LIGHT INSTALLATION

02   'SHIP LIFT STATION', 14

03   HIGH-POWER PROJECTORS
            TRANSFORMED MORE
            THAN 3,000 M² INTO A
            BRIGHTLY COLOURED
            CANVAS.

PANIRAMA'S GOAL WAS TO
LIGHT THE BUILDING AS
A WHOLE AND EMPHA-
SIZE ITS MONUMENTAL
STRUCTURE.

Berliner Dom Berlin,
Germany

CLIENT

CITY INITIATIVE BERLIN

LIGHTING DESIGN

PANIRAMA

MANUFACTURER

PANIRAMA

LIGHT SOURCES

6 PANI BP, 6 TURBO

DURATION OF

CONSTRUCTION

3 DAYS

COMPLETION DATE

OCTOBER 2006

PHOTOGRAPHER

STEFAN DAUTH

WWW.STEFANDAUTH.COM

During Berlin's Festival of Lights, initiated by the City Foundation Berlin and project partner DIFA under the artistic direction of Andreas Boehlke, landmarks such as the TV and Radio Towers, historic buildings including the Brandenburg Gate, the Berliner Dom and the Olympic Stadium and even entire streets, are illuminated to create a city alive with colour.

For the city's second festival in 2006, lighting designers Panirama were invited to illuminate the Berliner Dom – the city's impressive cathedral – with high-power projectors. Free to develop the project without the restrictions of a brief, lighting designers Kai-Uwe Schwenck and Ingo Dietzel created a unique lighting concept, inspired by the history of the city's largest church, for the 3,000 m2 West Portal. The goal of the illumination was to focus attention on the building with its rich and varied history - from the first Stiftsbau dating from 1465, to its current form. The cathedral as it stands today - a Baroque-influenced style of the Italian High Renaissance - was completed in 1905 after 11 years of construction. Flanked by four corner towers, the dome rises 114 m above street level and is the most prominent structure on Berlin's Museumsinsel – a small island in the Spree River protected as a UNESCO World Heritage Site, and regarded as one of the most important museum complexes in the world. The structure, decorated inside and out with lavish images from the New Testament and the Reformation, originally cost 11.5 million Marks to build. Architects estimate that a similar project today would cost approximately 180 million Euro. Criticism of the building began even before it was dedicated and continues to this day. The cathedral is accused of being too showy, too glitzy and a Byzantine expression of imperial extravagance. However, even in the midst of all this controversy, the cathedral continues to gain new admirers. Its imposing architecture has a festive and exhilarating effect and once inside, visitors are greeted with a place for quiet prayer amidst the hustle and bustle of central Berlin.

When planning their concept for the 2006 Festival of Lights, lighting designers Schwenck and Dietzel decided against accentuating any single individual component of the architecture. Instead, their goal was to light the building as a whole and make a feature of its monumental structure. During the development of their plans, the designers used the symmetry and aesthetics of the building as a guide. Their primary impetus was a desire to combine a sense of lightness with the scale of the building, whilst simultaneously emphasizing and celebrating the imposing architecture. In order to accurately plan their lighting design, Panirama used a camera obscura to create a 'scan' of the Dom's façade which, once uploaded to a PC,

allowed them to scale their images accordingly. An urban chameleon, the contrasts and colours of the Dom's multiple light skins were worked out during weeks of preparations resulting in a sequence of bold, kaleidoscopic images. Despite being based on the history of the building, the sheer scale of the images left them open to interpretation; abstracted to a greater or lesser extent depending on the location of the viewer. Up close, the images became blurred mists of colour, whereas further back on the Lustgarten (the park in front of the cathedral), the detail was as sharp as the glossy advertisements masqueraded on nearby buildings. Purple backdrops with yellow and red patterns, a mass of orange circles – like hundreds of digitalized embryos, and a yellow, black and white pattern forming a vertical field of daisies, were amongst the images projected over the festival's two-week course. Bringing the inside out, Panirama's creation provided a visual feast to passers-by - who may not normally venture inside the various museums arrayed around the edges of the park.

The lighting design employed six latest-generation PANI high-performance turbo projectors. Three of the projectors were set up only 30 m from the portal and the other three 100 m away.

The art of creating a uniform whole from six projected images under difficult projection conditions was an additional challenge for the two designers. However, when asked if they encountered any technical problems with the project, manager Thomas Treubel's answer was simple: 'We are professionals! No technical problems at all'.

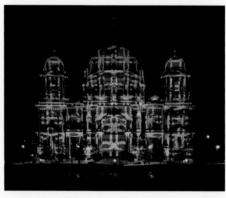

THE CONTRAST AND
COLOURS OF THE DOM'S
MULTIPLE LIGHT SKINS
RESULTED IN A SEQUENCE
OF BOLD KALEIDOSCOPIC
IMAGES.

The cathedral is accused of being too showy, too glitzy and a Byzantine expression of imperial extravagance

UP CLOSE, THE PROJECTED IMAGES BECAME BLURRED MISTS OF COLOUR WHEREAS FURTHER BACK ON THE LUSTGARTEN, THE PATTERNS BECAME VERY SHARP.

MBLD

Staff: 13
Management: Maurice Brill, Rob Honeywill, Tapio Rosenius
Key designers: Maurice Brill, Rob Honeywill, Tapio Rosenius, Lee Sweetman, Claudia Espinosa, Rebecca Harris, Christian Wendel, Zjeenja Gouwerok, Victoria Jones, Thanh Tran
Founded: 1982
Operates: Worldwide
Membership: PLDA

AWARDS
FX Awards, Winner, 2005
IALD Award of Excellence, 2004
The Lighting Design Awards, Winner, 2004

KEY PROJECTS
Broadgate, London/UK, ongoing
National Assembly, Bahrain
201 Bishopsgate & Broadgate Tower, London/UK, 2008
Fairmont Nile City & Heliopolis, Cairo/Egypt, 2008
One & Only Kanuhura, Kanuhura/Maldives, 2006
Sketch Restaurant, London/UK, 2002
Grand Hyatt, Berlin/Germany, 2000
Burj al Arab Hotel interior, Dubai, 1999
Peninsula Hotel, Hong Kong/China, 1994

PROFILE
A major aim of MBLD is to maximize the impact of the space around us, whether in hotels, shopping centres, museums or outdoor environments. The team strives to achieve its aesthetic objectives and to fulfil the design requirements of the brief with a high degree of technical competence and imagination, while remaining aware of the psychological effects of lighting. Light is used to enhance space, to define its authority, and to evoke the right mood for people in and around the building. MBLD can dramatically transform the experience of space in response to the business needs of its clients.

01

02

01   THE ASPIRATION WAS
02   TO MAKE REGENT'S
      PLACE TRITON SQUARE IN
      LONDON A FOCAL POINT
      DURING THE DAY AND AN
      EXCITING DESTINATION
      AT NIGHT. THE SQUARE
      – FRAMED BY ART IN
      MANY FORMS – BOASTS
      A COLOUR-CHANGING
      FLOOR FEATURE AS ITS
      CENTREPIECE.

03   THE RADISSON LUXURY
      RESORT COMPRISES 296
      ROOMS AND SUITES,
      FOUR RESTAURANTS,
      THREE BARS, A SPA WITH
      POOL DECK AND A BEACH.
      MBLD'S CONTRIBUTION TO
      THE PROJECT INCLUDED
      LIGHTING DESIGN FOR ALL
      AREAS OF THE RESORT.

03

THE INGROUND LIGHTING
INSTALLATION USES CO-
LOUR-CHANGING LEDS TO
TURN THE SQUARE INTO A
DYNAMIC SPECTACLE.

Broadgate London, UK

CLIENT
BRITISH LAND
ARCHITECT
SKIDMORE, OWINGS &
MERRILL
LIGHTING DESIGN
MBLD
PROJECT MANAGEMENT
M3 CONSULTING
MAIN CONTRACTOR
BOVIS LEND LEASE
ENGINEER
JB & B
MANUFACTURERS
ARTISTIC LICENSE, WE-EF
LIGHT SOURCES
ARTISTIC LICENSE
(CUSTOM-MADE RGB LED
FLOOR TROUGH), WE-EF
(INGROUND UPLIGHTS)
COMPLETION DATE
ONGOING

PHOTOGRAPHERS
TAPIO ROSENIUS, ROB
HONEYWILL
WWW.MBLD.COM

TOM BRILL
MAIL@TOMBRILL.CO.UK

JOHN ATTWELL
WWW.JOHNATTWELL.COM

The Broadgate Estate in the City of London provides some 360,000 m² of office, retail and leisure accommodation spread over 13 hectares. The area employs 30,000 people and has a mix of bars, restaurants and public spaces. In 1997 MBLD was commissioned to study the area and to draft a lighting report, outlining ways of improving Broadgate's night-time appearance. The report proposed to 'open' the complex by creating lit gateways, 'footprints' and night-time destination areas. This report later became the brief for the lighting scheme designed by MBLD, which comprises high- and low-rise building façades, landscaping, artwork and special dynamic lighting features. A large proportion of the scheme has now been completed.

A recent addition was Finsbury Avenue Square, which went on to win two lighting-design awards in 2004: the IALD Award of Excellence and the LIF Exterior Lighting Award. The judges described the lighting design as 'quite simply one of the outstanding schemes of recent years' and 'a technically demanding creation'. The project is still ongoing for MBLD, with new areas and buildings being added into the scheme and full completion envisaged some time in 2009.

The latest addition to Broadgate's buildings is 10 Exchange Square. The new building provides a gateway on the western edge of the Broadgate Estate. A series of textured cast-glass walls defines the space and visually conducts pedestrians through the new urban area. A generous stair mitigates the change in levels from the street to Exchange Square. The entrance stair extends into the lobby to provide alternative indoor and outdoor routes, while also allowing the external space to appear more expansive. At night, light is cast from the base of the walls, providing a subtle glow that frames the space and lends further ambiguity to the definition between inside and outside. Innovative LED lighting detail was developed for the main façade lighting. Stainless-steel spandrel panels were modified to accept discreet channel with blue LEDs indirectly illuminating the super-brushed finish of the steel. The linear detail expresses the curvature of the façade and the mass of the building in a subtle yet effective way, with no visible luminaires. The scheme is very low maintenance – with an estimated seven-to-ten-year lamp replacement cycle – and consumes a fraction of the energy typically required for lighting a ten-storey-high façade.

Finsbury Avenue Square represented a significant milestone in MBLD's lighting master plan for Broadgate. The inground lighting installation, one of the world's largest exterior lighting projects using colour-changing LEDs, turns the square in the Broadgate complex into a dynamic, ever-changing spectacle. The square was formerly an unprepossessing space at night, which users skulked through on their way to nearby Liverpool Street station. The project originated in a Broadgate lighting survey commissioned by property owner British Land in the late '90s. 'One of our proposals was that we could use lighting to create a series of features or focal points, which would help people find their way around,' says MBLD creative director Maurice Brill. Eventually, the idea for an illuminated inground matrix of lights emerged for Finsbury Avenue Square. The concept began as the brainchild of SOM Architects. 'There were five main technical requirements,' explains Brill. 'The installation had to be waterproof, low power, low maintenance, fully automatic – and it had to create dynamic, changing, colour shows.' The £750,000 scheme has a total of 650 DMX-controlled IP68 units, in five lengths, containing over 100,000 individual LEDs in RGB clusters to offer a full range of colours. These form a 20-x-20-m central grid matrix with 'arms' extending 5 to 10 m farther out on each side. Each 'intelligent fixture' has two-way remote device management (RMD), which allows the fixture to be dimmed locally, and three diagnostic sensors that 'talk back' to the central control system if there's water leakage, overheating or LED failure. There are currently ten lighting scenes – washes, chases, rapid colour changes, line movements and so forth – which are run in seven blocks, two shows a night, to provide a different programme every night. Visual result, which turns this formerly staid business square into a piece of dancing magic, seven nights a week, is unique in its colourful intensity, sharp movement and variety of effect.

A clean, bezel-less finish was required and was designed in two parts: an outer load-bearing drainage channel in steel, with the RGB LED units mounted in an aluminium extrusion hung inside it. The top glazing – 32-mm-thick laminated toughened glass with an opal finish, silk-screened with an anti-slip pattern – is bonded onto the steel body.

UBS BUILDING FAÇADE AT
BROADGATE.

ACCENT LIGHTING FOR
GATE AT BROADGATE.

SIGNATURE WALL LUMI-
NAIRE FOR BROADGATE.

10 EXCHANGE SQUARE
FAÇADE WITH DISCREET
LED ILLUMINATION.

FINSBURY AVENUE
SQUARE URBAN LIGHT
SHOW.

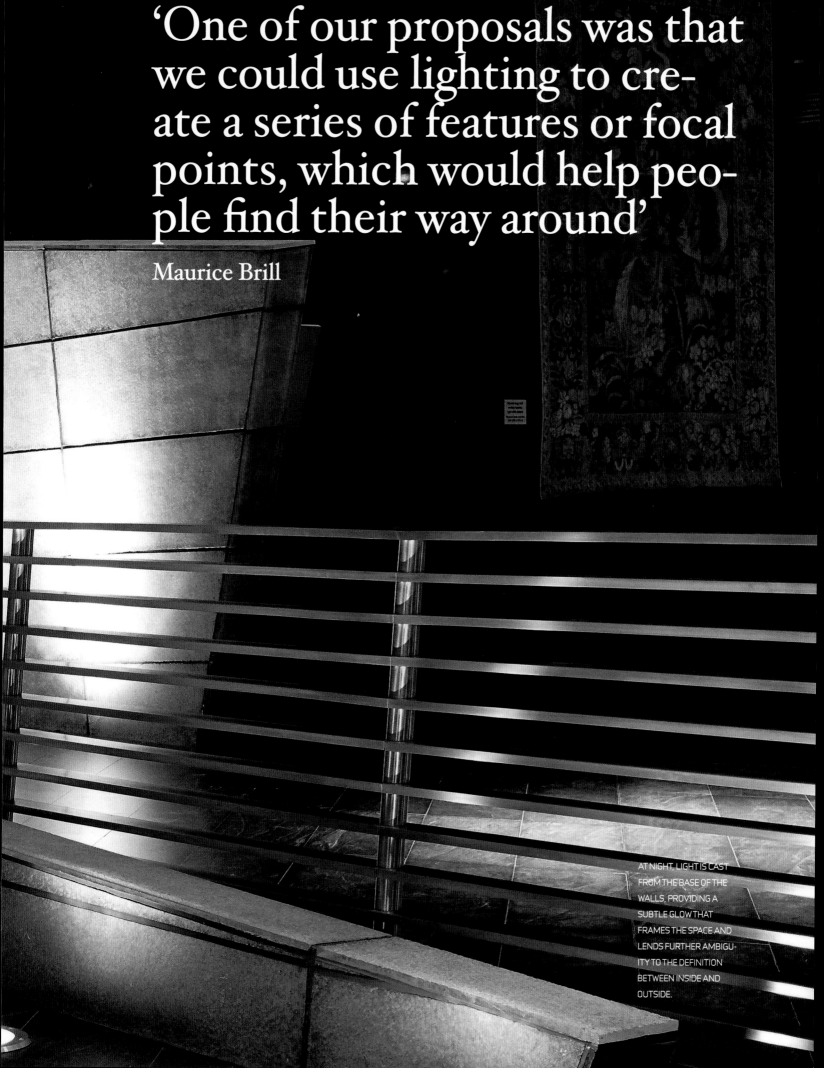

'One of our proposals was that we could use lighting to create a series of features or focal points, which would help people find their way around'

Maurice Brill

AT NIGHT, LIGHT IS CAST FROM THE BASE OF THE WALLS, PROVIDING A SUBTLE GLOW THAT FRAMES THE SPACE AND LENDS FURTHER AMBIGUITY TO THE DEFINITION BETWEEN INSIDE AND OUTSIDE.

THIS IS THE INTERACTIVE SECTION

IMMERSIVE REACTIVE EXPERIENCES THAT DEPEND ON HUMAN BEHAVIOUR TO CONVEY MESSAGES THROUGH LIGHT, THE INTERACTIVE WORKS IN THIS SECTION OF THE BOOK UTILIZE CUTTING-EDGE TECHNOLOGIES SUCH AS THERMAL IMAGING CAMERAS, TRACKING DEVICES AND BLUETOOTH SENSORS.

UNITED
VISUAL
ARTISTS

01

02

03

01 ECHO – AN 8 MINUTE, LIVE
PERFORMANCE PIECE –
WAS COMMISSIONED BY
VAMP, FOR A LAUNCH IN
THE TURBINE HALL OF THE
TATE MODERN IN 2006.
THE PROJECT WAS PRO-
DUCED IN COLLABORA-
TION WITH MIMBRE – AN
ACROBATIC PERFORM-
ANCE THEATRE COMPANY.

02 DIGITAL REPRESENTA-
TIONS OF INFORMATION –
REAL-TIME NEWS, GLOBAL
STATISTICS AND SPAM
EMAILS – FORMED THE
BACKDROP OF MASSIVE
ATTACK'S GLOBAL TOUR
IN 2003. TRANSLATED
INTO 36 LANGUAGES, THE
DISPLAY WAS PERFECTLY
SYNCHRONIZED WITH THE
BAND'S COMPUTERS.

03 PROVIDING THE MAIN
SOURCE OF LIGHT AT
LONDON'S KABARET
PROPHECY CLUB, A LOW-
RESOLUTION LED WALL
ALTERNATES BETWEEN
SERENE DIGITAL WALL-
PAPER AND INTENSELY
RHYTHMIC, GRAPHIC
VISUALS.

VOLUME CREATES A
TRULY IMMERSIVE FIELD
OF SOUND AND LIGHT,
PROVOKING A PERSONAL,
MEDITATIVE EXPERIENCE.

Volume London, UK

CLIENTS

VICTORIA & ALBERT
MUSEUM, SONY
COMPUTER ENTERTAIN-
MENT EUROPE

ARTIST

UNITED VISUAL ARTISTS

LIGHTING DESIGN

LITESTRUCTURES

PHYSICAL STRUCTURE

LITESTRUCTURES

LED RENTAL

XL VIDEO UK

LIGHT SOURCES

BARCO O-LITE LED PANELS

TOTAL SURFACE

90 M²

**DURATION OF
CONSTRUCTION**

3 MONTHS

COMPLETION DATE

2006

PHOTOGRAPHER

JOHN ADRIAN

WWW.SUPERMATIC.CO.UK

Volume was commissioned by the Victoria & Albert Museum as part of the Sony Playstation season. The project was conceived by United Visual Artists (UVA), and the production company onepointsix - Neil Davidge and Robert Del Naja of Massive Attack - was brought on board to create the musical elements.
The brief was to create an immersive, digital and interactive installation as a site-specific response to the John Madejski Garden at the centre of the Victoria & Albert Museum. UVA succeeded in the task of increasing visitor numbers for the garden, which struggles to draw in the crowds during the winter months, despite its impressive architecture and feel.
The light-based installation resulted in extraordinary visitor figures compared to the same season in 2006/2007.
Required to appeal to all visitors - from children to pensioners - UVA's installation also had to be able to run unassisted, in an outdoor location, for a two-and-a-half-month period as well as being completely weather resistant. Inspired by the practice's previous site-specific installation for the Transvision event – organized by onedotzero – which occupied the same space in March 2006, a form of responsive, LED-based sculpture was used as the starting point in the design and commissioning process. The original project, which consisted of a single band of colour and simple, analogue synth sounds, becoming harsher and more aggressive as you approached, was developed to create an all-enveloping field of light and sound. Comprising 46 columns, Volume was arranged in a grid measuring 10.5 x 9 m. Columns were housed within custom-built aluminium extrusions (designed and made by Litestructures) to ensure minimal visibility for the framework. Each column contained a high-output, low-resolution Barco O-Lite LED grid and a single Sony audio speaker at its apex. Placed on a precisely contoured flat platform of Litedeck, cut to follow the concave floor of the garden's former pond, the installation formed a regular sound and light field, whose elements dynamically responded to the location of audience members. Each column was finished in glossy black, creating varied reflections contributing to the play of light.
Utilizing an infrared, high-resolution camera system, the installation was able to respond to people's movement through the space in any lighting or weather condition. As people walked through the space, their proximity to the columns added energy to the interactive system, which in turn responded in light and sound. The combination of a novel, high-intensity lighting system and 3-dimensional sound system made for a truly immersive and reactive experience. The aim wasn't to produce a game, or a system of punishments and rewards but rather a unique experience. One of UVA's key objectives was to take people outside of their everyday experience - to bring them into 'the

moment'. One of the most pleasing results of the installation period was the number of photographs and other imagery that people chose to upload to various internet file-sharing systems. A search on the web-based photo album service, Flickr, for 'Volume' demonstrates the ongoing popularity of the piece. The musical elements - composed and produced by onepointsix - were distributed across the grid and triggered when visitors entered the space. Visitors activate the columns closest to them; the overall musical experience was therefore dependent on the number and position of visitors. In this way, people could choose between two roles; either a passive 'audience' standing back from the installation, or actively participating 'performers', walking into the space to modulate the piece.
Visual and musical aspects, generated in real time, allowed complex feedback patterns between audio and visual elements. At the same time, the decision was taken to keep the interaction model very simple, making it possible for visitors to discover it without instruction. The experience was structured with a main musical and visual sequence lasting eight minutes, broken up by six shorter interludes, each with different visual, audio and interaction models.
Volume won a Yellow Pencil in the Digital Installation Category at the D&AD Awards 2007 and, due to high demand, UVA are currently preparing the installation for tour.

VISITORS ACTIVATE THE
COLUMNS CLOSEST TO
THEM.

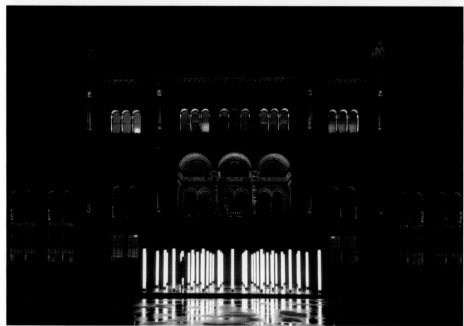

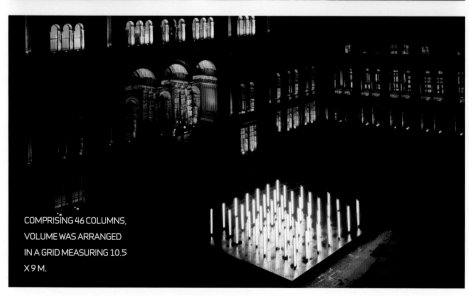

COMPRISING 46 COLUMNS,
VOLUME WAS ARRANGED
IN A GRID MEASURING 10.5
X 9 M.

UVA'S INSTALLATION
HAD TO BE COMPLETELY
WEATHER RESISTANT TO
BE ABLE TO RUN IN AN
OUTDOOR LOCATION FOR
A TWO-AND-A-HALF-
MONTH PERIOD.

One of UVA's key objectives was to take people outside of their every day experience to bring them into 'the moment'

AS THE NUMBER OF VISITORS INCREASED, VOLUME BECAME A MORE SOCIAL EXPERIENCE, ENCOURAGING PEOPLE TO INTERACT AND EXPERIMENT.

ARCHITEN
LANDRELL
ASSOCIATES

ARCHITEN LANDRELL ASSOCIATES
Staff: 50
Project management: Christopher Rowell, Adam Hall
Key designers: Paul Beales, Ceri Richards
Founded: 2006
Operates: Worldwide
Membership: IFAI

AWARDS
Numerous awards in different categories.

KEY PROJECTS
The O2 Store and Riverwalk, London/UK, 2007
Opera Holland Park, London/UK, 2007
Palace Exchange Shopping Centre, Enfield/UK, 2007
Barclays Bank Atrium, London/UK, 2004
McArthur Glen Ashford, Ashford/UK, 2000
Dalton Park Shopping Centre, County Durham/UK, 2002

KEY CLIENTS
Barclays Bank

BBC
Imperial War Museum
O2
National Assembly of Wales
National Tennis Centre
Robbie Williams/Rolling Stones
Vodafone

PROFILE
Established when tensile fabric structures were still a new concept within the construction industry, Architen Landrell is a leading manufacturer of bespoke fabric architecture with over 20 years of experience in the design, manufacture and installation of tensile structures. The company has completed over 5,000 projects worldwide, within a huge variety of construction sectors, and prides itself on the unparalleled design capability, originality and innovation to be found in its work. The company's 'can-do' approach to each project, strives to come up with intelligent answers to untried ideas and see these through from conception to completion.

01

02

01   SITUATED ON A ROUNDA-BOUT IN AN OLD MINING SITE, THIS FORMER PIT WHEEL IS LIT WITH COLOUR-CHANGING LEDS TO FORM A DRAMATIC CENTREPIECE WHICH MARKS THE ENTRANCE TO A MAJOR REGENERATION SITE.

02   A KEY FEATURE OF THE PALACE EXCHANGE SHOPPING CENTRE IS THE ENFIELD WORD WALL. APPROXIMATELY 120 M IN LENGTH, THE WALL DOMI-NATES THE DEVELOPMENT AND FEATURES PASSAGES OF PAST AND PRESENT CONVERSATION FROM THE TOWN.

A COVERED WALKWAY
LINKS THE 'O2' TO THE
QUEEN ELIZABETH II PIER
ON THE THAMES.

O2 Store and Riverwalk London, UK

CLIENT

AEG (RIVERWALK), O2

(STORE)

DESIGNERS

BARR GAZETAS (RIVER-

WALK), JPDA (STORE)

ENGINEER

TONY HOGG DESIGNS

MANUFACTURER

ARCHITEN LANDRELL

ASSOCIATES

LIGHT SOURCES

COLOUR-CHANGING LEDS,

PHAROS LPC (RIVERWALK

AND STORE)

TOTAL SURFACE

1100 M² (RIVERWALK),

90 M² (STORE)

TOTAL COST

£ 362,784 (RIVERWALK),

£ 90,000 (STORE)

DURATION OF

CONSTRUCTION

6 WEEKS (RIVERWALK),

1 WEEK (STORE)

COMPLETION DATE

JUNE 2007 (RIVERWALK),

MAY 2007 (STORE)

PHOTOGRAPHER

CHRISTOPHER ROWELL

WWW.ARCHITEN.COM

Early in 2007, Architen Landrell was awarded a number of projects at the redevelopment of the 'O2', formerly known as the Millennium Dome, London. AEG and O2 have transformed the Dome into a wholly new entertainment complex incorporating shops, restaurants, music and sporting venues. One of the projects included the design, manufacture and installation of a covered walkway linking the Dome to the Queen Elizabeth II Pier on the Thames. Another was to add fabric and lighting features to the O2 flagship store.

Stretching to around 150 m, and leading from the riverside to the entrance of the entertainment complex, a walkway was designed to provide all-weather protection. Encased in a willow wall, designers Barr Gazetas intended the walkway to give as much privacy as possible, creating an exclusive entrance to the Dome. A 'wow factor' was also important to the client and though the walkway was impressive in itself, the addition of interactive lighting ensures a truly stunning arrival. Architen's Lighting Division was tasked with the design and supply of an interactive system that lights the walkway in an array of vibrant colours. A whole host of impressive programmes and effects were created using the latest Tryka colour-changing LEDs and Pharos LPC control systems. Also included in Architen's project was the refurbishment of the old lighting system which involved replacing over 1000 light bulbs and extensive servicing of the control equipment.

Two additional inverted-umbrella canopies, located on the pontoon, were also added to the Architen brief, as was the installation of a further three inverted-cone canopies on the canting bridge.

Fabric was an obvious choice for the designers. Not only does it provide a lightweight structure with graceful form, it also ties in well with the natural surroundings and promotes the ethos of the Greenwich Peninsula which dates from the original days of the Millennium Dome.

'At the client's request, we recycled existing steelwork that was redundant. We managed the complete design of fabric, steelwork and lighting in-house, and we were able to deliver the whole package from steelwork and fabric to lighting and control systems, including maintenance of the existing structure', explains an Architen spokesperson. Working over water proved a challenge. The installation crew had to adhere to strict Port of London regulations which prohibited dropping anything in the Thames or upsetting the balance of this ecosystem in any way. A barge crane was used during a very low tide.

More engineering was carried out at the installation of the O2 flagship store inside the Dome. Architen worked alongside designers JPDA to realize a store that reflected the 'soft and tactile' feeling of the brand and encouraged visitors to touch, explore and experiment with the technology. Soft translucent fabric was chosen and the design slowly evolved into the inflatable colour changing pillow system which was finally installed. The client's needs were at the forefront of all design modifications – most importantly, that the control system was adaptable; allowing for very quick and simple programme changes as required.

The final design resulted in large, inflated, PVC-coated polyester pillows installed over two entire walls to form the basis of the installation. Architen's Lighting Division lit the pillows with LED colour changers mounted on the frame behind. The effect created was a pulsing sensation - slightly hypnotic - and intended to draw people into the store from the entry plaza of the Dome. The high quality of light was achieved by using 60 projectors made up of 18 high-power, high-output LEDs (6 red, 6 green and 6 blue). Each colour circuit can be individually controlled to create a vast array of possible colours and effects. Interactivity was an important element in the designer's scheme and the lighting allowed this to be uniquely integrated. Proximity sensors located behind each column interact with customers and change the effect of the lighting as people draw near or step away. All these functions are controlled by a central lighting control system which also monitors air pressure. These funky colour changing pillows help realize the designer's desire to create a laboratory space which encourages people to interact with the phones and their environment.

Without being able to fix anything directly to the floor, the whole installation – fabric, lights, steelwork and control systems – had to be suspended from the existing wall. A great deal of engineering work had to be carried out to ensure that the design would support the loads.

THE 150-M WALKWAY IS LIT UP BY AN ARRAY OF VIBRANT COLOURS.

A WEATHER-PROOF VIP ENTRANCE.

THE WALKWAY TIES IN WELL WITH THE FABRIC STRUCTURE OF THE UMBRELLAS ON THE CANTING BROW.

A WHOLE HOST OF IMPRES-
SIVE PROGRAMMES AND
EFFECTS WERE CREATED
USING THE LATEST TRYKA
COLOUR-CHANGING LEDS
AND PHAROS LPC CON-
TROL SYSTEMS.

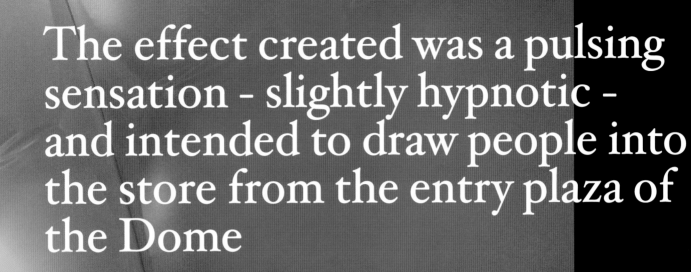

The effect created was a pulsing sensation – slightly hypnotic – and intended to draw people into the store from the entry plaza of the Dome

PVC-COATED POLYESTER
PILLOWS INSTALLED
OVER TWO ENTIRE WALLS
FORM THE BASIS OF THE
INSTALLATION OF THE O2
FLAGSHIP STORE.

LAB[AU]
LABORATORY FOR ARCHITECTURE AND URBANISM

LAB[AU]

Staff: 4
Members: Manuel Abendroth, Jérôme Decock, Alexandre Plennevaux, Els Vemang
Founded: 1997
Operates: Worldwide

AWARDS

Prix Mediatine, 2007
Arcadi, Best Information Architect, 2002
Grand Prix International Vidéo Danse C.I.D/UNESCO, 2002
Culture 2002 Award
Tech-Art prize, Vlaamse Ingenieurs Kamer, 1999

KEY PROJECTS

Touch, Brussels/Belgium, 2007
EOD02, Brussels/Belgium, 2006
12m4s, Leuven/Belgium, 2006
Man in e.Space, 2006
Point and line to plane, Leuven /Belgium, 2005
the 10th sphere, Brussels/Belgium, 2003
space navigable music, 2001-2007
Cityscapes, Graz/Austria, 2001
i.skin, Avignon/France, 2000

RGB Pavilion, Cannes/France, 2000
Gamevillage, Lyon/France, 1999
Lightscapes, the Heysel, Brussels/Belgium, 1999

KEY CLIENTS

Electrabel/Sibelgas
PSA, Peugeot Citroen
Infogrames
Unilever
Casinos Austria
Dexia

PROFILE

Established in 1997, LAb[au]: laboratory for architecture and urbanism has developed a transdisciplinary and collaborative approach to its work, based on various artistic, scientific and theoretical methods for examining the transformation of architecture and spatiotemporal structures according to the technological progress. Involved mainly in the creation of art, audiovisual performances and scenographies, LAb[au] develops its own software and interfaces. The members of the LAb[au] team – Manuel Abendroth, Jerome Decock, Alexandre Plennevaux and Els Vemang – also run MediaRuimte, a digital-design gallery in central Brussels that opened in 2003.

01

02

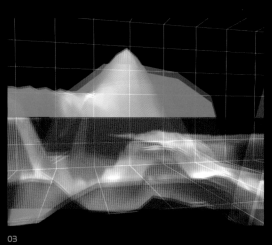

03

01 THIS 75 M² PAVILION CON-
CEIVED TO BE DISPLAYED
DURING THE 'FESTIVAL IN-
TERNATIONAL DU FILM DE
CANNES'. IN ADDITION TO
BE THE MAIN ENTRANCE
AND A TICKET DESK, THE
PAVILION WAS INTENDED
TO HOST AN EXHIBI-
TION OF EXPERIMENTAL
CINEMA.

02 '12M4S' IS BASED ON A
SPACE OF 12 METERS AND
A TIME OF 4 SECONDS,
CORRESPONDING TO A
HUMAN WALKING AT
ORDINARY SPEED. IN THIS
SPACE-TIME CONTINUUM,
HUMAN MOVEMENTS ARE
TRACKED TO GENERATE A
VISUAL AND SONIC SCAPE
IN REAL-TIME.

03 URBAN ENLIGHTENING
STUDY FOR THE HEIZEL
PLATEAU IN BRUSSELS.

THE FAÇADES OF THE
DEXIA TOWER, WITH THEIR
4200 WINDOWS, WERE
USED AS A GIANT SCREEN.

Dexia Tower/Touch Brussels, Belgium

CLIENT

DEXIA

ARCHITECTS

PHILIPPE SAMYN &
PARTNERS, M & J.M.
JASPERS, J. EYERS &
PARTNERS

ARTIST

LAB[AU]

LIGHTING ENGINEER

BARBARA HEDIGER

COMPLETION DATE

DECEMBER 2006

PHOTOGRAPHER

LAB[AU]

WWW.LAB-AU.COM

LAb[au] proposed the public finance company Dexia to use the latter's main office – the 145-m-high Dexia Tower in Brussels – as a canvas for a seasonal installation that would encourage creativity and social activity among the general public. The Belgian digital-design and art lab set up an urban installation allowing users to interact in real time with the entire light skin covering the tower – a lighting infrastructure conceived by Barbara Hediger. The result was Touch.

Instead of approaching the exterior walls as flat surfaces on which to display pre-rendered video loops, LAb[au] used the architectural characteristics of the tower and its urban context as the basis for the project. The orientation, volume and scale of the building became parameters for setting up a spatial and temporal concept, allowing people to engage directly with the tower. Participants were invited to create a composition by choosing colours to light up the windows, which were equipped with individually controlled RGB LED bars attached to the window frames. 'While working on this urban interactive installation, our main focus was to create a relationship between the user and the tower – and to transform the user's perception of the tower as a publicity screen into an experience related to urban art in the form of a lighting project,' explains Manuel Abendroth of LAb[au]. 'The challenge was to integrate participation and identification into a project that would encourage the user to get involved.'

A control station positioned at the foot of the building from late December 2006 to mid-January 2007 encouraged passers-by to interact either individually or collectively with the visual display through the use of a multi-touch screen. Both static (touch) and dynamic (gesture) input was recognized and used to generate an elementary graphic language of points, lines and planes, which combined with physical movement to determine the colours of the façade. Participants entered the coordinates needed to define the background colour and used directional controls (positive or negative) to select the colour of graphic elements (black or white). Having completed a composition, the 'artist' could capture it in a photo of the tower taken by a camera located some distance away and mail the photo in the form of an electronic postcard. Photographs were also uploaded onto the project website, where they could be found, forwarded by email or printed in PDF format and used as Christmas or New Year's greetings. 'The ephemeral work of art made in this manner,' says Abendroth, 'can be recorded and serve as the basis of a personalized greeting card.'

As the largest installation ever controlled by DMX cables, Touch required 25 km of cable, which ran from the base of the building through to the 39th floor, connecting a circuit of 4200 RGB LED bars for the windows. There were also 22 custom fittings in monochromatic blue light and 40 3W LEDs for the columns. Illuminating the perimeter of the main entrance and front doors were 60 Ath-Luxor custom LED bars of different lengths. A central computer on the 9th floor controlled each level individually, allowing colours on the different floors to be isolated or merged with colours on other floors, depending on the size of the desired pattern. Following the overall concept of the installation, the design of the interactive control station was based on the idea of folding and unfolding space. Thanks to the process involved, the spatial design could be combined with the time-based parameters inherent to the dynamic and sequential concept of the illumination of the tower itself. Divided into three parts, the sculptural station – located in front of the Dexia Tower on Brussels' north-south axis – framed part of the city skyline through a sequence of lustrous white arches, which the designers refer to as 'folds'. 'Each of the three folds that constituted the control station was related to a specific function, while following the principles of the entire design,' says Abendroth of a project in which light was used to convey 'information on an urban and artistic level'. The first fold allowed people to interact on a multi-touch screen, and the second displayed user interaction – finger drawing – on a projection screen. Establishing a direct relationship with the luminous display on the tower, the screen also engaged those outside the control station, providing a visual narrative of audience participation and enticing passers-by. Together, variables such as width (finger, hand, arm), direction (horizontal, vertical, diagonal), duration (introducing growth) and speed (introducing velocity and weight) used architecture to create a dynamic, abstract presentation composed of graphic elements. Able to process multiple-input data, the installation explored individual and collective experiences, transforming the Dexia Tower into a work of art in which software became the architecture of the space.

25 KM OF CABLE WAS
USED TO CONNECT A
CIRCUIT OF 4200 RGB LED
BARS FOR THE WINDOWS.

A CONTROL STATION
POSITIONED AT THE FOOT
OF THE BUILDING ENCOUR-
AGED PASSERS-BY TO
INTERACT WITH THE
VISUAL DISPLAY (THE
TOWER) THROUGH THE
USE OF A MULTI-TOUCH
SCREEN.

COLOURS OF DIFFERENT
FLOORS COULD BE
ISOLATED OR MERGED
WITH COLOURS ON OTHER
FLOORS.

TOUCH SCREEN = UNFOLDED TOWER

COORDINATE SPACE > COORDINATE COLOUR

UNFOLDING ON INTERFACE

UNFOLDING OF COLOUR-LIGHT ON TOWER

Fingertap = points / particles

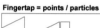

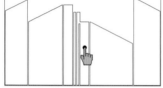

Duration touch = increase size = surface

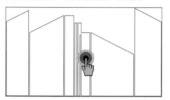

Introduce movement > push & move points, surface, lines

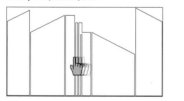

Draw lines

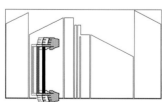

FROM GESTURE TO ARCHITECTURE.

HAVING COMPLETED A COMPOSITION, THE 'USER' COULD CAPTURE A SNAPSHOT OF THE SCENE TAKEN BY A CAMERA LOCATED SOME DISTANCE AWAY AND WHICH HE COULD MAIL FROM THE SPOT AS AN ELECTRONIC POSTCARD.

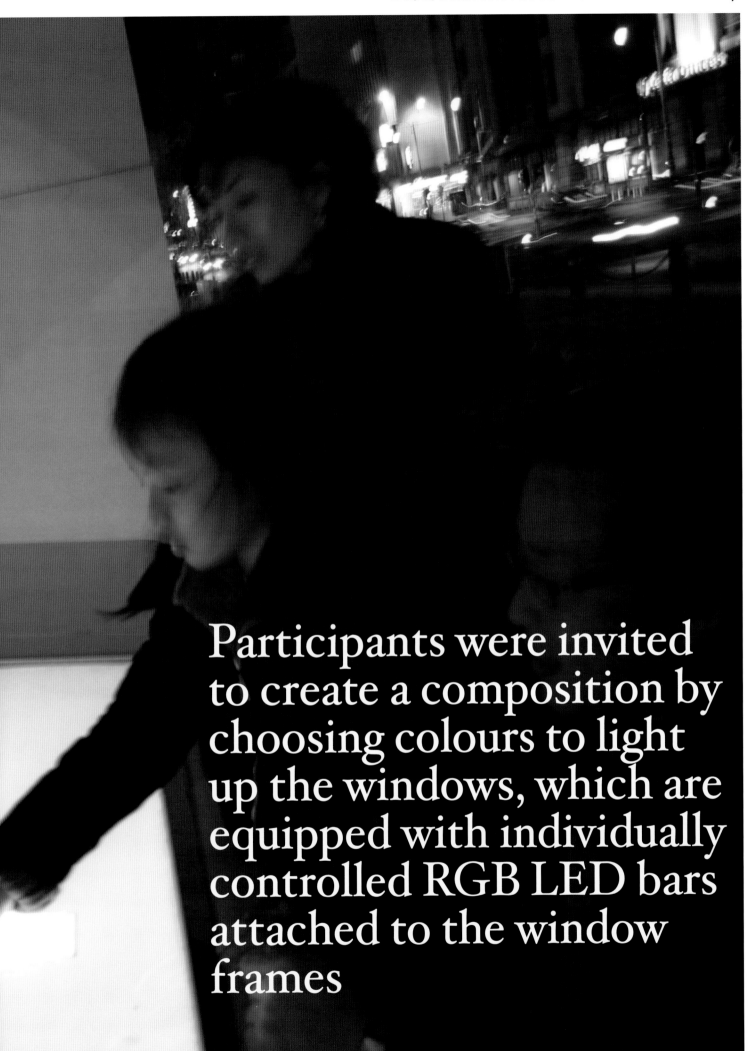

Participants were invited to create a composition by choosing colours to light up the windows, which are equipped with individually controlled RGB LED bars attached to the window frames

ELECTROLAND

Staff: 2
Management: Cameron McNall, Damon Seeley
Founded: 2002
Operates: Worldwide

KEY PROJECTS

La Face, Los Angeles/USA, 2007
Enteractive, Los Angeles/USA. 2006
Lumen, New York/USA, 2006
Indianapolis Gateways Competition Scheme, USA, 2006
Target Interactive Breezeway, New York/USA, 2005
Interactive Walkways, Fort Lauderdale/USA, 2005
City National Plaza Towers, Los Angeles/USA, 2005
New Indianapolis Airport proposal, USA, 2005
Urban Nomad Shelter
NoHo Commons, North Hollywood/USA, 2005
Axial Rings Stage 2 Competition Entry, Krems/Austria,
2004

Big Time, Los Angeles/USA, 2002 – present
Interactive Media, Los Angeles/USA, 2002 – present
R-G-B, Los Angeles/USA, 2001
Hollywood Shadow Project, Hollywood/USA, 2001
Terra Metallum, New York/USA, 1991

PROFILE

Working at the forefront of new technologies, Electroland
creates interactive experiences, including large scale public art
projects and electronic installations. Inviting visitors to interact
with buildings, spaces and each other in new and exciting ways,
Electroland uses spectacle as an effective strategy to reach large
audiences. Small visitor actions to a project may trigger a large
environmental response, or complete strangers may be temporar-
ily connected through light, sound, or electronics. A sensibility
expressed through whimsy and play, the practice's projects are
capable of engaging both casual and more curious visitors.

01

02

01   THE INTERACTIVE
      BREEZEWAY ENGAGES
      PEDESTRIANS IN AN
      EPHEMERAL INTERACTIVE
      ENCOUNTER WHERE THEIR
      POSITION AND PATHS ARE
      TRACED BY COLOURFUL
      AVATARS AND EFFECTS.

02   ELECTROLAND PROPOSED
      AN INSTALLATION TO RE-
      ASSERT THE PROMINENCE
      OF THE CITY NATIONAL
      PLAZA TOWERS ON THE
      LOS ANGELES SKYLINE.

THE BUILDING FAÇADE
PROJECTS LIGHT PAT-
TERNS GENERATED BY
THE INTERACTIVE CARPET
BELOW.

Enteractive at 11th & Flower Los Angeles, USA

PROGRAMMING

KEVIN TANAKA

MANUFACTURER

SPECIAL T LIGHTING
INCORPORATED

LIGHT SOURCES

176 LED TILES,
41,200 LEDS

COMPLETION DATE

2006

PHOTOGRAPHER

ELECTROLAND

WWW.ELECTROLAND.NET

Expert in orchestrating interactive experiences, Electroland's Enteractive project provides the perfect expression of the company's goal: to entice passers-by to interact with their environment in a new way. The site is located on and in front of the Met Lofts building at 11th and Flower Streets in downtown Los Angeles and is an apartment building designed by architectural firm Johnson Fain. The electronic artwork designed to emphasize the building's clean lines – inspired by 20th-century Bauhaus design – energizes the skyline of South Park LA with a bright grid of red light. Combining environmental intelligence and surveillance of human activity with a video game sensibility, the large 'interactive carpet' of LED tiles located at the building's entrance detects visitors and displays interactive light patterns in response to this data. Synchronized with the activity on the street, the building's façade - fitted with a structure of LED light fixtures - projects the same light patterns to the surrounding city. Visitors on the carpet can see the effects of their actions beneath their feet and in a view of the building's face. Both these can be seen simultaneously via a video transmission from across the street. Covered by a layer of glass, the electronic carpet is a bright square of red LEDs and composed of 176 LED tiles, each 16" square, with a total of 23,200 LED lights. Weight sensors under each tile corner are read 30 times per second by a master CPU. This central computer runs custom software designed to analyze the weight data in real time to determine where people are standing and in what direction they are moving. Based on this data, the software generates sequences of light, scaling the patterns and interaction according to levels of activity on the carpet. As a result, different visitors produce different patterns, and the experience changes throughout the day. When unoccupied, echoes of previous participants play on the carpet and building face.

Corresponding to each floor, the building face on Flower Street features 18 red square light fixtures in 6 rows. This matrix of fixtures, including a total of 18,000 LED lights, was specially designed to project extremely bright light towards the west, and yet remain within carefully designed U channels to prevent light projecting back into tenant units. Electroland was careful to produce a lighting scheme considerate of the people both outside and inside the building. Deemed appropriate by the designers due to its location – opposite a large entertainment complex – the project gives a very bright and aggressive presence to the street. The uncanny way in which one can sense the presence of human activity - movement betrays the underlying human motion - gives the lights a special resonance.

An urban video game, capturing passers-by in an electronic field, the project has provoked interesting reactions. Tenants of Met Lofts love the project, and relish the opportunity to demonstrate it to visitors who are uninformed as to why people are frantically jumping around the square. Distracted by the fun of the experience, the greater implications of people-tracking do not assert themselves. As a result, participants do not feel that there is anything ominous about being closely tracked and followed by a faceless intelligent agent. However, it seems that LA inhabitants are not so uninhibited when it comes to Big Brother and continue to refuse Electroland's request to install a video camera across the street from the installation – the last stage in the proper completion of the project. 'The city is just terrified by the notion of lawsuits stemming from "video surveillance" and will not allow us to place a camera anywhere,' explains an Electroland spokesperson. 'Technologically we exist in this interesting moment in time where our keystrokes are recorded on the web, our voices are recorded in telephone conversations, our images are recorded as we enter buildings, and our locations can be pinpointed via mobile phones - all for the purposes of business efficiency and social order. But the prospect of a video transmission for an art project is still too threatening.'

VISITORS CAN SEE THE
EFFECT OF THEIR ACTIONS
BENEATH THEIR FEET.

THE MATRIX OF FIXTURES
FEATURING 18,000 LED
LIGHTS IS SPECIALLY
DESIGNED TO PROJECT
EXTREMELY BRIGHT LIGHT
TOWARDS THE WEST BUT
WITH NO LIGHT PROJECT-
ING BACK INTO TENANT
UNITS.

TILES RESPOND TO SENS-
ING DATA WHICH TRACKS
VISITOR LOCATION AND
DIRECTION OF TRAVEL.

The large 'interactive carpet' of LED tiles located at the building's entrance detects visitors and displays interactive light patterns in response to this data

VEHOVAR + JAUSLIN ARCHITEKTUR

Staff: 10
Management: Stefan Jauslin, Mateja Vehovar
Key designers: Stefan Jauslin, Mateja Vehovar
Founded: 1997
Operates: Europe
Membership: SIA

AWARDS
Best Architects 08, 2007
Silver Medal at Prague Quadrennial, 2003
Swiss Prize for Fine Arts, 1999

KEY PROJECTS
Sihlcity Church, Zurich/Switzerland, 2007
Restaurant Swisscom Mobile, Bern-Liebefeld/Switzerland, 2006
Arteplage Yverdon Expo.02, Neuchatel/Switzerland, 2002

PROFILE
Transcending the traditional boundaries of architecture, Swiss architects Mateja Vehovar and Stefan Jauslin work simultaneously on both traditional building projects and artistic installations. In addition to practical projects, the duo also teaches architecture, design and video and both pursue research in the areas of architecture and urbanism.

DELUX

Staff: 12
Key designer: Rolf Derrer
Founded: 1980
Operates: Worldwide

AWARDS
Deutscher Designpreis, 2000/2001
Hans-Reinhart-Ring, 1995

PROFILE
Combining expertise and creative flair, Delux designs and develops lighting concepts and creates set designs for a range of multimedia productions. Working on both internal and external spaces, the company has been involved with exhibitions, museums, public architecture, parks and squares

01

01 EXPLORING THE POS-
SIBILITIES OF ARTIFICIAL
INTELLIGENCE, THE ADA
EXHIBITION IS AN ARTIFI-
CIAL ORGANISM CAPABLE
OF RESPONDING TO ITS
SURROUNDINGS.

02 MADE FROM CLUSTERS OF
COLOUR-CHANGING LEDS,
THE CHRISTMAS LIGHT-
ING DISPLAY FOR THE
HEADQUARTERS OF CAN-
TONAL BANK OF ZUG IS AN
ANIMATED INSTALLATION,
INCONSPICUOUSLY INTE-
GRATED INTO THE FRONT
OF THE BUIDLING.

02

THE INSTALLATION FOR
GENEVA'S LIGHTING FES-
TIVAL STRETCHES 80 M
ALONG THE RIVER RHONE.

L'echo du Silence
Geneva, Switzerland

CLIENT

CITY OF GENEVA

ARCHITECT

VEHOVAR + JAUSLIN
ARCHITEKTEN

LIGHTING DESIGN

DELUX

MANUFACTURERS

NEONILLUMA, SCHNICK-
SCHNACK-SYSTEMS

LIGHT SOURCES

HIGH-OUTPUT, RGB LEDS

TOTAL SURFACE

80 M²

**DURATION OF
CONSTRUCTION**

1 WEEK

COMPLETION DATE

OCTOBER 2006

PHOTOGRAPHERS

ALAIN GRANDCHAMP/
DOCUMENTATION
PHOTOGRAPHIQUE
VILLE DE GENÈVE

NIKLAUS SPOERRI
WWW.NIKLAUSSPOERRI.CH

VEHOVAR + JAUSLIN
ARCHITEKTUR
WWW.VJA.CH

Collaborating with global lighting design company, Delux, to create an installation for Geneva's 2006 lighting festival 'Les yeux de la nuit', architects Vehovar + Jauslin were given carte blanche to pursue their own direction. Free from the restraints of a brief, the installation 'L'écho du Silence' represents a 3-dimensionalization of the architects' futuristic vision.

The piece explores intelligent space, the interplay of built space, nature and human beings. It is a response to static and insensitive architecture that relies on humans to adapt to their environment.

Dissecting the landscape with a series of luminescent bars, the installation provides a clearly defined path along an 80 m stretch of the River Rhone, bathing intersecting bridges in colourful pools of light. These bridges are not often highlighted in the dark of night, and their illumination creates diffuse waves of colour that appear to float on the river's surface. The installation became an integrated part of its surroundings. Constructed from 24 translucent polycarbonate pillars, measuring 3 m in height and 20 cm in diameter, each pillar, equipped with twelve segments of colour-changing LED strings, was controlled via a standard computer. The computers ran custom-made software to generate light moods of various colour combinations. In addition to solid bars of light, individual segments of the poles could also be illuminated. By lighting the top and bottom of successive posts a wave effect was created – evocative of the installation's water-front location. In addition to the lighting, more software was used to interpret visitors' reactions and create an instantaneous soundscape based on this data. Indeed, music as a non-verbal form of communication became the installation's secondary element. The arrangement used different instruments to accumulate information about its environment: infrared sensors and a system to track water movements monitored the space, while microphones captured sound within the installation. Combined, these inputs provoked 'emotional states' within the system such as happiness, sadness, reclusiveness, disappointment, pride, amorousness, etc. These in turn triggered pre-programmed 'moods' expressed via co-ordinated use of the available media resulting in a dynamic, 3-dimensional, and immersive light-space. Imagery was manipulated in real time, and the soundscape created is best described as 'life-composed'. The installation enabled intelligent interaction between space, environment, and humans. Visitors' feelings are stimulated through light and sound, and yet the piece also expresses its own 'emotions', drawn from the flow of water, the movement of visitors inside as well as other surrounding conditions. Unlike past attempts to create intelligent buildings and rooms - most of which use strongly predetermined systems that cannot be adapted to the behaviour of the user - the level of visitor/piece interaction encountered with 'L'echo du Silence' was far beyond anyone's expectations. Seducing visitors with a mystical show of colour, the installation's ambience of light and sound guides audiences safely along the river.

Utilizing technology based on the growing comprehension of perceptual and cognitive abilities in biological systems, 'L'écho du Silence, unlike conventional rule-based computer systems, is based on models of biological nervous systems. Insistent that the inclusion of natural systems leads to new functional qualities in architecture and artefacts, the team at Vehovar + Jauslin believe that buildings should not be confined to reacting only to weather, brightness or pollution. Instead they believe that buildings will become more and more capable of interpreting these conditions, adapting and exchanging knowledge with others. They believe that assimilation, communication with other natural and artificial systems and the ability to learn all signify that architecture and artefacts can display the characteristics of a living organism. Artefacts will begin to interpret and interact with their social and physical environments, becoming able to meaningfully react to them.

Exploring the visual aesthetics of architecture and artefacts that act like organisms and adapt to their users' needs, Vehovar + Jauslin's work is at the cutting edge of both the theoretical and applied worlds of art. Their fields of operation have therefore extended to include architecture, media arts, and various scientific disciplines.

THE INSTALLATION
BATHED INTERSECTING
BRIDGES IN COLOURFUL
POOLS OF LIGHT.

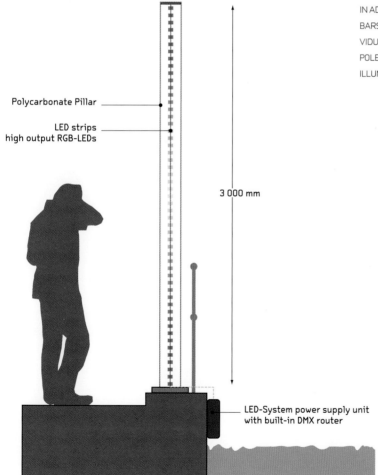

Polycarbonate Pillar

LED strips
high output RGB-LEDs

3 000 mm

LED-System power supply unit
with built-in DMX router

SECTION OF THE PILLAR.

IN ADDITION TO SOLID
BARS OF LIGHT, INDI-
VIDUAL SEGMENTS OF
POLES COULD ALSO BE
ILLUMINATED.

THE 24 TRANSLUCENT PO-
LYCARBONATE PILLARS,
EQUIPPED WITH TWELVE
SEGMENTS OF COLOUR-
CHANGING LED STRINGS,
WERE CONTROLLED VIA A
STANDARD COMPUTER.

THE ILLUMINATION CRE-
ATED DIFFUSE WAVES OF
COLOUR THAT APPEARED
TO FLOAT ON THE RIVER'S
SURFACE.

L'echo du Silence is a response to static and insensitive architecture that relies on humans to adapt to their environment

IN ADDITION TO THE LIGH-
TING, MORE SOFTWARE
WAS USED TO INTERPRET
VISITOR'S REACTIONS AND
CREATE AN INSTANTANE-
OUS SOUNDSCAPE BASED
ON THIS DATA.

TRAXON TECHNOLOGIES LIMITED

TRAXON TECHNOLOGIES LIMITED

Staff: Over 100
Management: Mr. Nicolai Wiest, CEO
Founded: 1992
Operates: Worldwide
Memberships: PLDA, IALD, ESNA

AWARDS

Melda, 2007
Design for Asia Award, 2006
Luminaire of the Year Award, 2005
IF Design Award, 2004
DCC Award, 2004
Red Dot Design Award, 2003
Roeder Award, 2003
POPAI, 2003

KEY PROJECTS

Tower Bridge, London/UK, 2007
Guggenheim Museum, New York/USA, 2007
Nagoya Lucent Tower, Nagoya City/Japan, 2007
Clarion Hotel Bergen Airport, Bergen/Norway, 2007
Diesel, Hong Kong, 2007
Lacoste, Hua Hin/Thailand, 2006
Anne Fontaine, Tokyo/Japan, 2006
Miramar Shopping Centre, Hong Kong, 2006
Diesel, Italy, 2006
Cirque du Soleil, Las Vegas/USA, 2006
Hugo Boss, Berlin/Germany, 2005
Louis Vuitton, Worldwide, 2004

PROFILE

Combining state-of-the-art technology with award winning
design, Traxon - a leading systems and solutions provider - creates
solid-state lighting systems for a diverse range of clients and applications. Establishing a decisive and competitive advantage, Traxon
designs and develops its own products, developing sophisticated
and innovative LED lighting systems that have received numerous
international product and design prizes. With proven expertise
in creating customized solutions for virtually any lighting scenario, Traxon collaborates with renowned lighting designers and
architects as well as multinationals including Coca-Cola, Hilton
Hotels, Philips and Swarovski.

01

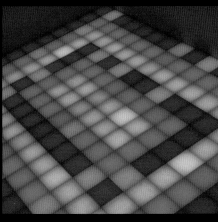

02

03

01 EMBEDDED IN STRAIGHT LINES IN THE STONE FLOOR, TRAXON'S COVE LIGHT 12 SMD RGB ILLUMINATES THE WALKWAY OF THE NAGOYA LUCENT TOWER, JAPAN, IN A RAINBOW OF COLOUR.

02 PROVIDING THE TECHNICAL EXPERTISE BEHIND PIOTR UKLANSKI'S REMAKE OF UNTITLED (DANCE FLOOR) FOR THE GUGGENHEIM MUSEUM IN NEW YORK, TRAXON TRANSFORMED A GLASS FLOOR OF OVER 60 M² INTO AN INTERACTIVE LIGHT INSTALLATION.

03 INSTALLED IN THE MIRAMAR SHOPPING CENTRE, HONG-KONG, AN LED MIRROR 64PXL WASH PANEL FAÇADE WITH OVER 9,000 INDIVIDUALLY CONTROLLABLE PIXELS PROVIDES A REVOLUTIONARY THREE-STOREY-HIGH SCREEN.

THE TOWER BRIDGE WAS
ILLUMINATED FOR THE
'SWITCHED ON LONDON'
EVENT.

Tower Bridge London, UK

CLIENT
SWITCHED ON LONDON,
FESTIVAL OF LIGHT
ENGINEER
JONATHAN HODGES/JA-
SON BRUGES STUDIO
MANUFACTURER
TRAXON TECHNOLOGIES
LIMITED
LIGHT SOURCES
4PXL COLOUR BEAMER
DMX
TOTAL SURFACE
61 LINEAR M
TOTAL COST
£ 30,000
DURATION OF
CONSTRUCTION
4 DAYS
COMPLETION DATE
FEBRUARY 2007

Invited to participate in 'Switched On London' by organizer Paul James, editor of architectural lighting magazine mondo*arc, Traxon Technologies partnered with interactive design company Jason Bruges Studio to transform London's iconic Tower Bridge into an interactive light sculpture. The festival was curated by Sharon Stammers and organized within just six months to coincide with the annual ARC07 lighting exhibition – a two-day conference dedicated to architectural lighting. The committee, made up of renowned lighting designers, manufacturers and members of the media trade, hosted lighting installations throughout the Capital. Reflecting the very best of urban lighting, James was keen to counteract the bad publicity surrounding architectural lighting. 'The perception', he explains 'is that architectural lighting leads to wasted energy and light pollution. However, the majority of the lighting industry continually strives to tackle the issue of energy. Our hope is that Switched On London will have value beyond simple decoration. It is an opportunity to use light to educate the public and media journalists alike. It is essential to illuminate better, not less'.

Asked simply to illuminate an iconic building in the Pool of London, either side of the river Thames, to demonstrate London as a forerunner in urban lighting concepts, Traxon Technologies used the largest of the sites available as an opportunity to demonstrate the power of sustainable lighting sources and the potential applications of new lighting technologies. Like a simulation of the racing headlights below, the high walkways of Tower Bridge were illuminated with sporadic flashes of colour. Fitted with over 300 Traxon Technology 4-pixel, LED colour beamers mounted 65 m above the Thames, the installation was programmed to react individually to Bluetooth signals received by sensors. The colour and speed of the animations displayed were determined by pedestrians crossing the Thames with electrical devices. Bluetooth signals captured by Bluetooth data-loggers transferred data via wireless technology to a DMX controller that converted the signals into unique pixels. Each identification number emitted was assigned a different colour. Travelling across the span of the bridge the flecks of colour ran parallel and concurrent with their corresponding transmitting device. Capturing the pace of city life, the speed and bustle of pedestrians, reproduced along the bridge, cast an effervescent reflection on the river below. Bruges describes the effect: 'Each person had their own colour, so you would get this dancing performance of light'. An unexpected addition to the light show was the clusters of Bluetooth signals, created by passengers on double-decker buses which produced a double layered effect. The tip of a technological iceberg, the project inspired Bruges and his team to explore the idea of mapping patterns, which he hopes will lead them to transform the façades of buildings with similar animations, 'I suspect there'll be structures that will become their own buildings, start to become part of the city... the agenda is really about making a difference in city environments, in terms of their general delight and richness'.

Switched on from 4pm until midnight on nine consecutive evenings throughout February, the project allowed anyone owning a Bluetooth device to contribute to the display. Despite the construction, installation and dismantling process amounting to nearly as long as the festival itself, the piece remained sympathetic to the city's landmark, with the low-energy luminaires almost invisible in the light of day.

In addition to the designers and manufacturers taking responsibility for their own projects, the festival's overall environmental impact and energy consumption – which was estimated at a mere £20 – was also audited throughout the event. Highlighting the need for light in our night-time urban environment, James intends to organize an accompanying exhibition for future festivals that will reflect the motives and energy usage of each project.

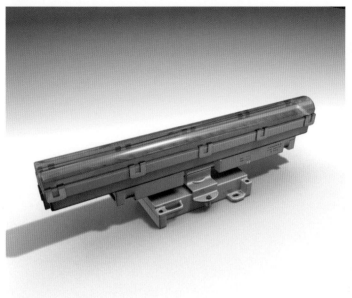

THE TRAXON COLOR BE-
AMER 4PXL DMX ALLOWS
FOR THE GENERATION OF
A HUGE SPECTRUM OF DIF-
FERENT COLOURINGS AND
COLOUR-CHANGING LIGHT
SCENARIOS, ADDING AN
UNIQUE LIGHTING TOUCH
TO PLAIN FAÇDES AND
SURFACES.

THE COLOUR AND SPEED
OF THE ANIMATIONS
DISPLAYED WERE DETER-
MINED BY PREDESTRIANS
CROSSING THE THAMES
WITH ELECTRICAL DEVI-
CES. BLUETOOTH SIGNALS
WERE CONVERTED INTO
UNIQUE PIXELS.

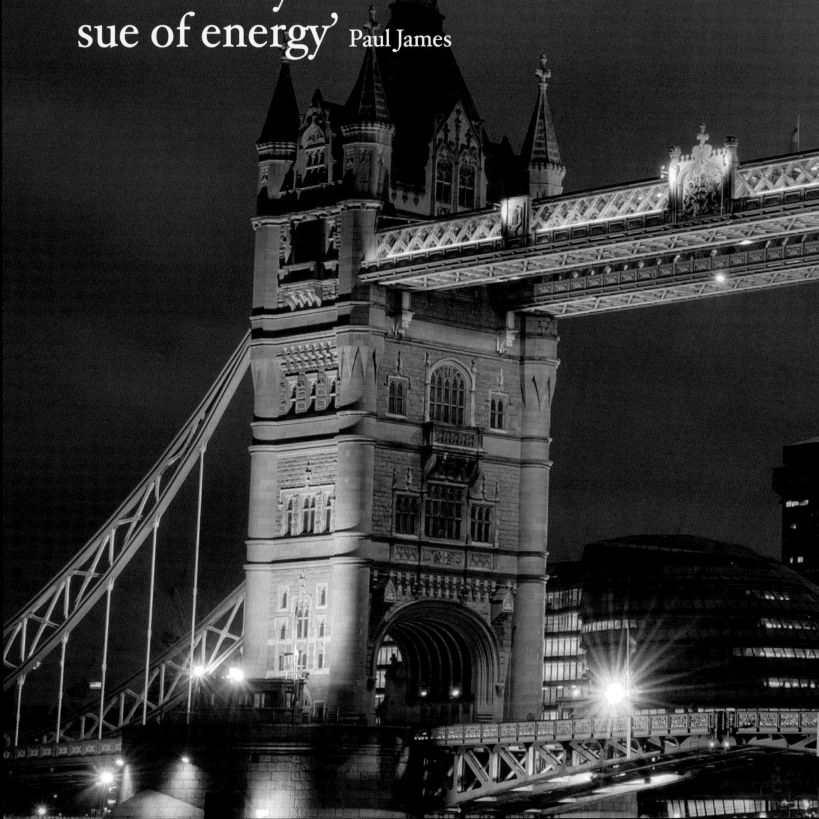

'The perception is that architectural lighting leads to wasted energy and light pollution. However, the majority of the lighting industry continually strives to tackle the issue of energy' Paul James

FITTED WITH OVER 300
TRAXON TECHNOLOGY
4-PIXEL AND LED COLOUR
BEAMERS MOUNTED 65M
ABOVE THE THAMES,
THE HIGH WALKWAYS OF
TOWER BRIDGE WERE ILLU-
MINATED WITH SPORADIC
FLASHES OF COLOUR.

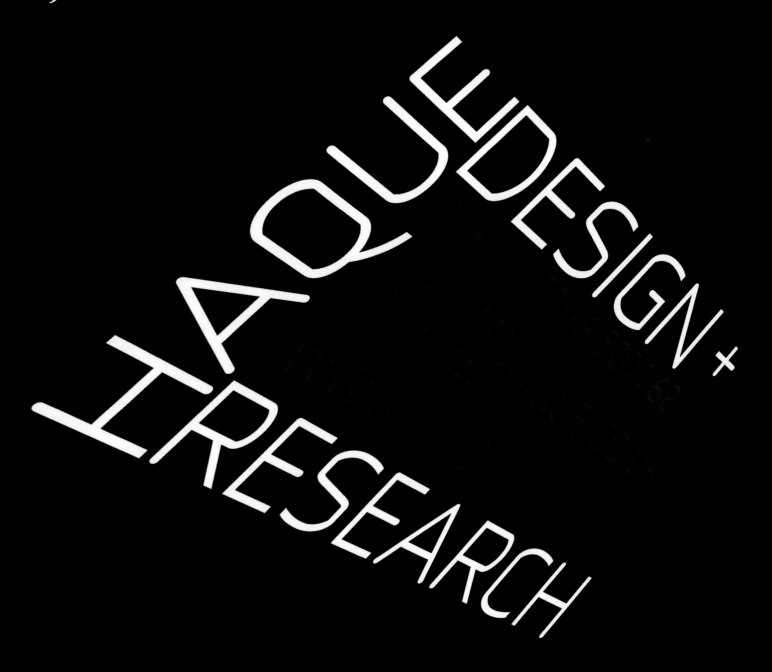

HAQUE DESIGN + RESEARCH

Staff: 4
Key designers: Usman Haque, Ai Hasegawa
Founded: 2002
Operates: Worldwide

AWARDS

Japan Media Arts Festival Excellence Prize, 2004
Asia Digital Art Grand Prize, 2005

PROFILE

Haque Design + Research specializes in interactive architecture systems. Removing architecture from its static and immutable connotations, Haque Design + Research sees the discipline as a dynamic and responsive interlocutor, transformed by developments in interaction research, wearable computing, mobile connectivity, people-centred design, contextual awareness, RFID systems and ubiquitous computing. Exploring this new and exciting territory, Haque Design + Research works with advanced technology, multisensory systems and carefully-crafted algorithms.

01

02

01   VIEW OF SKY EAR ABOVE
THE NATIONAL MARITIME
MUSEUM, GREENWICH.

02   SKY EAR, A NON-RIGID,
CARBON-FIBRE 'CLOUD',
EMBEDDED WITH 1000
GLOWING HELIUM BAL-
LOONS AND SEVERAL
DOZEN MOBILE PHONES,
LISTENS FOR ELECTRO-
MAGNETIC FIELDS IN THE
SKY.

OPEN BURBLE IN SINGA-
PORE. COLOURS (FORMED
BY LEDS INSIDE THE BAL-
LOONS) INDICATE BLOCKS
DESIGNED BY THE PUBLIC.

Burble Singapore,
Singapore

CLIENT

SINGAPORE BIENNALE
2006

ENGINEERS

ANOMALOUS RESEARCH /
ROLF PIXLEY, SENSEINATE
/ SETH GARLOCK

MANUFACTURER

HAQUE DESIGN +
RESEARCH

LIGHT SOURCES

LED, CUSTOM-BUILT
ELECTRONICS

TOTAL SURFACE

2400 M²

TOTAL COST

£ 120,000

DURATION OF
CONSTRUCTION

4 MONTHS

COMPLETION DATE

SEPTEMBER 2006

PHOTOGRAPHER

HAQUE DESIGN +
RESEARCH
AI HASEGAWA AND ENG
KIAT TAN
WWW.HAQUE.CO.UK

A frequent site of pageantry, Singapore's Pangdang - a green space located at the heart of the city's central business district - became the temporary host for Usman Haque's installation, Burble. Almost threatening to float away into the night sky, the interactive piece, constructed from extra-large helium balloons, was commissioned for the opening ceremony of the Singapore Biennale 2006 (SB2006). This was the first of Singapore's international contemporary art biennales. The events were curated by Fumio Nanjo, with the aim of creating an event that 'conveyed amusing and thought-provoking experiences through the dynamism, excitement and relevance of art within contemporary culture'. Instead of recreating 'Sky Ear' – a cloud of glowing helium balloons, responsive to the electromagnetic fields created by mobile phones, installed in London's Greenwich Park in 2004 – as requested by Nanjo, Haque – who is not one to repeat a project - suggested Burble as a similar but conceptually different alternative. Inviting members of the public to contribute at an urban scale to a structure that occupies their city, albeit for only one night, Burble competes visually with the silent skyscrapers that usually surround inhabitants. Never too old for a fairytale, Haque was inspired by 'Jack and the Beanstalk' - the story of a magical seed which grows into an enormous structure, reaching for the skies - and his own childhood memories of watching the columns at Dulles Airport.

Soaring upwards like a plume of smoke, the installation was constructed from a set of 140 modular and configurable carbon-fibre units, 2.5 m in diameter. Each unit was supported by seven extra-large helium balloons - a total of approximately 1,000 individual pixels - which contained custom-built sensors, LEDs and microcontrollers, which coordinated the balloons and units, creating patterns of colour that rippled upwards, towards the sky. Each balloon was equipped with a single sensor board and powered by two button-cell batteries. Just as the participants were composers of Burble's tall form, they were also the ones to control it. Holding on to it using handles consisting of 22 articulated segments - each with an ST Micro accelerometer chip, akin to the ones found in Nintendo's Wii controller, which sent infrared signals to the balloons – they could position the Burble as they liked. Balloons could curve in on themselves, or be pulled into a straight line, making the shifting form a combination of the crowd's desires and the impact of wind currents varying throughout the height of the Burble. Graduated illumination created a giant luminescent structure; the balloons looked like atoms in an over-sized molecular chain; appearing to dance, rustle and fold in on themselves, creating turbulence as the wind caught the structure like a sail. Ignited with colour and sparkling in the evening sky, people on the ground shaking and pumping the handle bars, saw their movements represented as colours through the entire system and were able to identify their own individual fragments and perhaps even their design choices. These contributions formed an integral part of the spectacular, ephemeral experience which was ultimately a collective piece of art.

Referring to the piece as a 'massively complex dance', Haque describes the extraordinary creation as 'part installation, part performance'. Insistent on the importance of experimentation and testing, the designer used both physical and virtual prototypes to overcome the various problems which arose throughout the course of the installation's development. Time issues proved a particular challenge for the designer, who had to consider design and fabrication times as well as actual installation times. 'Once inflation starts, 10% of the helium lift is lost in the first five hours or so; and the battery life depends entirely on how long each LED has been on for', explains Haque. Another challenge was size. Designed and manufactured in the Haque Design + Research studio in London, everything had to be transportable. All the parts had to fit into carrying cases that did not exceed the standard sports equipment length of the aeroplane's baggage hold.

Involved in the conceptual development of the project, Haque was assisted by Seth Garlock and Rolf Pixley; a working relationship which the designer explains is based on a 'passion for second-order cybernetic systems'.

THE BURBLE IGNITES WITH COLOUR AS PEOPLE ON THE GROUND BEGIN TO MOVE THE SEGMENTED HANDLEBAR.

PREPARATION OF THE CARBON FIBRE HEXAGONAL 'CLOUDS'. EACH CLOUD IS SUPPORTED BY SEVEN 36" BALLOONS (HERE DEFLATED).

DIAGRAM INDICATING ONE PARTICULAR CONFIGURATION OF THE BURBLE CARBON FIBRE 'CLOUDS'.

THE BURBLE FULLY
IGNITED AGAINST THE
SINGAPORE SKYLINE.

THE BURBLE IS CONSTRUCTED FROM

- OVER 1 KM OF 6.35 MM CARBON-FIBRE RODS
- OVER 1 KM OF EXCEL D12 HIGH-PERFORMANCE SAILING ROPE
- APPROX. 1000 LATEX BALLOONS (36")
- APPROX. 1000 FISHING LOCK-SWIVEL CLIPS
- APPROX. 1000 SKY EAR BOARDS

THE HANDLE BAR, WHICH CONTROLS THE BURBLE CONSISTS OF
- 30 M OF HARD, BLACK BAMBOO
- 22 CONSOLES

COLOURS POUR THROUGH
THE SURFACE OF THE
BURBLE IN RESPONSE
TO MOVEMENTS OF THE
HANDLE BAR BELOW.

Never too old for a fairytale, Usman Haque was inspired by 'Jack and the Beanstalk', the story of a magical seed which grows into an enormous structure, reaching for the skies

THE BURBLE MOVES IN
RESPONSE TO A SUDDEN
GUST OF WIND.

LOOP.PH

Staff: 2
Designers: Rachel Wingfield, Mathias Gmachl
Founded: 2003
Operates: Worldwide

AWARDS

Red Dot Design Award, 2007
V&A Permanent Collection, 2004
Short-listed for best newcomer, 100% Design Blueprint Awards, 2003
Peugeot Design Awards, 2002

KEY PROJECTS

BioWall, London/UK, ongoing
Sonumbra, Sunderland/UK, 2006
Weather Patterns, York/UK, 2005
Digital Dawn, London/UK, 2000

KEY CLIENTS

Central Saint Martins School of Art and Design
Design Museum, London
Droog Design
Philips Design
Sunderland City Council
Victoria & Albert Museum
York City Council

PROFILE

Loop.pH is a London-based design and research studio that aims to bridge the gap between design and the natural sciences. Directed by designers Rachel Wingfield and Mathias Gmachl, the company specializes in the conception, construction and fabrication of environmentally responsive textiles for the built environment. Emphasis is placed on learning from both traditional, craft-based practices alongside the cutting edge of scientific and technological discovery. Drawing on its deep understanding of the complex and cyclic nature of ecological systems, the company places value on both the physical process of design and fabrication as well as its preparatory research of methodologies and theories. Loop.pH works on public space commissions and is available to consult on design and research projects, running workshops in the field of responsive textiles and digital media.

01

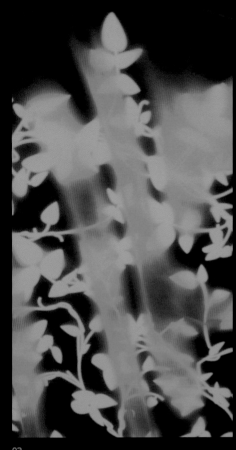

02

03

01   BLUMEN WALLPAPER
      USES ELECTROLUMINES-
      CENT TECHNOLOGY TO
      TRANSFORM TRADITIO-
      NAL DECORATIVE SURFA-
      CES INTO A RICH, DYNAMIC
      DISPLAY OF BOTANICAL
      LIFE.

02   A REACTIVE WINDOW
      BLIND, DIGITAL DAWN
      USES PRINTED ELEC-
      TRONIC TECHNOLOGY TO
      EMULATE THE PROCESS OF
      PHOTOSYNTHESIS.

03   PATTERN IS HEARD AND
      EXPERIENCED SIMULTANE-
      OUSLY IN 'SONUMBRA'; AN
      INSTALLATION FABRICA-
      TED FROM ELECTROLU-
      MINESCENT WIRES, RES-
      PONSIVE TO THE PHYSICAL
      PRESENCE OF PEOPLE.

THE FIVE WEATHERPROOF
WINDOW UNITS CONTAIN
PRINTED ELECTROLU-
MINESCENCE PANELS,
SANDWICHED BETWEEN
TOUGHENED GLASS AND A
MIRROR.

Weather Patterns York, UK

CLIENT

YORK CITY COUNCIL

LIGHTING DESIGN

LOOP.PH

MANUFACTURERS

DAVE FALCON STUDIO,

ELUMIN8 SYSTEMS

LIGHT SOURCES

PRINTED ELECTROLUMI-

NESCENT DISPLAY, 250

INDIVIDUAL ANIMATED

SEGMENTS

TOTAL SURFACE

10 M²

TOTAL COST

£ 25,000

DURATION OF

CONSTRUCTION

10 DAYS

COMPLETION DATE

DECEMBER 2005

PHOTOGRAPHER

LOOP.PH

WWW.LOOP.PH

Weather Patterns is part of Loop.pH's ongoing exploration dealing with the effects that humans have on the environment. 'Scientific and technological progress has given us powerful tools to expand our knowledge, but they have also allowed us to work on a scale far beyond human', explains designer Mathias Gmachl. 'The whole world has become a laboratory. It is increasingly difficult to judge whether our experiments are well designed or not,' he continues.

Within this area of research, global climate change is one of the most prominent and widely acknowledged issues. In response to increased media exposure and public concern regarding this topic, Loop.pH created an installation allowing people to experience changes in our weather and to rethink their relationship with the fragile situation that secures life on this planet. Designed as a permanent light installation for York Art Gallery, Weather Patterns is an architectural intervention commissioned by York City Council for the façade of the gallery. It aims to improve the appearance of the building during both daylight and night time hours. Combining traditional surface decoration with modern display technologies, the building communicates local weather cycles during the hours of darkness using a language of animated patterned light. The Art Gallery - a listed building which first opened its doors to the public in 1879 - is a structure designed in the Italian Renaissance Style. On the first floor, five window cavities remained empty. This was because most of the proposed carved-stone and tile decorations for the building were never executed. Developed under the close observation of local conservation officers, it was these empty windows that Loop.pH used to house the installation. Five weatherproof window units, designed to emit light at night and allow sunlight to reflect during daytime where successfully installed. The units contain printed electroluminescence (EL) panels sandwiched between toughened glass and a mirror. Each window is constructed from 2 prints, each 90 x 100 cm, with either 8 or 16 lamp channels. A computer reads data from a dedicated on-site weather station and uses this information to animate the printed EL pattern. Loop.pH's design duo developed dedicated software and hardware solutions to interface the EL panels with the weather station. In addition, an animated language was designed to communicate environmental information.

For Weather Patterns, Loop.pH reworked the classic dot-matrix display, creating a spiral-based pattern capable of reproducing basic movement, rotation and growth without the pixelated aesthetics of most low-resolution displays. The matrix is inspired by natural growth patterns easily recognized in the spiral designs of sunflowers and pinecones, applying their mathematical abstractions including concepts like 'the golden ratio'. Despite only occupying five small windows in the structure's grand façade, the electroluminescent displays, which appear to dance in the dark, provide the gallery with a presence deep into the night. Favouring Weather Patterns over Loop.pH's other proposal – which was to cast light onto the façade of the building using projection – the gallery was the first ever building to feature these unique window lamps. As a result, planning officers had to be contacted and, as with all Loop.pH's work, extensive prototyping and testing was imperative.

Initially fitted in 2005, the installation was highlighted as part of Illuminating York 2007 - an event aimed at enticing residents and visitors alike to explore the city after dark.

THE YORK ART GALLERY
DURING DAYTIME.

THE YORK ART GALLERY
AT NIGHT, DISPLAYING THE
WEATHER PATTERNS.

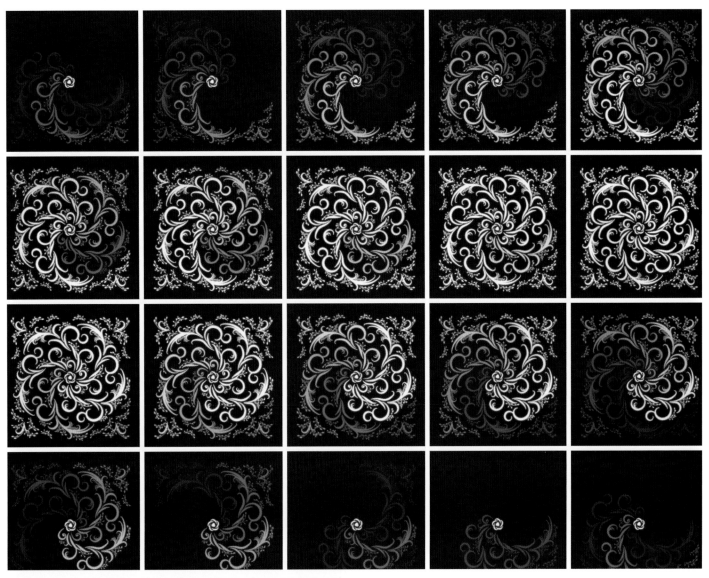

THE MATRIX IS INSPIRED
BY NATURAL GROWTH
PATTERNS EASILY REC-
OGNIZED IN THE SPIRAL
DESIGNS OF SUNFLOWERS
AND PINECONES.

'The whole world has become a laboratory' Mathias Gmachl

THE BUILDING COMMUNI-
CATES LOCAL WEATHER
CYCLES DURING THE
HOURS OF DARKNESS
USING A LANGUAGE OF
ANIMATED PATTERNED
LIGHT.

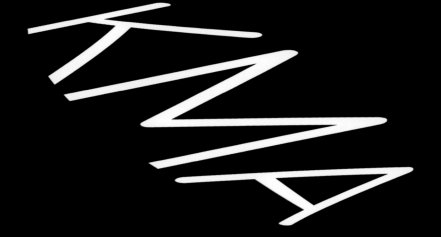

KMA

Staff: 2
Key designers: Kit Monkman, Tom Wexler
Founded: 2004
Operates: Worldwide

PROFILE
Digital artists KMA (Kit Monkman and Tom Wexler) develop
kinetic scenery, installations and light sculptures that are rooted
in the modelling of the physics of nature; using the mathemat-
ics of swarm behaviours, springs and masses, cellular automata
and chaos. KMA's work has been used both indoors - in galleries,
arenas and traditional theatre spaces - and outdoors - in site-specific works. In addition to their installation pieces, Monkman
and Wexler also undertake work in urban planning and design,
continuing to develop innovative new media, film and TV projects
for organizations including Channel 4 and the BBC.

01

02

01   ILLUMINATING THE PAVE-
02   MENT DURING ITALY'S ES-
      TERNI FESTIVAL IN 2006,
      ABSTRACT, ORGANIC
      PATTERNS RESPOND TO
      THE MOVEMENTS OF PAS-
      SERS-BY; LINKING THEM
      TO OTHERS AND PULLING
      THEM INTO A RELATION-
      SHIP WITH THE ARTWORK.

A PROJECTOR AND THERMAL IMAGE CAMERA WERE MOUNTED TOGETHER ON A CRANE 20 M ABOVE THE SQUARE AND OPTICALLY ALIGNED.

Flock London, UK

CLIENT

ICA

LIGHTING DESIGN

KMA

ENGINEER

XL VIDEO

LIGHT SOURCES

CHRISTIE ROADSTER
S+20K - SXGA+ 20000
LUMEN 3-CHIP DLP
DIGITAL PROJECTOR

TOTAL SURFACE

625 M²

TOTAL COST

£ 45,000

**DURATION OF
CONSTRUCTION**

3 WEEKS

COMPLETION DATE

FEBRUARY 2007

PHOTOGRAPHER

KMA

WWW.KMA.CO.UK

Commissioned by the Institute of Contemporary Arts (with support from The Royal Opera House, London) to explore the relationship between technology and 'liveness', digital duo, Monkman and Wexler of KMA, collaborated with choreographer Tom Sapsford to create Flock, inspired by Tchaikovsky's Swan Lake. The interactive installation – which ran on three consecutive evenings in February 2007 – transformed the 625 m2 area of London's famous Trafalgar Square into a virtual stage. Inspired by the white act in classical ballet, in which the hero comes into a realm where fantasy and reality merge, Flock uses the encounter in Swan Lake between the Prince and an enchanted band of Princesses – swans by day, women by night - as the basis for its visual imagery. Combining the romance and emotion of fairytale with the classical groupings and lines of precisely drilled dancers, this corps de ballet showcase is the archetypal image of ballet to many people. Re-imagining the experience of a dancer working as part of a large production to Tchaikovsky's bombastic notes, KMA and Sapsford created an installation in which the audience members themselves (commuters, tourists, shoppers and passers-by) became the dancers. Thus offering London's pedestrians the chance to mix the choreography of the crowd (that subconscious ducking and weaving all urban pedestrians know so well) with formal, classical choreography. Peoples' movement in the 625 m2 square were detected by a thermal imaging camera, triggering spotlights which then tracked them until they stepped out of the active area. The space - constantly filled with projections of dancing figures - relied on people's individual spotlights to cross their paths and illuminate them before they disappeared again into the surrounding darkness. (One dancer was filmed making the movements, then the images were built up, layer upon layer.) Following these figures, which moved with the music – another component triggered by the audience – allowed participants to mirror their movements in their own way; whether in high heels or work boots, they entered the dance. As more people moved into the space, more dancers appeared and the music became louder. If the space was empty, then nothing was seen or heard. The concept conjured images of a ghostly, miniature ballet being played out under the pavement and brought to life by the presence of people. At peak times, when filled with participants, the square became transformed into a big, brassy, camp experience; typical of the Capital's hotspots. At other times, when the space was occupied by just one dancer, the audience could see only fleeting figures accompanied by the very faintest of music. What was a seemingly personal experience for the participant became something more wide-reaching when viewed from afar, and by onlookers who formed its audience. Each participant's journey through the space became intricately connected to the group as a whole and ultimately created a coordinated corps de ballet of pedestrian performers, as engaging to the bystander as the performer in the installation.

Captivating the audience in an immersive experience, Flock resembled a life-sized, 3-dimensional computer game in which the players (pedestrians) were individually in control of their engagement but also working together to enhance the experience. Former Director of the ICA's Performing Arts and Digital Media Programme, Vivienne Gaskin, who originally commissioned the piece claims that it was 'a very significant piece in the transition of technology-based work becoming public art and understanding all the challenges this entails in the maturity of live, digital art.'

Flock was not simple in its construction and thus posed a number of technical challenges. Notable amongst these was generating a real-time, high-definition image that responded to pedestrians' movements with a fast enough frame rate so as not to create time delays impeding people's engagement with the work. The piece was programmed using Max/MSP and Jitter, and ran on a fast Quad G5 Macintosh computer. The projector and thermal image camera were optically aligned and mounted together on a crane 20 m above the square. The projection was directed downwards by a custom-built mirror and audio was handled by a PA system at ground level.

KMA's installation, Flock, will open China's first, and the world's largest, digital arts festival in Shanghai's Pudong Century Square in October 2007.

AS PEOPLE WALKED INTO THE STAGE AREA, A THERMAL IMAGING CAMERA REGISTERED THEIR HEAT SIGNAL. THIS TRIGGERED A SPOT-LIGHT TO FALL ON THEM AND TRACK THEM.

THE PROJECTIONS OF
DANCING FIGURES COULD
ONLY BE SEEN WHEN
PEOPLE CROSSED THEIR
PATHS AND THEIR SPOT-
LIGHT ILLUMINATED THEM
FOR A MOMENT.

At peak times, when filled with participants, the square became transformed into a big, brassy, camp experience; typical of the Capital's hotspots

A 625-M SQUARE AREA OF TRAFALGAR SQUARE WAS PRIMED AS THE VIRTUAL STAGE.

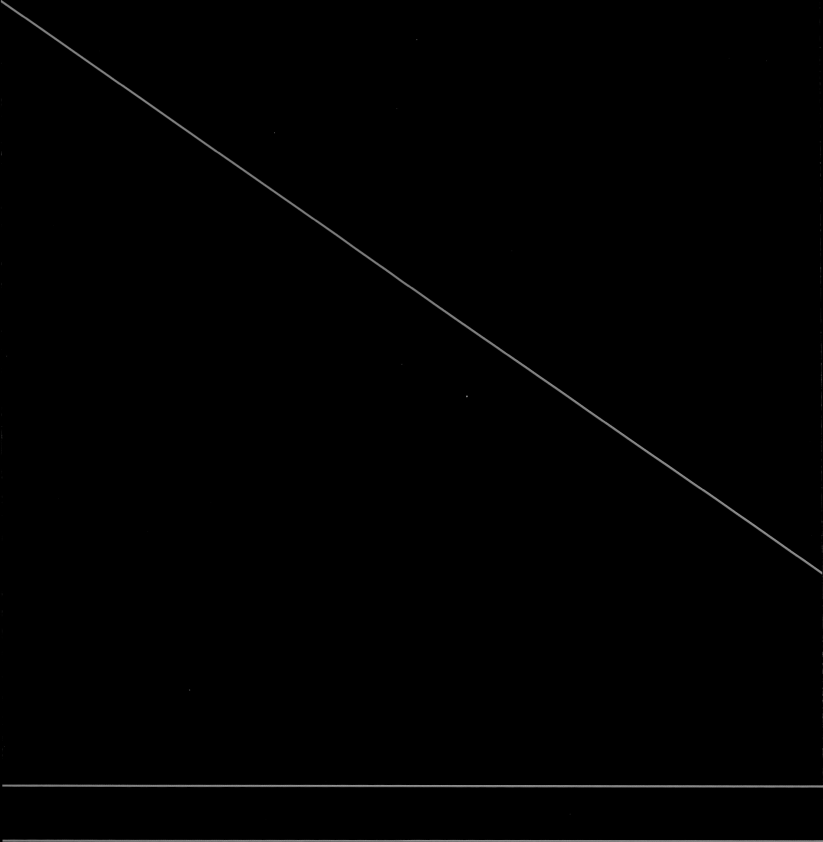

LIGHTING GUIDE

SOURCE: ERCO

1 TYPES OF OUTDOOR LIGHTING

2 OUTDOOR LIGHTING LUMINAIRE GROUPS

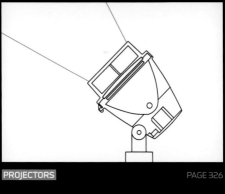

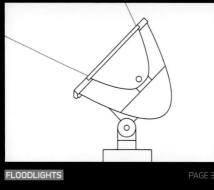

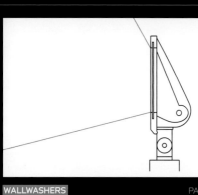

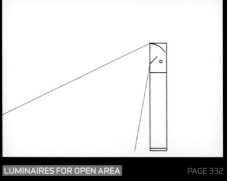

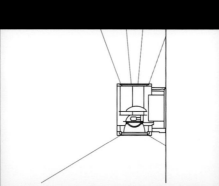

CEILING AND WALLMOUNTED LIGHTS PAGE 336

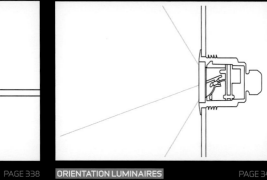

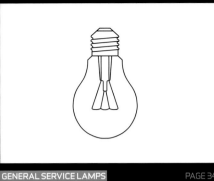

GENERAL SERVICE LAMPS PAGE 342

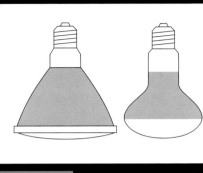

R AND PAR LAMPS PAGE 343

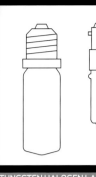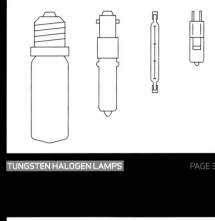

TUNGSTEN HALOGEN LAMPS PAGE 344

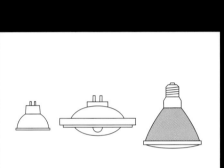

HALOGEN REFLECTOR LAMPS PAGE 345

FLUORESCENT LAMPS PAGE 346

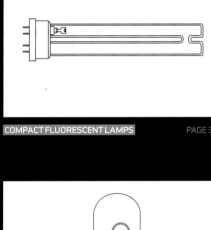

COMPACT FLUORESCENT LAMPS PAGE 346

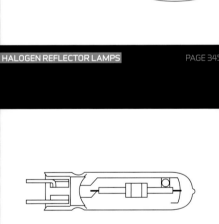

METAL VAPOUR LAMPS PAGE 347

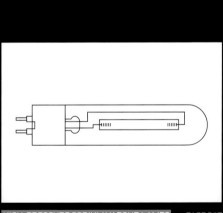

HIGH-PRESSURE SODIUM VAPOUR LAMPS PAGE 347

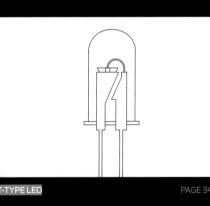

T-TYPE LED PAGE 348

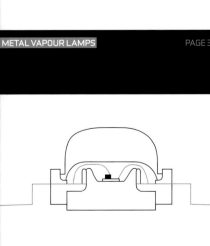

SMD LED PAGE 349

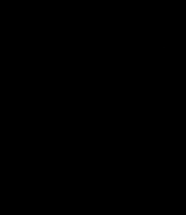

COB LED PAGE 349

1

TYPES OF OUTDOOR LIGHTING

The effect of rooms, façades, objects and vegetation greatly depends on the type of lighting. This ranges from general lighting through to specific highlighting.

1.1 GENERAL

General lighting designates an even illumination related to a horizontal working plane or pedestrian traffic zones. Quantitative aspects are often a primary consideration. Direct lighting permits both diffuse and directed light.

1.1.1 DIRECT, AIMED

The directed light produces good modelling and brilliance. The uniformity on the working plane increases as the mounting height increases or as the beam angle widens. Directed light enables good appreciation of form and surface texture. The visual comfort increases as the cut-off angle increases. A feature of direct illumination is its highly efficient use of energy.

APPLICATIONS:

» entrance areas
» arcades
» passages
» atria

PREFERRED LUMINAIRE GROUP:

» downlights

REPSOL PETROL STATION, SPAIN.

1

TYPES OF OUTDOOR LIGHTING

1.1.2 DIRECT, DIFFUSE

Direct, diffuse light produces a soft illumination with little shadow and reflection. The limited formation of shadow results in weak modelling capabilities. Shapes and surface textures are only slightly emphasised. One feature of using fluorescent lamps for the general lighting is an efficient use of energy.

APPLICATIONS:

» entrance areas
» overhanging or cantilevered roofs
» floor lighting on access driveways, paths and public squares

PREFERRED LUMINAIRE GROUPS:

» downlights
» wall-mounted downlights

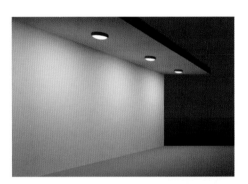

PRIVATE RESIDENCE, RAVENSBURG.

1

TYPES OF OUTDOOR LIGHTING

1.2 WASHLIGHTING

Washlighting illumination refers to an architecture-related and object-orientated illumination. It is characterised by high uniformity and a soft gradient of light intensity distribution. The primary purpose is to make visible the room proportions and room limits.

1.2.1 SYMMETRICAL

Symmetrical washlighting produces an even illumination on objects or surfaces. The directed light produces good modelling abilities and enables good appreciation of form and surface structure. Washlighting illumination can serve as a background for accent lighting.

APPLICATIONS:

» wall lighting
» façades
» entrance areas
» cantilever roofs
» trees
» park and garden complexes
» sculptures
» objects

PREFERRED LUMINAIRE GROUP:

» floodlights

PRIVATE RESIDENCE, SOUTHERN HIGHLANDS, AUSTRALIA.

1

1.2.2 **ASYMMETRICAL**

With asymmetrical washlighting, areas of a room can be defined and thus have attention attracted to them. It can also serve as a background for accent lighting or form the ambient brightness for the work place. To obtain a uniform light intensity distribution the correct positioning of the luminaires is of great importance.

APPLICATIONS:

» façades
» entrance areas
» passages
» atria
» cantilever roofs
» park and garden complexes

PREFERRED LUMINAIRE GROUPS:

» floodlights
» washlights
» wallwaschers
» recessed floor luminaires

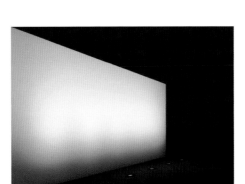

REGIONAL GOVERNMENT OF LOWER SAXONY AND SCHLESWIEG HOLSTEIN IN BERLIN.

1

TYPES OF OUTDOOR LIGHTING

1.3 ACCENTUATION

Highlighting emphasises individual objects or architectural elements. This makes it possible to establish a hierarchy of how noticeable each item is and to attract attention. Accent lighting enables good appreciation of form and surface structure. The focused light produces pronounced shadows and good modelling ability, as well as brilliance. A narrow beam and a high brightness contrast to the surroundings give the object particular emphasis. Highlighting emphasises individual objects or architectural elements. This makes it possible to establish a hierarchy of how noticeable each item is and to attract attention.

APPLICATIONS:

» façades
» entrance areas
» arcades
» park and garden complexes
» objects

PREFERRED LUMINAIRE GROUP:

» projectors
» directional luminaires

ERCO LIGHTPARK, LÜDENSCHEID.

ERCO P3 AUTOMATED WAREHOUSE, LÜDENSCHEID/GERMANY.

1

TYPES OF OUTDOOR LIGHTING

1.4 **ORIENTATION**

Orientation lighting can be achieved by luminaires that function as sources of illumination or as signals. Illuminating the room is of secondary importance here; instead, a row of these luminaries is typically arranged to form an orientation line. Small luminaires with high luminance clearly set themselves apart form their surroundings.

APPLICATIONS:

» architectural lines
» steps and exclusion zones
» entrances
» routes
» emergency exit routes

PREFERRED LUMINAIRE GROUPS:

» floor washlights
» wall-mounted downlights
» recessed floor luminaires
» orientation luminaires

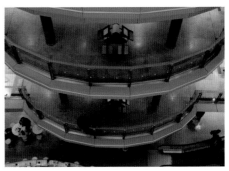

SEVENS DEPARTMENT STORE, DÜSSELDORF/GERMANY.

BATHING PLATFORM KASTRUP SOBAD, COPENHAGEN.

2 OUTDOOR LIGHTING LUMINAIRE GROUPS

Luminaires are available in a wide variety of types, each intended to fulfill different lighting requirements. For external applications it is primarily permanently mounted luminaires that are used.

2.1 PROJECTORS

Projectors illuminate a narrowly constrained area. The type of mounting and the orientation are variable. Projectors are offered with different beam emission angles and light distributions. Projectors have narrow-beam light distribution with a rotationally symmetrical beam.

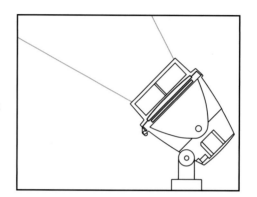

CRITERIA:

» choice of lamp determines light colour, brilliance, functional life, light intensity
» emission angle determines the beam of light and is defined by the reflector and the lamp
» cut-off angle limits glare and increases visual comfort
» rotatable and tiltable

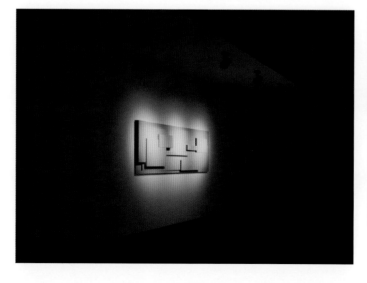

2 OUTDOOR LIGHTING LUMINAIRE GROUPS

APPLICATIONS:

» facades
» entrance areas
» arcades
» park and garden complexes
» objects

ERCO LICHTWIESE (LIGHT GARDEN), LÜDENSCHEID/GERMANY.

NORWEGIAN AVIATION MUSEUM, BDDO.

2

2.2   **FLOODLIGHTS**

Floodlights have a wide-beam characteristic. They are offered with a axially symmetrical or asymmetrical light distribution.

CRITERIA:

» choice of lamp determines light colour, functional life, efficiency, light intensity
» uniformity: optimised reflector for even illumination of areas
» gradient: soft edge to the beam of light
» light output ratio is increased by optimised reflector technology

FLOODLIGHTS WITH AXIALLY SYMMETRICAL LIGHT DISTRIBUTION PROVIDE EVEN ILLUMINATION OF OBJECTS OR AREAS. LIGHT DISTRIBUTION WITH FOCAL EMPHASIS.

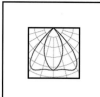
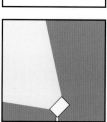
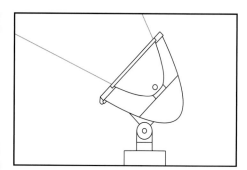

FLOODLIGHTS WITH ASYMMETRICAL LIGHT DISTRIBUTION PROVIDE EVEN ILLUMINATION OF AREAS. THE LUMINARIES CAN BE MOUNTED ON WALLS, CEILINGS OR FLOORS AND IN ADDITION CAN ALSO BE TILTED.

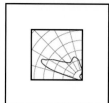
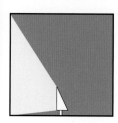
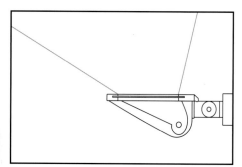

2 OUTDOOR LIGHTING LUMINAIRE GROUPS

APPLICATIONS:

» wall lighting
» façades
» entrance areas
» overhanging or cantilevered roofs
» park and garden complexes
» sculptures
» objects

SRI SENPAGA VINAYAGAR TEMPLE, CEYLON ROAD/SINGAPORE.

CENTENARY HALL, BOCHUM/GERMANY.

2

OUTDOOR LIGHTING LUMINAIRE GROUPS

2.3 WALLWASHERS

Wallwashers have a wide-beam characteristic. They are offered with an asymmetric light distribution. Wallwashing is an important component of architectural lighting for adding emphasis to façades.

CRITERIA:

» choice of lamp determines light colour, functional life, efficiency, light intensity
» uniformity: optimised reflector for even illumination of areas
» gradient: soft edges to the beam of light
» light output ratio is increased by optimised reflector technologymised reflector technology

RECESSED-MOUNTED WALLWASHERS WITH ASYMMETRIC LIGHT DISTRIBUTION PROVIDE AN EVEN ILLUMINATION OF AREAS.

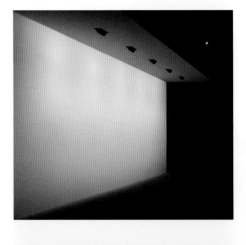
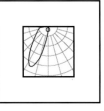
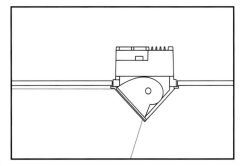
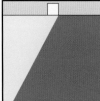

SURFACE-MOUNTED DOWNLIGHTS CAN BE MOUNTED ON WALLS, CEILINGS OR FLOORS AND IN ADDITION CAN ALSO BE TILTED.

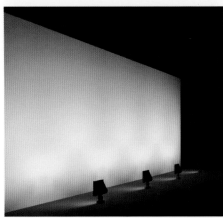

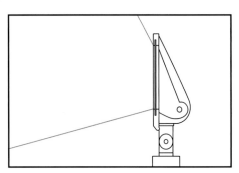

2 OUTDOOR LIGHTING LUMINAIRE GROUPS

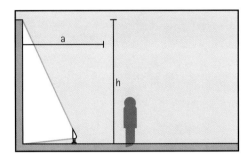 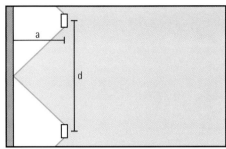

The offset from the wall should be at least one third off the wall height. Alternatively, the light's angle of incident should be 20° to the vertical. An optimum evenness is obtained when the luminaire spacing is the same as the offset from the wall, or at least does not exceed it by more than 1.5 times. Wallwashers only develop their optimal evenness as of a minimum number of three luminaires.

APPLICATIONS:

» façades
» entrance areas
» passages
» atria
» overhanging or cantilevered roofs
» park and garden complexes

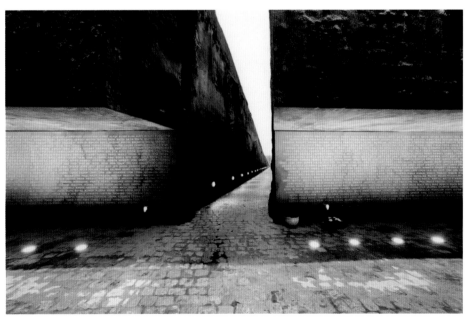

CONCENTRATION CAMP MEMORIAL, BELZEC/POLAND.

2

OUTDOOR LIGHTING LUMINAIRE GROUPS

2.4 LUMINAIRES FOR OPEN AREA AND PATHAWAY LIGHTING

Luminaires for open area and pathway lighting have a widebeam characteristic. They are offered with an asymmetric light distribution.

CRITERIA:

» choice of lamp determines light colour, functional life, efficiency, light intensity
» uniformity: optimised reflector for even illumination of areas
» gradient: soft edges to beam of light
» cut-off angle increases visual comfort and limits glare and light pollution
» light output ratio is increased by optimised reflector technology

PATHWAY LIGHTING LUMINAIRES WITH ASYMMETRIC LIGHT DISTRIBUTION PROVIDE UNIFORM ILLUMINATION ON PATHWAYS. THE LIGHT IS SPREAD IN ITS WIDTH SO THAT PATHWAYS CAN BE EVENLY ILLUMINATED. THEIR SMALL DESIGN MAKES THESE LUMINARIES SUITABLE FOR LIGHTING STEPS.

LIGHT FOR ILLUMINATING OPEN SPACES IS GENERATED BY AN ASYMMETRIC REFLECTOR-FLOOD SYSTEM. A SCULPTURE LENS ACTING AS SAFETY GLASS DIRECTS THE LIGHT DEEP INTO THE OUTDOOR AREA.

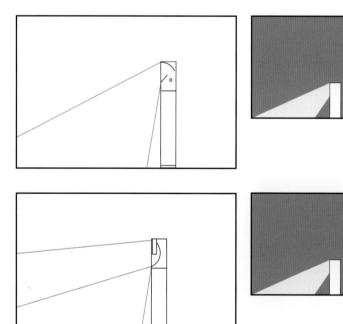

2 OUTDOOR LIGHTING LUMINAIRE GROUPS

FLOOR WASHLIGHTS
WITH ASYMMETRIC LIGHT
DISTRIBUTION PROVIDE
AN EVEN ILLUMINATION
OF BUILDINGS.

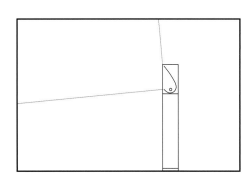 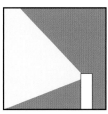

APPLICATIONS:

» façades
» entrance areas
» arcades
» passages
» floor lighting on access driveways, paths
  and public squares
» orientation lighting on pathways, drives,
  entrances and steps
» park and garden complexes

PRIVATE RESIDENCE, BERLIN/GERMANY.

PANTICOSA RESORT, PANTICOSA.

2

OUTDOOR LIGHTING LUMINAIRE GROUPS

2.5 DOWNLIGHTS

Downlights emit a beam that is directed downwards at either a perfectly vertical or an adjustable angle. They are usually mounted on the ceiling and illuminate the floor or walls. They are offered with narrow-beam, wide-beam, symmetric or asymmetric light distribution. The cut-off angle of narrow-beam downlights means they are largely free of glare. On downlights with Darklight reflector, the lamp's cut-off angle is identical to that of the luminaire. This gives a luminaire with the widest beam possible while simultaneously having an optimized light output ratio. The use of a diffuser reduces the luminance in the luminaire and thereby improves the visual comfort and the evenness.

CRITERIA:

» choice of lamp determines light colour, functional life, efficiency, light intensity
» emission angle determines the beam of light and is defined by the reflector and the lamp
» cut-off angle limits glare and increases visual comfort
» light output ratio is increased by optimised reflector technology

DOWNLIGHTS HAVE A ROTATIONALLY SYMMETRIC BEAM THAT IS DIRECTED VERTICALLY DOWNWARDS.

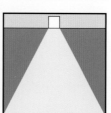
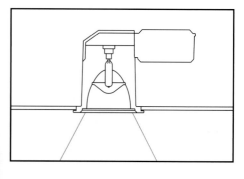

DIRECTIONAL LUMINAIRES PROVIDE HIGHLIGHTING FOR INDIVIDUAL AREAS OR OBJECTS WITH A MEDIUM TO NARROW LIGHT DISTRIBUTION.

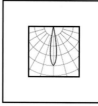

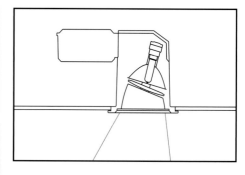

2

OUTDOOR LIGHTING LUMINAIRE GROUPS

APPLICATIONS:

» entrance areas
» arcades
» passages
» atria

CONGRESS PALACE, VALENCIA.

2

OUTDOOR LIGHTING LUMINAIRE GROUPS

2.6 ▌CEILING AND WALL-MOUNTED DOWNLIGHTS

Ceiling and wall-mounted downlights are defined first and foremost by their type of mounting and not by their light characteristics. They are available with narrow-beam, wide-beam, symmetrical or asymmetric light distribution. Some luminaries can be positioned either on the wall or on the ceiling.

CRITERIA:

» choice of lamp determines light colour, functional life, efficiency, light intensity
» uniformity: optimised reflector for even illumination of areas
» cut-off angle increases visual comfort and limits glare and light pollution

FAÇADES LUMINAIRES ARE OFFERED WITH NARROW-BEAM, WIDE-BEAM, SYMMETRICAL OR ASYMMETRIC LIGHT DISTRIBUTION. THE LIGHT CAN BE DISTRIBUTED EITHER VIA A SINGLE-SIDED OR DOUBLE-SIDED LIGHT APERTURE.

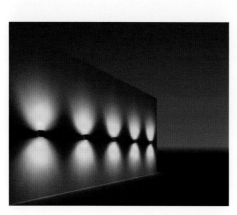
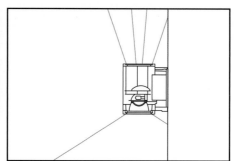
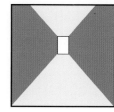

WALL-MOUNTED DOWNLIGHTS, WITH THEIR DIFFUSE BEAM IN THE ROOM, PROVIDE GOOD VISUAL COMFORT. THEY CAN ALSO BE MOUNTED ON THE CEILING.

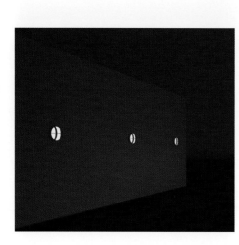
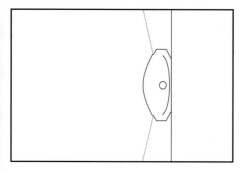
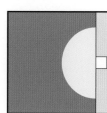

2

OUTDOOR LIGHTING LUMINAIRE GROUPS

WALL-MOUNTED DOWN-
LIGHTS WITH HALF-SHIEL-
DED FACE OFFER GOOD
VISUAL COMFORT AND
ILLUMINATE THE FLOOR
AREA IN PARTICULAR.

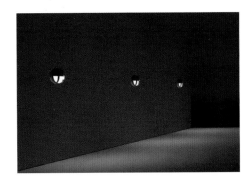

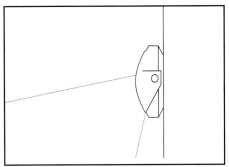

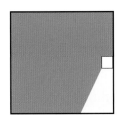

APPLICATIONS:

» façades
» entrance areas
» overhanging or cantilevered roofs
» floor lighting on access driveways, paths
  and public squares

MUSEUM NORVEG, RØRVIK.

PRIVATE RESIDENCE, RAVENSBURG/GERMANY.

2

OUTDOOR LIGHTING LUMINAIRE GROUPS

2.7 RECESSED FLOOR LUMINAIRES

Recessed floor luminaires emit their beam upwards. They are offered with narrow-beamed, wide-beamed, symmetric or asymmetric light distribution.

CRITERIA:

» choice of lamp determines light colour, functional life, efficiency, light intensity
» uniformity with wallwashers: optimised reflector for even illumination of areas
» range of tilt for directional luminaires with high glare protection
» light output ratio is increased by optimised reflector technology

UPLIGHTS FEATURE AN UPWARDS DIRECTED BEAM WITH SYMMETRICAL LIGHT DISTRIBUTION. THE NARROW, ROTATIONALLY SYMMETRICAL BEAM IS USED FOR HIGHLIGHTING OBJECTS.

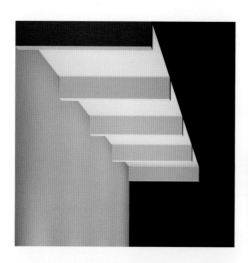

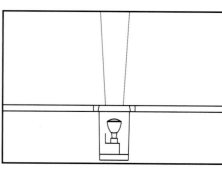

LENS WALLWASHERS FEATURE AN UPWARDS DIRECTED BEAM WITH ASYMMETRICAL LIGHT DISTRIBUTION. THEY PROVIDE AN EVEN ILLUMINATION OF WALLS.

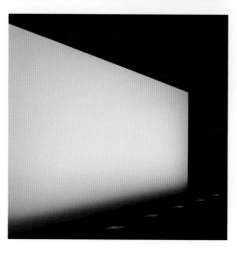

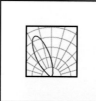

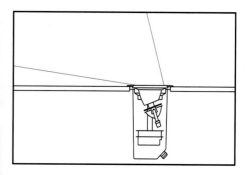

2 OUTDOOR LIGHTING LUMINAIRE GROUPS

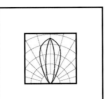

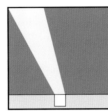

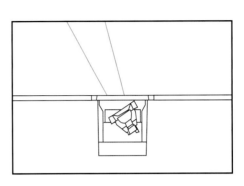

DIRECTIONAL LUMINAIRES PROVIDE HIGHLIGHTING FOR INDIVIDUAL AREAS OR OBJECTS WITH A MEDIUM TO NARROW LIGHT DISTRIBUTION. THE BEAM CAN BE TITLED.

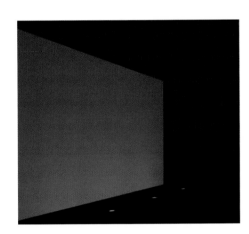

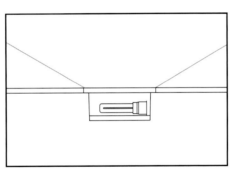

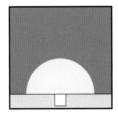

RECESSED FLOOR LUMINAIRES WITH DIFFUSE LIGHT INTENSITY DISTRIBUTION ARE USED FOR MARKING PATHS OR EMPHASISING ARCHITECTURAL LINES.

APPLICATIONS:

» façades
» entrance areas
» arcades
» passages
» atria
» overhanging or cantilevered roofs
» park and garden complexes

GLASS PAVILION, GLASS TECHNOLOGIE COLLEGE, RHEINBACH.

2

2.8 **ORIENTATION LUMINAIRES**

Orientation luminaires are defined first and foremost by the task of providing orientation. This can be achieved by luminaries that function as sources of illumination or as signals.

CRITERIA:

» luminance: noticability of the luminaires in their surroundings

ORIENTATION LUMINAIRES WITH POINT-FORM FRONT LENS ACT AS A LOCAL ORIENTATION LIGHT.

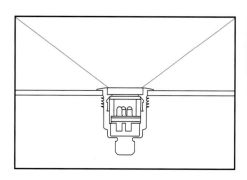
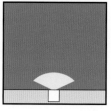

FLOOR WASHLIGHTS FORM POINTS OF LIGHT ON THE WALL AND SERVES AS AN ORIENTATION LIGHT ON THE FLOOR SURFACE.

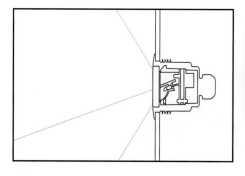
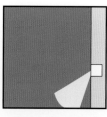

2 OUTDOOR LIGHTING LUMINAIRE GROUPS

APPLICATIONS:

» architectural lines
» steps or restricted areas
» entrances
» routes
» emergency exit routes

HILTON HOTEL, DUBAI/DUBAI.

PRIVATE RESIDENCE, PALAMOS.

3

The electric light sources can be divided into three main groups, divided according to how they convert electrical energy into light. One group is that of the thermal radiators, this contains incandescent lamps and tungsten halogen lamps. The second group is made up of the discharge lamps; this consists of a large spectrum of light sources, e. g. all forms of fluorescent lamps, sodium vapour lamps and metal halide lamps. The third group consists of the semiconductors with the LEDs.

3.1 THERMAL RADIATORS

Thermal radiators generate light by using an incandescent metal filament. As the temperature increases the spectrum of light shifts from the red heat of the filament to warm white light. Characteristic features are low colour temperature, excellent colour rendition and brilliance as a point light source.

3.1.1 GENERAL SERVICE LAMPS

A low colour temperature is characteristic for the general service lamp. It is perceived as being warm. The continuous spectrum of the incandescent lamp results in an excellent colour rendition. As a point light source with high luminance it produces brilliance. Incandescent lamps can be dimmed without problem. They do not require any additional equipment for their operation. The disadvantages of incandescent lamps are low luminous efficacy and a relatively brief nominal service life.

Incandescent lamps are available as A-lamps (All-purpose lamps) in many forms. Their bulbs can be clear, matt or white. The light is emitted in all directions.

3
LAMPS

3.1.2 R AND PAR LAMPS

A low colour temperature is characteristic for the reflector and parabolic aluminised reflector lamps. The continuous spectrum of the incandescent lamp results in an excellent colour rendition. As a point light source with high luminance it produces brilliance. They do not require any additional equipment for their operation. The disadvantages of incandescent lamps are low luminous efficacy and a relatively brief nominal service life.

The R (Reflector) lamps are blown from soft glass and direct the light due to their shape and a partial mirror coating on the inside.

REFLECTOR LAMP WITH PRESSED GLASS BULB AND POWERFUL PARABOLIC REFLECTOR

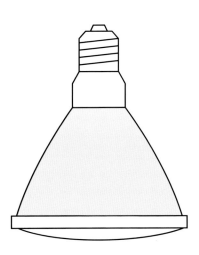

The PAR lamps are manufactured from pressed glass in order to achieve high resistance to temperature change and high accuracy of shape. The parabolic reflector is available with different half peak spreads and produces a defined beam emission angle. On coolbeam lamps, a subgroup of the PAR lamps, a dichroic mirror coating is used. Dichroic reflectors focus the visible light but allow a large part of the thermal radiation to pass through unaffected. This allows the thermal load on the illuminated objects to be reduced by approximately half.

REFLECTOR LAMP WITH SOFT GLASS BULB AND ELLIPSOID REFLECTOR WITH MODERATE FOCUSING POWER.

3

3.1.3 **TUNGSTEN HALOGEN LAMPS**

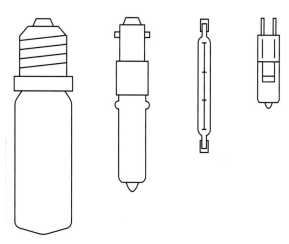

The tungsten halogen lamp emits a whiter light than conventional incandescent lamps. Its light colour is in the range of warm white. Due to the continuous spectrum, the colour rendition is excellent. Its compact form makes the tungsten halogen lamp an ideal point light source. The particularly good directability of the light produces brilliance. The luminous efficacy and life of tungsten halogen lamps is above that of ordinary incandescent lamps. Tungsten halogen lamps can be dimmed and do not require any additional control gear; low-voltage halogen lamps, however, must be powered via transformers.

Tungsten halogen lamps are available for operation on mains voltage. They usually have a special fixing. Some feature a screw fixing and an additional external glass capsule and can be used just like conventional incandescent lamps. The advantages of the low-voltage halogen lamp primarily concern the high luminous power for its small dimensions. The lamp enables compact luminaire designs and a very narrow focussing of the light. Low-voltage halogen lamps are available for different voltages and in various shapes and must be powered via transformers. The lamps emit light in all directions. Halogen lamps with low-pressure technology are permitted for all corresponding luminaires. Halogen lamps without low-pressure technology are only permitted in luminaires with protective cover. The advantages of the low-pressure version are improved luminous flux throughout the entire service life.

3 LAMPS

3.1.4 HALOGEN REFLECTOR LAMPS

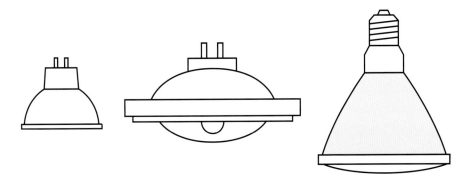

The tungsten halogen reflector lamp emits a whiter light than conventional incandescent lamps. Its light colour is in the range of warm white. Due to the continuous spectrum, the colour rendition is excellent. Its compact form makes the tungsten halogen reflector lamp an ideal point light source. The particularly good directability of the light produces brilliance. The luminous efficacy and life of tungsten halogen reflector lamps is above that of ordinary incandescent lamps. Tungsten halogen reflector lamps can be dimmed and do not require any additional control gear; low-voltage halogen reflector lamps, however, must be powered via transformers. Narrow or wide beam reflectors are available. Lamps with coolbeam reflector place less thermal loading on the illuminated objects. Lamps with an integrated cover glass permit operation in open luminaires.

Tungsten halogen reflector lamps are available for operation on mains voltage. They usually have a special fixing. Some feature a screw fixing and an additional external glass capsule and can be used just like conventional incandescent lamps. The advantages of the low-voltage halogen lamp primarily concern the high luminous power for its small dimensions. The lamp enables compact luminaire designs and a very narrow focussing of the light. Low-voltage halogen reflector lamps are available for different voltages and in various shapes and must be powered via transformers. They are available with different half peak spreads. The versions with coolbeam reflectors radiate the heat away to the sides and reduce the thermal loading in the focused beam. The halogen parabolic reflector lamp combines the advantages of halogen technology with the technology of the PAR lamps.

3.2 DISCHARGE LAMPS

Discharge lamps comprise those light sources whereby the generation of light does not rely, or does not solely rely, on the temperature of the materials. Depending on the type, a differentiation is made between photo luminescence and electroluminescence. The light is generated principally using chemical or electrical processes. The discharge lamp group is subdivided into low-pressure and high-pressure lamps.

3.2.1 FLUORESCENT LAMPS

With fluorescent lamps, the light is emitted from a large surface and is mainly diffuse light with little brilliance. The light colours of fluorescent lamps are warm white, neutral white and daylight white. Fluorescent lamps feature a high luminous efficacy and long life. Both starters and control gear (chokes) are necessary for operating fluorescent lamps. They ignite immediately and attain their full luminous power after a brief moment. An immediate re-ignition is possible if the current is interrupted. Fluorescent lamps can be dimmed depending on the control gear.

Fluorescent lamps are usually shaped as a straight tube, whereby the luminous power depends on the length of the lamp. Special forms such as U-shape or ring-shape fluorescent lamps are available.

3.2.2 COMPACT FLUORESCENT LAMPS

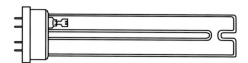

By blending or coiling the discharge tubes, compact fluorescent lamps are made shorter than ordinary fluorescent lamps. They have fundamentally the same proportions as the conventional fluorescent lamps, above all these are high luminous efficacy and long life. The relatively small volume of the discharge tubes can produce a focused light using the luminaire's reflector. Compact fluorescent lamps with integrated starters cannot be dimmed. However, there are types with external starters available, which can be operated on electronic control gear and allow dimming. Compact fluorescent lamps are primarily available as a straight tube. Starters and fluorescent lamp chokes are necessary for their operation; on two pin lamps, however, the starters are already integrated into the end cap. In addition to these standard forms, there are also compact fluorescent lamps with integrated starter and control gear. These feature a screw-in fixing and can be used just like incandescent lamps.

LAMPS

3.2.3 METAL VAPOUR LAMPS

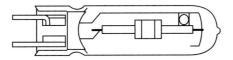

Metal halide lamps feature excellent luminous efficacy while simultaneously having good colour rendition; their nominal service life is high. They represent a compact light source. The light can be optically well directed. The colour rendition is not constant. Metal halide lamps are available in the light colours warm white, neutral white and daylight white and are not dimmed. Metal halide lamps require both starters and chokes for their operation. They require an ignition time of several minutes and a longer cooling-down phase before re-igniting. On some forms an immediate re-ignition is possible using special starters or the electronic control gear.

Metal halide lamps are available as single-ended or doubled-ended tubular lamps, as elliptical lamps and as reflector lamps. Metal halide reflector lamps combine the technology of the metal halide lamps with that of the PAR lamps.

3.2.4 HIGH-PRESS. SOD. VAP. LAMPS

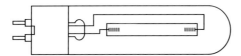

High-pressure sodium vapour lamps have excellent luminous efficacy and a high nominal service life. Their colour rendition is moderate to good. High-pressure sodium vapour lamps are operated with a control gear and a starter. They require an ignition time of several minutes and a cooling-down phase before being re-ignited. On some forms an immediate re-ignition is possible using special starters or the electronic control gear.

High-pressure sodium vapour lamps are available as clear lamps in tubular form and as coated lamps in ellipsoid form. Furthermore, there are also double-ended compact straight tube lamps, which allow immediate re-ignition and represent a particularly compact light source. One part of the high-pressure sodium vapour lamps has a coated outer capsule. This coating serves only to reduce the lamp luminance and to give a more diffuse light emission, it does not contain any fluorescent substances.

3

LAMPS

3.3   ELECTROLUMINESCENT LUMINAIRES

In electroluminescent luminaires, the electrical energy produces visible radiation. One of the characteristic aspects of light emitting diodes, LEDs, is their narrow banded spectrum, while their advantages include a compact form, high colour density, a long life, and low power consumption.

3.3.1   LED

Light emitting diodes, LEDs, have extremely long life, impact resistance and low energy consumption. When dimmed, the light colour remains constant. When connected to the mains, they require control gear to ensure the correct operating current. The point light source provides for precise light control while the plastic encapsulation of the diode acts as protection and lens. The output of the LED decreases with increasing temperature. Consequently, good heat dissipation is important for smooth operation. Direct solar radiation should be avoided so too installation near other sources of heat. With an average rated life of 50,000 hours, LEDs are suitable for long operating times. As they start instantly and react directly to control, they are ideal for quick, dynamic light scenes. The development of LEDs currently focuses on more compact designs, a higher luminous flux, and better luminous efficacy as well as a more economical production process. A further goal is the reduction of production-related colour deviations. Manufacturers sort LEDs by luminous flux and dominant wavelength and give them a bin code and a rating. This sorting of LEDs is called binning.

T-TYPE LED

The standard T-type LED has a plastic housing measuring 3-5mm for the wired LED. The shape of the lens determines the light emission angle. As a light source with a low luminous flux it is used as an orientation or a signal luminaire.

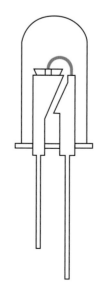

SMD LED

With the 'Surface Mounted Device' (SMD) type, the component is glued directly to the circuit board and the contacts are soldered.

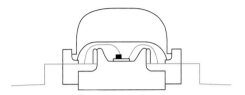

COB LED

The 'Chip on Board' (COB) technology places the chip directly on a circuit board without its own housing. The anode and cathode contact can be made using thin wires. The chip is sealed to protect it.

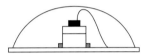

HIGH-POWER LED

High-power LEDs are LEDs with a power consumption of over 1W. This includes both SMD and COB LEDs. The key factor is their special construction that ensures very low thermal resistance between the chip and the circuit board. High-power LEDs are usually used on metal core circuit boards requiring special thermal management in the luminaire.

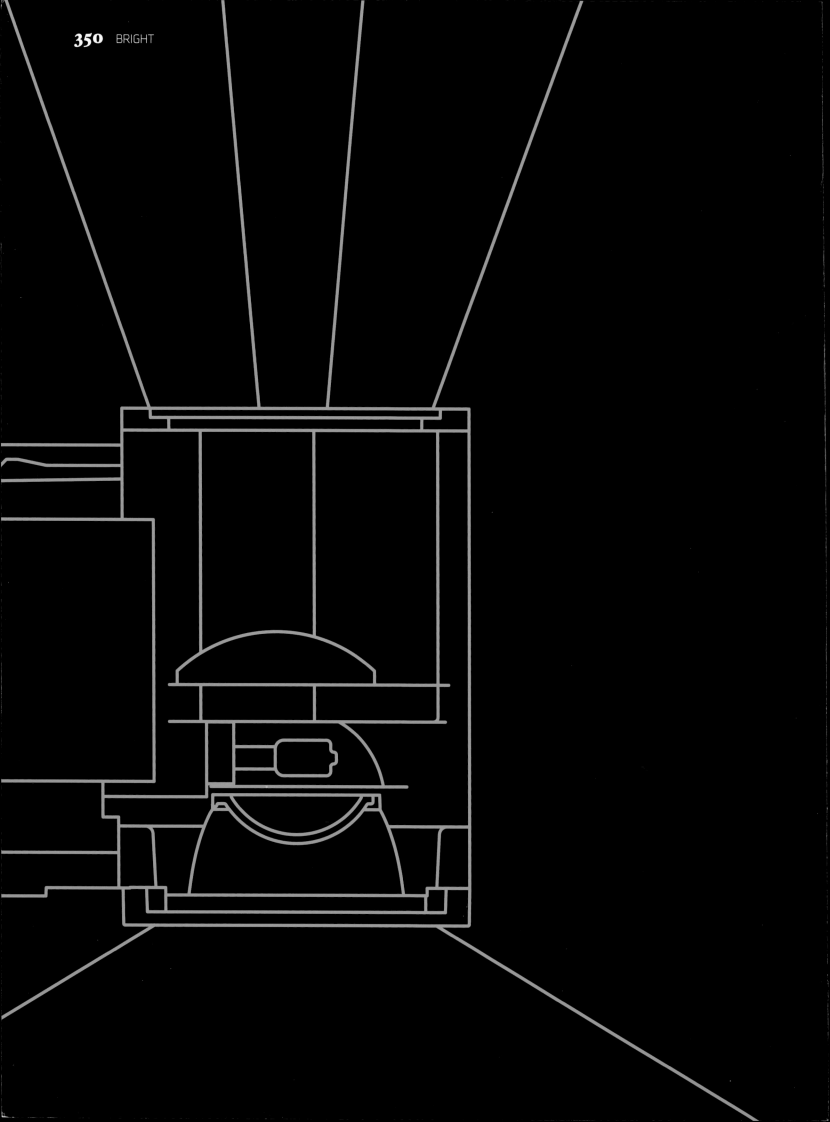

Lighting Associations
Overview

ALD
Association of Lighting Designers
www.ald.org.uk

AIA
The American Institute of Architects
www.aia.org

BDA
Bund Deutscher Architekten
www.bda-architekten.de

CAUS
The Color Association of the United States
www.colorassociation.com

ESTA
Entertainment Services & Technology Association
www.esta.org

IALD
International Association of Lighting Designers
www.iald.org

IESNA
Illuminating Engineering Society of North America
www.iesna.org

IESANZ
Illuminating Engineering Society of Australia and New Zealand
www.iesanz.org

KÖLNDESIGN
www.koelndesign.de

LDE
Light Design Engineering
www.lde-net.com

PLDA (ELDA)
Professional Lighting Designers' Association
www.pld-a.org

SIA
Schweizerischer Ingenieur- und Architektenverein
www.sia.ch

SBSE
Society of Building Science Educators
www.sbse.org

SLG
Schweitzer Licht Gesellschaft
www.slg.ch

TEA
Themed Entertainment Association
www.teaconnect.org

USGBC
U.S. Green Building Council
www.usgbc.org

Bright

Architectural Illumination and
Light Installations

PUBLISHERS
Frame Publishers
www.framemag.com
Die Gestalten Verlag
www.die-gestalten.de

EDITING
Clare Lowther, Sarah Schultz

INTRODUCTION
Rogier van der Heide, Arup

GRAPHIC DESIGN
Lava Grafisch Ontwerpers, Amsterdam
(Florian Gläser and Jorgen Koolwijk)
www.lava.nl

COPY EDITING
TransL Vertaalbureau (Rebecca Parker)
Jane Smith
Donna de Vries-Hermansader

TRANSLATION
Ella Wildridge

COVER PHOTOGRAPHY
XAL GmbH

COLOUR REPRODUCTION
Graphic Link BV

PRINTING
D2Print, Singapore

SPONSOR
ERCO Leuchten GmbH

INTERNATIONAL DISTRIBUTION
dgv – Die Gestalten Verlag GmbH & Co. KG
Mariannenstrasse 9 – 10, 10999 Berlin, Germany
www.die-gestalten.de
sales@die-gestalten.de

ISBN: 978-3-89955-301-7

© 2008 Frame Publishers, Amsterdam
© 2008 dgv – Die Gestalten Verlag GmbH & Co. KG, Berlin

Bibliographic information published by the Deutsche Nationalbibliothek
The Deutsche Nationalbibliothek lists this publication in the Deutsche Nationalbibliografie;
detailed bibiographic is available on the internet at http://dnb.d-nb.de

Printed on acid-free paper produced from chlorine-free pulp. TCF ∞

987654321